ONENESS AND SEPARATENESS: FROM INFANT TO INDIVIDUAL

by Louise J. Kaplan, Ph.D.

A Touchstone Book
Published by
Simon and Schuster

For my children, Ann and David

Copyright © 1978 by Louise J. Kaplan, Ph.D.

Published by Simon and Schuster
A Division of Gulf & Western Corporation
Simon & Schuster Building
Rockefeller Center
1230 Avenue of the Americas
New York, New York 10020
TOUCHSTONE and colophon are trademarks
of Simon & Schuster

Manufactured in the United States of America

4   5   6   7   8   9   10   11

5   6   7   8   9   10   11   Pbk.

LIBRARY OF CONGRESS CATALOGING IN PUBLICATION DATA

KAPLAN, LOUISE J.
ONENESS AND SEPARATENESS.
INCLUDES BIBLIOGRAPHICAL REFERENCES AND INDEX.
1. INFANT PSYCHOLOGY.   2. MAHLER, MARGARET S.
I. TITLE.
BF723.I6K33   155.4′22   77-27960

ISBN 0-671-22854-4
ISBN 0-671-24061-7 Pbk.

Acknowledgments

Foremost among those who made this book possible is Margaret S. Mahler. Mahler's extraordinary scientific discoveries supplied a great deal more than the inspiration for *Oneness and Separateness*. Several years before I had the opportunity to work with Mahler, her theories on the etiology and treatment of childhood disorders had already influenced the course of my career as a child psychologist. Mahler's conviction about the central importance of direct child observation for an understanding of human development and her scientific strategies of uncovering the psychological processes underlying overt behavior would shape my own research and teaching style. In Mahler's work, I found an alternative to the prevailing tradition of academic research, which emphasizes hypothesis-testing and laboratory manipulation. I was able to give a higher priority to putting the right questions to observations of ordinary human behavior occurring in naturalistic settings.

There is a personal history to my eventually becoming familiar with the precise details of Mahler's work. On this score, I am enormously grateful to my friend and colleague Anni Bergman. It was she who recommended me to Mahler and Dr. John B. McDevitt as the psychodiagnostician for the separation-individuation follow-up study. Anni's devotion and loyalty to her child patients and her original way of organizing what she sees before her own eyes have become a model for my approach to working with children and parents, and students.

Another invaluable personal influence was Dr. Robert Evans, who was Director of the Children's Day Treatment Center and

School during the years that I was Chief Psychologist and Educational Supervisor. In our age of a therapeutic zeal that opts for "fast cure," it was my unusual good fortune to work with a child psychiatrist who put his authority behind the belief that scholarship and thoughtful diagnostic assessment are as essential to the training of clinicians as therapeutic activity. While working with him, I began to appreciate the clinical relevance of Mahler's theories. Bob also had a knack for selecting a staff that could measure up to his standards for disciplined, scholarly work. I therefore wish to thank my colleagues at the Children's Day Treatment Center, from whom I learned so much.

When I came to New York University, Professor Donald P. Spence was the first advocate of my research and teaching ambitions. It was on his advice that I proposed the setting up of a research nursery for the study of normal separation-individuation. Professor Samuel Feldman, who was then Chairman of the Psychology Department, agreed to sponsor my proposal. Sam's psychology background and mine are worlds apart. He is a "hard-nosed" experimental, physiological psychologist, and I, one of those "soft" psychoanalytically oriented, observational researchers. Even so, Sam knew the value of observational research for the education of psychologists, and he arranged the initial financing and necessary laboratory space for the New York University Mother-Infant Research Nursery.

The Nursery could never have gone on to become a reality if it had not been for the enthusiasm and dedication of the students who worked with me. Their observational skills and clinical insights were more vital to me than they probably realized. And to the lively, charming children and devoted parents who were, after all, the heart of our research and also of this volume, I owe my enduring appreciation.

Certainly, in the personal history that led to the writing of *Oneness and Separateness,* my husband, Dr. Donald M. Kaplan, has been the most constant source of my inspiration. Our twenty-eight years of partnership and camaraderie and our twenty years of shared parenthood are what furnish *Oneness and Separateness* with its vitality and essence.

And, though they did not live to read this book, my parents, Matilda Davidson Miller and Joseph Miller, would have comprehended their roles in creating it. My childhood home was a place where individuality and a respect for other human lives could flourish side by side.

After the inspiration and the research, next came the difficult work of writing and arriving at a tone suitable to the ideas I hoped to communicate. Here my appreciation for the assistance, recommendations and encouragement of my friends is extensive: It goes to Mary Ann Dishman, who typed the manuscript, calmly and faithfully keeping pace with my schedules and deadlines; to Professor Marvin Hurvich for our stimulating collaboration on the beginnings of a different version of the story of separation-individuation; to my dear friends Katherine Rees, Joanna Pisello Herman and Professor William Herman, who read some of the opening chapters with warm reactions; to Rhoda Wolf, who immediately saw the value of the book, and to Dan Wolf, who found for me the ideal editor at Simon and Schuster—Nan Talese. It was Nan's intuitive and intelligent understanding of the dilemmas of oneness and separateness that enabled me to transform abstract theories and complex observational data into palpable ideas. A special note of thanks to Rita Kramer, who put aside her own writing to read my final manuscript when time was precious to her. Rita is an exacting critic; her affirmation meant everything to me. And, to Katherine Ross, whose enthusiastic reactions and sensitive editorial suggestions on the initial drafts of the manuscript sustained my spirit and energies through the inevitable doubts and uncertainties of authorship.

New York
July, 1977

Contents

Foreword

Margaret S. Mahler, M.D.

I greet this work with particular joy, satisfaction and pleasure, as I have been desirous ever since I discovered and described the ubiquitous process of psychological birth to make these findings available to the widest possible circles of readers. My work needed Dr. Kaplan's unique talents, coupled with her firsthand experience with mothers and babies, to translate those concepts for which I coined the terms that became household words, into generally readable English. Here is a text appealing to the educated public, unencumbered by the original technical and heavy scientific attributes.

Dr. Kaplan's book, however, is much more than the translation of my concepts into readable English. It also integrates for the reader the fundamental concepts of Spitz and Winnicott, to name only a few of the great names of developmental psychology; with her basic knowledge of Piaget's work on cognition, it encompasses the understanding of many other architects of the edifice of the psychoanalytic, existential, and behavioral sciences.

Foremost of the virtues of this book are the messages it brings to mothers and fathers in so many respects. It conveys the rhythm, the flavor, and deeply reverberating miracle of the newborn's growing from limbo to attachment to the "mothering one." It describes how the mother's presence is implicated in the baby's profoundest pleasures, creating impressions in the baby of boundless perfection and well-being. The holding mother becomes the measure by which the infant's inborn energies begin to prompt him to reach out into the "not-mother" world, when the maturational forces motivate him to abandon "lapdom," until he gradually reaches the acme of his illusion of having become the upright, walking-away conqueror of the ever-widening expanses of his world. For this to happen under optimal circumstances, the mother has to remain the fairly reliable home base of the infant, available for emotional refueling.

In the course of Kaplan's elaboration of these processes, she convinces you about the importance of the mother's—but also the father's—attainment of or retention of their faith in the solidity and rightfulness of their own, every-so-often turbulent, emotional reactions to the rapidly changing choreography of their infant's growth from limbo to his subjective grandeur (at eleven to fifteen or sixteen months), a conqueror who has the illusion that the world is his oyster. The parents' self-confidence is especially needed during the second part of the second year of the child's life, which I named "rapprochement," and which flows into the open-ended period of "constancy" during the third year and beyond.

I always found that the most difficult task for the chronicler of psychological birth was to convey, without laborious technical terms, the essence of the toddler's ending the love affair with the world, when he is bound—destined as it were —to enter the fifteen- to sixteen-month-old's *thinking* world. Imperceptibly, to the noninitiated, the toddler begins to have a mind that can create words (symbols), images and finally concepts. An inner (intrapsychic) life takes over gradually the hitherto predominantly action-body-mind.

With this fateful step, with this new mind, the toddler does not have to have an actual "mother in the flesh" right before his eyes. He may act as though he is Mommy; he is able to pretend playfully. By acting as though he is Mommy, however, the toddler reveals his growing awareness that he and his mother are different and separate beings. The grandiose conqueror who felt one with the world is more or less suddenly overwhelmed by his sense of aloneness, small-ness and separateness.

Dr. Kaplan describes in detail the struggle which dominates the second half of the second year of life that strives to restore the senior toddler's waning belief in his omnipotence by sharing with Mother and Father and concomitantly building up his own autonomous, individual self. The mother's and father's comforting presence is recaptured in the toddler's *make-believe*—with which he assures himself that aloneness can be coped with. The inside mother becomes more and more part of him.

Within a month or two of his dawning awareness of separateness, a more or less dramatic, shorter- or longer-lasting crisis occurs even in the most normal child with the best ordinary, devoted mother. Knowledge about this normative, unavoidable crisis at around eighteen months, I feel, is the most crucial finding that psychoanalytic child observation has unearthed. Dr. Kaplan graphically describes this crisis in Chapter Six, in the section titled "Clinging and Pushing Away, Shadowing and Darting Away, Holding On and Letting Go." The insight which this book gives the reader about the happenings inside the child's mind, and the various and varied reactions of individually different mothers, is one of the most fascinating renderings of this cardinal juncture of the growing-up process.

Kaplan describes how, in most instances, "the tumultuous choreography of the crisis calms down, leaving a wake of expanded space for growth and further movement into self-hood. The eighteen- to twenty-four-month-old child is on the crest of a new mode of organizing experiences.

That Dr. Kaplan was able, in addition, to encompass the anthropological, historical data that highlight the uni-versality of human symbiosis and strivings for separate individual entity and identity is one more testimony to her gifts. Not least, she has achieved a difficult integration of the psychological and the cultural without falling into the error of reductionism.

We are reminded at every step of the way that to proceed from the psychology of mother-infant interaction to adult cultural forms we must take account of innumerable, complex transformations—transformations which artists and scientists alike have only just begun to appreciate.

MARGARET S. MAHLER, M.D., Sc.D. (Med.)
December 5, 1977

Introduction

In the first three years of life every human being undergoes yet a second birth, in which he is born as a psychological being possessing selfhood and separate identity. The quality of self an infant achieves in those crucial three years will profoundly affect all of his subsequent existence.

Nearly two decades ago, Margaret S. Mahler, a world-renowned child psychoanalyst, first described the stages leading to the acquisition of the sense of self.

Mahler was born in a town at the border between Austria and Hungary. She took her psychoanalytic training in Vienna. Like many European analysts, she was a refugee from the Nazi holocaust. Trained as a pediatrician, while still in Vienna she had changed course to become a psychoanalyst with a particular interest in child analysis and the psychoanalytic investigation of child development. After a brief period in London, she emigrated with her husband to the United States.

Shortly after arriving in the United States in the early 1940s, Mahler began to discover a relationship between the tic syndrome in children and the child's intolerance for separation from the mother. Underlying this intolerance in most children who suffered from tics, Mahler found, was a fear of acquiring a sense of separate identity. Mahler's 1943 paper on the tic syndrome was instantly recognized as a classic.

By 1948 Mahler had uncovered a parallel set of conflicts

in her very young psychotic patients. Moreover, she was impressed by the similarities between these psychotic children and the normal infants she had seen as a pediatrician and head of a well-baby clinic in the 1920s. In spite of the immense differences between a normal infant and a psychotic child, Mahler realized that they were alike in that neither had been tuned in to the outside world: The normal infant has not yet achieved psychological birth; the psychotic child has remained in that twilight state of existence where he does not seem to know where he begins and where the other leaves off. Neither has achieved a sense of self.

To portray the normal state of oneness between mother and child, Mahler borrowed from biology the term *symbiosis*. She named the pathology of her young patients *symbiotic psychosis*. Her later studies of the stages of normal psychological birth grew out of her theory of the symbiotic origins of human existence.

Normally an infant learns to use his mother as a "beacon of orientation" during the first five months of life. The mother's presence is like a fixed light that gives the child the security to move out safely to explore the world and then return safely to harbor. She makes the world of time and space sensible and intelligible. As the child separates from the state of oneness with his mother, he continues to have an inner experience of a mothering presence which orients him in the world. A child who traverses the symbiotic phase normally has been able to build up an experience of an "inner mother." He therefore is able to take the necessary steps toward personal independence and separate identity.

Since the normal child carries a reliable inner mother, he does not fear that the attainment of a separate self will cast him adrift in a chaotic, alien world. The symbiotic psychotic child, on the other hand, has been unable to make effective use of the mother as a beacon of orientation. The few fragments of inner mother he carries with him are unreliable. Therefore, he is terrified to move ahead toward separation and separate selfhood.

But for the symbiotic psychotic child, oneness with mother is just as terrifying as separateness. In contrast to the primarily autistic child, who has never made any tie to the mother, the symbiotic psychotic child has had *some* of the benefits of the symbiotic relationship with his mother. He has taken *some* steps toward becoming a separate self, and what little sense of self he has acquired that is separate from his mother is already precious to him.

He is thus forever plagued by two related but contradictory fears: He fears separation because he has an inadequate inner mother orienting him to the world, and when the challenges of separate functioning arise, the child attempts to restore a feeling of oneness; but the merging of oneness is also terrifying because it threatens the loss of the separate self.

The symbiotic psychotic child comes to dread oneness as much as separateness, and these conflicts periodically strain to the breaking point the fragile structure of his personality. Rather than continue to struggle, he regresses even further in his development, to the stage that precedes oneness—the autistic stage. Here the child no longer has conflict and no longer struggles. His only relationship is with the inanimate, nonhuman environment. The break with humanness is total.

Mahler felt that it was necessary to understand more thoroughly the meaning of separateness and the establishment of selfhood. The findings of her studies of childhood psychosis led to her investigation of the steps by which the vast majority of infants emerge from the state of symbiosis. Mahler posed the questions: How do normal children separate their self-images from the images of the mother? How do they go through the gradual process of psychological birth?

In 1959 Mahler, along with Dr. Manuel Furer, embarked on a pilot study of the normal steps in the development of the self. Their research was conducted through virtually continuous daily observations of the interactions between normal babies and their average mothers during the first three years of the infant's life.

At the conclusion of the first part of this research project, Mahler was able to hypothesize the four stages of normal separation-individuation that followed the normal autistic and normal symbiotic periods of life. In 1963 she began the second phase of her observations of normal babies, which eventually led to the confirmation of her hypothesis.

Mahler's discovery of the phases of separation-individuation came at a crucial moment in psychoanalytic history. Many psychoanalysts had deemed the infant's earliest relationships inaccessible to psychoanalytic investigation because they occur during the "preverbal" period of life. In some circles it was argued that direct child observation was incompatible with a psychological method that based its interpretations on a patient's verbalized, fantasied reconstructions of childhood. Mahler was a pioneer in two respects: She believed in the vital significance of the preverbal mother-child interaction and in the value of direct child observation.

Increasingly, psychoanalysts were to become aware of the importance of the preverbal period, as the patients that came to their offices and clinics presented problems that could not be understood or properly treated by attending solely to the vicissitudes of the Oedipus complex. In fact, just around the time of Mahler's initial investigations, psychoanalysts were realizing that the Oedipus complex itself is shaped by the early mother-child relationship. Mahler illuminated the events that precede the oedipal resolutions. By demonstrating the primary significance of the mother and clarifying the differing reactions to separation of female and male children, Mahler has amplified and enriched the concept of the Oedipus complex. Her delineation of a child's moves from oneness into separateness and selfhood has extended the possibilities of the psychoanalytic method.

Between the devastation of outright symbiotic psychosis, which occurs only about once in ten million instances, and the classical psychoneurosis for which the psychoanalytic method was originally elaborated is the wide range of borderline and so-called narcissistic disorders that have come to typify the pathology of our contemporary societies. The sub-phases of separation-individuation provide a more precise way of understanding the vast number of today's patients whose chief symptoms are inadequate selfhood, narcissistic vulnerability and emotional detachment. These disturbances are now believed to originate in deficiencies and weaknesses in the separation-individuation process.

There is no question that in the near future Mahler's discoveries will leave their imprint on methods of child-rearing. The issues of separation-individuation touch upon every aspect of our ordinary daily lives and also on our illusions and dreams of human perfectibility. It can be hoped that an appreciation of the dilemmas and reconciliations of oneness and separateness will serve as a bulwark against the antihuman social forces that make us all a little deranged, detached, disenchanted, cynical.

In the end, Mahler discovered the process that begins the shaping of a human being. When this process goes wrong, a human being will have difficulties loving others, nurturing the young, taming his own aggression, knowing the boundaries of immediate time and space, mourning the dead and caring about the destiny of the human species.

To the Reader

In the Notes I express my indebtedness to Margaret Mahler, who first brought the story of oneness and separateness to light. Were it not for Mahler's formulations of the meaning of the symbiotic origins of human existence and her discovery of the separation-individuation process, the book you are about to read could not have been written.

The Notes also contain my acknowledgments to the many psychoanalysts, child psychologists, anthropologists and philosophers whose theories and observations helped to substantiate and amplify the full significance of Mahler's work. Since my main concern has been to convey the *spirit* of the inner psychological forces that are believed to govern the psychological birth of the human infant, I have not wished to interrupt the narrative to go into the controversies over some of the details of infant and child development that I have delineated. These are elaborated in the Notes.

Furthermore, there are numerous passages that a reader is likely to question—"How do we know this?" Usually the Notes will cite the studies that support these passages. Most of the studies are based on experimental or observational evidence. Others are primarily theoretical. In the latter instance the evidence is inferential.

Most significantly, the Notes contain some of the living qualifiers of my story of a *prototypical* process. Those who already understand what it's like to be a baby or a parent will recognize themselves in the main body of the narrative.

Nevertheless, no one child or mother or father could possibly follow the course of the second birth to the letter of the prototype I have described.

For all these reasons, I regard the Notes as an essential adjunct to the main narrative and not as a bibliography or reference list in the accepted scholarly tradition. I strongly recommend the Notes to your attention.

Finally, I have followed the convention of referring to the child with the pronouns "he" and "him" for clarity—in order to distinguish the baby from the mother.

L. J. K.

My God, but I can only say
I touch, I feel the unknown!
I am the first comer!
Cortes, Pisarro, Columbus, Cabot,
*   they are nothing, nothing!*
I am the first comer!
I am the discoverer!
I have found the other world!

The unknown, the unknown!
I am thrown upon the shore.
I am covering myself with the sand.
I am filling my mouth with the earth.
I am burrowing my body into the soil.
The unknown, the new world!

"New Heaven and Earth"
D. H. Lawrence

Tie the Strings to my Life, My Lord,
Then, I am ready to go!
Just a look at the Horses—
Rapid! That will do!

Put me in on the firmest side—
So I shall never fall—
For we must ride to the Judgment—
And it's partly, down Hill—

But never I mind the steepest—
And never I mind the Sea—
Held fast in Everlasting Race—
By my own Choice, and Thee—

Goodbye to the Life I used to live—
And the World I used to know—
And kiss the Hills, for me, just once—
Then—I am ready to go!

Emily Dickinson

Chapter One

Constancy

There were once well-defined, culturally standardized modes of adaptation to the events that comprise the life of a human being. Now we are confronted with increasingly complex styles of adaptation to major life events such as marriage, pregnancy, birth, parenthood, old age and death. We find ourselves stranded without credible social structures. Our own inner authority fluctuates. We face the major events of life with doubt and confusion.

When the emotional structure of the family was more certain, children accepted parental authority out of a sense of obligation and devotion. And from their parents they acquired the firm and rigid ideals that later allowed them to act, albeit inflexibly, with confidence and inner authority toward their own children.

Unfortunately, in the transition from an authoritarian family to an individualistic one that had been expected to encourage flexibility and freedom of choice, the soil of family structure shifted too rapidly and too frequently to nourish the positive values of individualism.

Uncertainty of authority did not bring about broader sensibilities. Opportunities for personal growth and self-realization shut down rather than opening up. With everyone clamoring for self-fulfillment and identity expansion, why do mournful sighs of emptiness and hopelessness pervade the modern consciousness? Why have our strivings for individuality made us feel unloved and unlovable?

No doubt answers could be gathered from an examination of our current educational, political, economic and religious institutions, which in addition to decaying from inner corruption, were apparently designed by a mad architect whose deliberate plan was to alienate us from one another and to wrench us from the soil that would nourish humanness and self-fulfillment.

An alternative is to explore the biological origins of our longings for human attachment and individuality, our possibilities for despair and disappointment. In these times when it has become fashionable to elevate social forces as the liberators of the human spirit, we have come to disparage biology as its fetter. Every now and then we need reminding that a healthy respect for our biological roots is the best protection against the invasion and domination of antihuman social forces.

Certainly nowhere is the disparagement of the biological more evident than in our current view of motherhood. Motherhood has come into conflict with our postindustrial mentality, a mentality that locates a person's most significant activity outside the home and therefore questions the possibility of self-realization through motherhood. The self-absorbing solitude of mother and infant is interpreted as a lamentable turning away from activity that is considered more socially productive. Legions of women who wish to have children and devote themselves for a time to the care of their children are shamed into believing that such a wish amounts to a capitulation to sexist and antiquated social values intended to exile them to a doll's house. In the rush to "return to normal," to "get on with the business of *real* life" and to compete in the race for career and social advancement, the modern mother is deprived of her rightful experience of mothering.

The confidence and pleasure that make it possible for a

woman to respond leisurely and sensitively to her baby's needs have been jeopardized. It is ironic that the vital importance of a human infant's *attachment* to his mother should be subverted by shame and impatience at the very moment in history when the complaints of human *detachment* are loudest. Modern social forces conspire to interrupt the elemental dialogue between mother and infant—the dialogue that insures our humanity.

The science fiction nightmares of robot humans, test-tube babies and mechanized love have not become a reality, but they loom everywhere—in television cartoons for children, contemporary fiction and cinema, genetic engineering, architecture and in our personal nightmares. As we plunge unthinkingly into the very emptiness we fear, something in us continues to resist. Our essential humanity demands attention. For the time being at least, the human dialogue goes on.

Where does the dialogue begin? In his first partnership outside the womb, the infant is filled up with the bliss of unconditional love—the bliss of oneness with his mother. This is the basic dialogue of human love. The next series of mother-infant dialogues concern the way the infant separates from the state of oneness with the mother. As he separates he will learn the conditions of actual love and acquire the sense that he is himself and nobody else. All later human love and dialogue is a striving to reconcile our longings to restore the lost bliss of oneness with our equally intense need for separateness and individual selfhood. These reconciliations are called *constancy*.

The reconciliations of constancy are manifold. We spend most of our adult life solving and re-solving the dilemmas of our second birth. Because we all began this second, or psychological, birth in a state of oneness with mother, and achieved selfhood by gradually recognizing our separateness from her, these dilemmas are the inevitable lot of every human being—of every human society.

As he moves out of the limbo of newbornness and into oneness with his mother, the infant molds his body to hers. From the infant's point of view there are no boundaries between himself and mother. They are one. This is how we first discovered merging bliss and inner harmony. This is how our psychological birth began. In molding oneness we were all-good and everything that surrounded us matched up with our inner sensations of pleasure and goodness. Yet all was not harmony in these early months. Disturbing tensions, feelings of loss of balance, extremes of heat or cold, digestive upsets, made us stiffen away from mother—away from bliss and body-molding oneness. Already our minds were marked with the dangers of separateness. Separateness was equated with pain. Why then did we ever leave oneness and strive to become our own separate self? As strong as the longings for oneness were equally powerful urges to move away, to seek distance, to explore the world outside the mother-infant orbit, to be a self.

No one had to tell us when to move out of the blissful kingdom of our mother's lap. The urges to separate were inside us—in our body-mind, in the liveliness of our own growth energies, in the vitality of our stiffening-away muscles, in our looking eyes, our listening ears, our reaching-out hands.

From the dialogue of oneness the infant gradually becomes aware of his mother's presence out-there, in the world. When he is five months old, her presence lights his way to the small familiar world outside their commonly shared orbit. In his wariness with strangers and in the way he checks back to his mother's face for reassurances, the eight-month-old tells us that he is still cautious about separateness. By twelve months his moves away from mother are more courageous. The child stands up and walks away. With these steps, as he walks away on his own, the child's body-mind has reached its moment of perfection. The world is his—and he, the mighty conqueror of all he beholds.

His joyousness and grandeur show in the exhilaration of his running, jumping and climbing, staring and naming.

However, at the height of this joyous period of his life, an infant is still not able to comprehend that he and mother are separate beings. His exhilaration is partly based on the illusion that the world is his mother—that her presence pervades the world. Not until he is around eighteen months, when his body-mind is joined by an imperfect thinking mind, will the child come to the full awareness that his mother has an existence apart from his own. Then he confronts the crisis of his second birth; he is thrown into turmoil. The joyous mood of the previous months will be replaced by letdown, anger and sadness. The child would want to return to the unconditional bliss of oneness, but now he cannot relinquish his sense of separateness, his overwhelming desire to claim his body and mind as his own. He begins his quest to comprehend the conditions of actual love. For the next year or two he will be learning that it is possible to be a separate self without giving up his sense of goodness and wholeness; that he can retain the love of his parents and his self-love and still possess his own mind and his own body.

By three years, a child will have achieved his initial sense of separateness and identity. However, the reconciliations of oneness and separateness have only begun. The three-year-old has but a small degree of constancy—just enough to allow him to feel safe in the world even though he now recognizes that his self is separate from the self of his mother. He can hold on to a positive image of his mother when he is away at school or visiting friends. He may occasionally long for her presence, but he does not turn separateness from mother into a fantasy that she is a bad, frustrating mother who has ceased to care about him or love him. A young child's sense of well-being comes from his having built up inside him enough good-mother and good-self experience to permit him to continue functioning as a separate self even when he might have angry/hateful thoughts about himself or his parents. The child who has a good-enough self image and a good-enough mother image isn't overwhelmed by his "bad" feelings. He doesn't begin to suppose that he has to be a perfect all-good child or a clinging, helpless nonentity in order to protect himself and his parents from his awful wickedness. When such a child becomes an adult he won't reject someone he loves and exchange her for another the moment she no longer is there to provide him with satisfaction. He will go on valuing her even when she disappoints him and lets him down.

Fundamentally, constancy is our emotional acceptance of the idea that we are neither saints nor demons but whole persons who are capable of ordinary human love *and* ordinary human hatred. By uniting our loving emotions with our emotions of anger and hatred, constancy confirms our sense of personal wholeness. We all strive to protect and uphold the good images of the self. When constancy is weak, the only way to protect the cherished parts of the self from the unwanted or bad parts is to split them apart and to keep them fenced off. When the good and the bad are split apart, the wholeness of the self fragments and disintegrates. And then it becomes impossible to appreciate and respect the wholeness of others.

Personal wholeness and integrity derive equally from both aspects of our psychological birth. The first, or core, experience of wholeness comes from the dialogue of oneness, the dialogue of unconditional love, the heavenly dialogue of merging, body-molding unity when self and other have not yet differentiated. The second experience of wholeness comes after the achievement of separateness, after the formation of the boundaries between the self and the other. This second source of personal wholeness is more complex than the first because it includes all the varied emotions, thoughts, fantasies and values that are involved when we relate to down-to-earth, in-the-flesh actual persons. In the perfection of oneness there is neither self nor other and therefore no true emotional relatedness. Relatedness requires a whole self and a whole other. Yet even as separate, whole persons we never forget that core experience of oneness. Whenever the challenges of separateness become too great we all long to bring back the primary bliss of oneness. This basic human longing to refind our core wholeness is the essence of religion and poetry and the essence of the ecstacies of perfect love.

Constancy then is much more than the capacity to unite love and aggression, or the capacity to maintain the wholeness of the self and the wholeness of the other, or the ability to go on valuing someone even when they no longer provide us with pleasure and satisfaction. Constancy is also the reconciliation of our everlasting longings for perfection with our down-to-earth daily existence. In this way constancy unites the serene harmonies of oneness with the vitality and rhythms of separateness. Though oneness is the essence of love, the vitality of love comes from the partnership of two whole, in-the-flesh human beings who respect each other's separateness. Ultimately every facet of human existence is reflected in the reconciliations of oneness and separateness.

By watching a child as he discovers the core and limits of his being, our comprehension of the meaning of existence is expanded. This special vision of childhood helps us to become more aware of the direction and movement of our adult life. To observe the sequences that transform a totally physical, unrelated, unthinking newborn into a three-year-old who is a self-aware, psychological being with the emotions and fantasies that give him a unique identity is to journey back into one's own infancy and childhood.

For those who can still recognize the child in themselves this is a fascinating journey. However, in the process of becoming adult many people learn that they must put away childish things, that they must cast out the foolishness and uncertainties of childish ways. The past is done and buried. They have no wish to reopen Pandora's box. They are ashamed to admit that they occasionally feel insecure and helpless, that they are needy and dependent, that they are still vulnerable to disappointment and humiliation. By their definition, the self-sufficient, successful adult is a person who has rid himself of childlike passions and fears. Is it possible that an adult clings to the safety of home and personal possessions the way an infant clings to his security blanket? Or that something inside an adult still quivers with apprehension when he meets a stranger? Or that when he bets on horses or becomes enthralled with ghost stories and melodramas he might be playing a peek-a-boo game with Fate? Or that his prowess in the boudoir often ends up as a catch-me game in which he is running desperately from some menacing catcher of babies?

There are reasons to reject such direct comparisons between the child and the adult. An adult is justified in turning away from the suggestion that his actions are mere replications of his childhood behavior. The complex behaviors of an adult can never be reduced to their infantile origins. An adult does not gamble because he played peek-a-boo as a child; a man does not run from his bed partner because he once was desperate to separate from his mother. By the time we reach adulthood the blunt passions of infancy have been enriched and transformed many times over. Our adult actions are but distant echoes, distorted reflections, metaphorical paraphrases of the events of our second birth. Even so, adulthood is not the end of childhood or the completion of a journey that goes only forward. The maturing adult is continually reliving and revising his memories of childhood, refinding his identity, reforging the shape of his selfhood, discovering new facets of his being.

Words like *identity, self, being* conjure mystery; they seem abstract and unfathomable. But the sequences that lead to the formation of a psychological self are to be seen in the quite commonplace actions of the infant and young child. Parents have always noticed these behaviors and even participated in them. What has been elusive and unknown is their exceptional and extraordinary meaning. We have not known that these everyday behaviors were expressions of the child's movement into selfhood and constancy; that each of us was made into a whole human being by the small miracles of everyday life; that we continue to grow and change when we can resonate with the miracles that constitute the round of our ordinary adult existence.

When such familiar aspects of childhood as security blankets, peek-a-boo and catch-me games, the first smile, learning to walk, no-saying and temper tantrums are viewed from the perspective of our second birth, we comprehend the child in our adult self. We understand why children give us hope and also why sometimes they frighten and bewilder us.

Hopefulness is the heartbeat of the relationship between a parent and child. Each time a child overcomes the next challenge of his life, his triumph encourages new growth in his parents. In this sense a child is parent to his mother and father. The mother who is not ashamed or frightened of childish things will recognize in her child's struggles for separate selfhood her own still-evolving reconciliations, her own longings for oneness, and her own continuing search for selfhood. It is easy for a mother to be hopeful when her child says "yes" to her milk, embraces, soothing gestures, educational advice, restrictions and values. However, it is difficult to appreciate the hopefulness in a child's no-saying. Only a fantasy child conforms to all the wishes and expectations of his parents. An actual child does not always respond affirmatively. He does not always gratify his parents' hopes and fantasies. An actual child challenges his mother to remember that she was once an actual child who struggled against her parents, a child who often turned her head the other way. If a mother can appreciate the meaning of these challenges, she does not begin to see in her child's rebellious turning-away everything she has come to despise in her own self. She does not become hopeless and despairing when her child does not accept her advice or live up to her expectations, when he turns from her gestures of love and goes his own way.

Frequently parents interpret a child's necessary steps to becoming a separate person as signs of rejection and as indications of their own inadequacy and failure. So much of the childhood behavior that engenders self-recrimination in a parent does not really represent failure in the parent but rather the child's need to establish his own sense of identity.

One of the most bewildering periods in the child's attainment of separateness comes toward the middle of his second year of life, when his defiance, sadness, willfulness and disappointed anger cast a dark shadow over the relationship with the mother. These unwelcome and frightening events are the signs that the child has at last come face to face with the decisive moments of his second birth, that he is recognizing that he is truly a separate being.

During this difficult time the immature mind of the child perceives experience in absolutes. He tends to associate his natural defiance and anger with the idea that he must be an all-bad monster child who is not worthy of love. Similarly the normal frustrations and restrictions imposed by the mother seem to turn her into an all-bad monster mother who will never again be capable of giving and loving. The child forgets that he was ever lovable or loved, and that his mother was ever good or gratifying. He longs for that magical time when he was an angel child with a mother he could control absolutely.

As he approaches the third year of life, the child begins to be able to piece together the thought that the mother who sometimes frustrates him is the same mother who also loves and cares for him. He also begins to realize that he does not turn into a worthless, all-bad child every time he has angry, hateful thoughts and emotions. He does not have to be perfect in order to feel that he is lovable. Such realizations are the first indications that the child is learning to be constant in the face of life's inevitable disappointments and frustrations.

Constancy is the enduring inner conviction of being me and nobody else. When constancy prevails we are able to respect and value the separateness of others. We go on loving them even when they cannot fill us up with the perfect harmonies of unconditional love. Through constancy the perfect is united with the real. Every move into separate selfhood from birth until three years makes its distinctive contribution to constancy and brings with it new potentials for love and hate, mastery and fear, trust and suspicion, elation and disappointment.

Subsequent life is a series of fresh opportunities to enlarge on the initial potential for constancy that emerges from the strivings of the second birth. Provided our beginnings have been good enough and the demands of the rest of life are not harsh or oppressive, constancy of self and constancy toward others will be enriched by the ordinary vicissitudes of human existence.

Those earliest days of our beginnings are never experienced exactly as they were. What happens is that they become subtly transformed by each subsequent opportunity of our life history. The rivalries and fears of the mother-child-father oedipal triangle, the period of learning to participate in the social world outside the home, the adolescent's broader vision of the family ties of his childhood, falling in love and out of love, choosing one's life work and then perhaps rechoosing, pregnancy, parenthood and the trials of middle age and old age, each will effect its peculiar modification of our memories of the first dialogues of oneness and separateness, and each modification will test the durability of our constancy.

However, the incessant variations that are superimposed

on the themes of the second birth do not entirely obscure them. The echoes of these earliest dialogues continue to be prominent in our dialogues with the world—not abstractly, but in the familiar and commonplace and in the illusions that hold us together as we venture forth to embrace the challenges of our everyday lives.

We go through the paces of daily life measuring our way with the logical actions and matter-of-fact thoughts that have gradually come to regulate our personal styles of act-ing in the world. But all the while the nonlogical body-mind with which our psychological life began makes itself known in the choreography of our gestures of love, our movements toward the world, turning away and returning, greeting, smiling, having conversations with our eyes. And, though we have become accustomed to waking and sleeping in tune with the orderly cycles of day and night, in truth the moments of our waking day are punctuated by states mid-way between full alertness and sleep; we are glassy-eyed and inward-turning, often lost in the musing reveries, day-dreams and silent fantasies that soften the stresses of waking life. Our sleep is marked off by periods of half-alert guarded-ness as once again we dream away the pressures of the day. And, every so often just before waking, just before sleeping, in moments of intimacy, while having conversations with our eyes, our bodies relax into that twilight of body-molding oneness with which we began our existence and which was soon interrupted by the impatient vitality of our stiffen-ing muscles pushing us eagerly toward the outer world and into that state of alert consciousness which we later learned had the name "waking."

Similarly, our conscious efforts to interpret and explain the world according to the sophisticated modes of language and thought that took us twenty years of growing to acquire is easily sabotaged by that discordant, two-year-old, not-yet-logical, imperfect, symbol-making mind of absolute goodness and absolute badness. Our two-year-old mind is still with us. And it will stamp its way to the fore whenever the delicate balances of constancy are upset. Then we think of our ordinary imperfections as absolute wickedness; our self-conscious blushes and hesitant words come to mean that we are naked and transparent; disappointment in a loved one becomes that sinking sensation of abandonment and falling into a bottomless abyss. Then separations from home, from loved ones, from our valued possessions, make us feel helpless and alone in the world. And that two-year-old mind follows us into our dream sleep, where angels and monsters rule supreme, where the logic of language becomes the logic of visual images, where visual images are the translations of stomach quiverings, adrenaline secretions, heart flutterings and genital excitements that we wake up to identify as images of standing naked, the roof falling in, drowning in the void, blissful embrace, ascending and falling.

The chairs, tables, books, plants, clothing, hairbrushes, perfumes, pots, dishes and paintings with which we furnish the niche in the world we call home are paraphrases of the dialogues of oneness and separateness. So deeply embedded is the archetype of home that we wonder no more about its genesis than we do about the landmarks between waking and sleeping. Yet the globe is covered with the marked-off circles of human homes. Even nomads who wander from base to base or the remnant tribes of aborigines, who might possess but an amulet, a piece of cloth and the mat on which they sleep, push their lives forward within the geometry of moving away and returning to the centers they call home.

Our attachment to this fixed point from which our lives radiate is a feature we share with all members of the human species in the same way that all humans dream and wake, make gestures of love, greeting and threat, and become self-aware. And, in the firmness or looseness of the boundaries that mark off our home base; in the manner in which we push away or dash away to explore the world outside its boundaries; whom we let through the boundaries and whom we fence out; whether we cling to base or fling ourselves to the far edges of the world as though to escape the bounds of our base—these become central aspects of our personal uniqueness and set us apart from other members of our species. The bravest explorers of Everest or the depths of the Black Sea carry with them an image or replica of home. The most clinging homebodies are alert to the possibilities that lie beyond the doorway.

The origins of our attachment to home are to be found in the infant's earliest attachment to his mother—the mother he begins to use as a home base from which to explore the world as soon as the aliveness of his muscles gird him to creep away from the safety of lapdom into ever-widening circles of the unknown. From then on, though he may roam but a few feet or venture across thresholds into new rooms, his body-mind is anchored by an image of home base.

The possessions that furnish our base pulsate with the dialogues of oneness and separateness. Attachment to possessions represents the infant's earliest conjectures about mine and yours, having and not having, giving and taking, collecting and tossing away, emptiness and fulfillment, as well as the transformations of these conjectures into the civilized motives of envy and power, generosity and loyalty.

Even after we become adult, some possessions are more alive with dialogue than others. These we count as our personal treasures; we do not share them, and if we lose them we are bereft. They testify to the security of home. Merely possessing them gives us the courage to roam. Assured that they will stay fixed on shelves and in closets, we carry their images with us in our minds. Other treasures we make certain actually to carry with us when we leave home base—the coral amulet, the steel-blue pen, the burnished briefcase, the sea-green sweater. As much as these special personal possessions signify the safety of home, they are equally an intimate aspect of our own being. Though they are inanimate we identify with them as though they were alive. The thought of their lying alone on some shelf kindles a sympathetic pang of loneliness. Once having invested a possession with the illusion that it is both a me and a not-me thing that is both animate and inanimate, this possession resonates with metaphor and can come to stand for a multitude of personal attributes and desires—safety, courage, risk-taking, fortune, success, wisdom, generosity or goodness. And though most of us may never create the metaphors of poetry and music, in these treasured possessions we have nonetheless created an illusion. Like all illusions, they help to relieve the strain of relating the wishful longings of our inner life with the imperfections of everyday reality. Like the security blanket or humming sound the young infant creates when the sensations of separateness begin to dawn, our treasured possessions become a perfect mother of oneness who never disappoints us. These possessions are also like the first mother of separation—the mother of home base who stays fixed and permanent no matter how far we wander.

Adult strivings for unity and wholeness continue to find expression in illusions. Illusions help us to maintain that delicate balance between longing and actuality, that anchoring equilibrium at the center of each of us which we call constancy. Though the constancy of the adult is far more complex than the constancy of the three-year-old, our adult versions of constancy echo the journey we once made—the journey we negotiated from the oneness of a body-mind infant to the separateness of an individual who recognizes his mother and the world as being outside the boundaries of the self.

As the body-mind infant created his security blanket when the contradictions between oneness and separateness first began to worry him, so the adult creates the illusions that reconcile his inner longings with the challenges of outer life. By conquering Everest, arranging color and line on canvas, tempering raw berries and flesh into a meal, composing a symphony, turning a possession into a cherished treasure, adoring the Madonna, naming our states of waking and sleeping, we create the illusion that what was torn asunder is once more united and whole.

Human life begins in illusion. It begins with the illusion created by a down-to-earth mother's devotion to her ordinary baby. In her ordinary way of holding him, a mother gives her baby the impression of a world that will hold him together and make sense of the unformed excitements and appetites raging inside him. The baby then has the illusion that his appetites are congruent with the new world he has just entered. As adults, the experience of being held is evoked when the world meets our desires half way. And on those occasions when the world holds us particularly well we may even fill up with the ecstatic harmonies of oneness. It is possible to feel held even when we are all alone and separated from those we love. Aloneness is cherished when it is accompanied by that singular experience of being held. Aloneness is dreaded when it is associated with abandonment and the sinking flutterings that overwhelm us when our desires have no place to go. Then we feel let down.

Although we sometimes suppose otherwise, the earth is not a perfect mother of oneness whose empathic readiness to make sense of our excitements and appetites can be counted on. Inevitably we confront our moments of letdown. Frequently our letdowns are preceded by our greatest expectations and confirmations; after the acclaims of opening night, after the birth of the breathlessly awaited baby, after the longed-for reunion with a lost lover, after the bliss of erotic surrender, after writing the poem's last line. How often we are raised to peaks of exhilarated anticipation by our fantasies of triumph only to come face to face with who we really are. Yet, with hopefulness and high expectation we risk melting our wings, as every once in a while we break out of the boundaries and edges of our usual selves. Given the opportunity, we do not choose to cling to the safety of the humdrum plains. We chance our letdowns as we entrust ourselves to the arms of others. We go on hoping and trusting even though our exaltations are brief and we realize that those we count on most surely will disappoint us most.

And we manage to hold together when the world lets us down. Although we feel temporarily abandoned and vulnerable, constancy prevails. We retain enough of a sense of our personal worth and the worth of others eventually to convert disenchantment and disappointment into challenge. Constancy enables us to bend with the shifting winds and still remain rooted to the earth that nourishes us. At times, we even yield to the sudden changes of the wind and allow ourselves to be swept away from the enchantments of the past and the security of home base. Though temporarily cast adrift, the permanence and constancy of our sense of self holds us and lights the way. Then the challenges of the unknown and unfamiliar are shaped into broader visions of who we are and who we might become.

Occasionally we are hurled upward to the white heavens of ecstasy or downward into the black caves of despair. The moods of ecstasy and despair are the extremes which make the world appear to be all-fulfilling or all-withholding. They blind us to the hues of ordinary life. But for the most part we stay rooted to the yellow-orange, blue-green, gray-blue, red-brown surface of the earth. The moods of constancy are as subtle and varied as the semiprecious colors of the earth. With such moods, we interpret the earth as a good enough, solid place and we comprehend its finite possibilities for giving nourishment and withholding it. And, with the emotions of constancy, such as love, surprise, anger, fear, contentment, joy, grief and remorse, we remain loyal to the earth.

For some the white and black moods, all-or-none emotions and primitive logic of the two-year-old continue to hold

sway. Out of the interrupted dialogues and half-consum-
mated appetites of their second birth emerged a self that
could not endure or prevail. The markings of the first outline
of separate identity are shadowy, too blurred and uncertain
to permit the succeeding transformations that reshape constancy and selfhood to exert their full influence. So in later
life each challenge is defended against as though it were a
violent invasion.

The fragment of yet-unforged constancy that such people
wrested from the second birth is easily shattered by disappointment. For them what begins as a simple low of letdown
will sink to an abyss of breaking down and falling to bits.
The world that momentarily lets them down is then perceived as an eternally uncaring, eternally withholding world.
In the months that follow the disappointment they pine
away with longings to restore the crystal harmonies of oneness or they sink into despair. Some are swept away in the
boundless fury of a hurricane rage which never settles down
into the calm of anger and grief.

Lacking the constancy that would allow them to reconcile
the contradictions between oneness and separateness, these
people regulate their lives by splitting experience into the
irreconcilable dichotomies of all-good and all-bad. Exalted
when they imagine they are completely filled up and perfectly held or when they omnipotently control the comings
and goings of others, they feel humiliated and worthless
when they fall from grace. They idealize those whom they
can coerce into becoming the all-giving, perfectly holding
partner who will sustain their image of self-perfection. Although they idealize their partners, they use them ruthlessly
as though they were mere extensions of the self; they use
them to manipulate and destroy potential enemies; they use
them in order to experience the pride that comes from
possessing a perfect partner.

Such greed with regard to other people breeds the everlasting emptiness that is the silent dread of those without

constancy. Inevitably they use up the all-perfect partner, who after all is just an ordinary person who sometimes frustrates, who can't gratify magical wishes, a person whose comings and goings cannot be omnipotently controlled. Frustration and disappointment evoke rage and fury—a wish to eradicate these contradictions of omnipotence. But if rage were to be expressed, the partner might turn into a powerful enemy, a retaliatory monster. The safer course is to make sure the frustrator is emptied of all power. It's easier to denigrate her, to see her as a worthless nothing, a nobody who has no value at all. To the extent that the partner was once overvalued, she is now devalued. Now that the all-perfect partner has been emptied out and cast away, the world becomes a barren terrain—until the next all-perfect partner comes along.

The unending search for a perfect partner whose comings and goings can be magically coerced is one way to cover up inner emptiness and feelings of vulnerability. Another way of masking vulnerability is not to care whether or not anyone comes or anyone goes. Such an alternative is exemplified by the haughty aloofness of the narcissist who loves only the reflections of the grand person he imagines himself to be, the spectacular person he once was, or the mighty person he would have wished to be. For love he seeks out his own mirror image: an adored face that reflects what he wished he could be or still wishes he might become, or simply an adoring face that will reflect his current grandiosity. When the mirroring partner no longer sustains him, she vanishes into nothingness. Yet her disappearance counts for nothing. The narcissist will turn his eyes to the next adoring/adored face. But, even the most successful of these haughty, uncaring lovers one day turns around to face emptiness. What he feared most—terrible aloneness in the world—becomes a reality.

Exclusively clinging or exclusively mirroring love splits apart the mutualities of constant partnership—devotion, loyalty and admiration. Constant love is the reconciliation between self-love and love for others. Those who love themselves just enough will trust themselves to the arms of others —without clinging to them in desperation.

Whereas splitting destroys the connections that make life whole, constancy is the magnet that holds our emotional world together. It sets us firm in the orbit of our separate selfhood. From this perspective we are able to appreciate and value the independence of other orbits.

Dazzled with the bliss of love, we imagine that our being is merged with the being of the one we love. Or, overcome with awful disappointment, we long to be held forever in the embrace of a powerful protector. And when the celebration dies down we lean toward someone whose eyes continue to reflect our glory. But those blissfully loving and all-protecting arms, those mirroring eyes, do not suddenly cease to exist, to count for nothing, when bliss recedes into ordinary devotion or when we can once again stand firmly on our own two feet.

Emotional constancy is analogous to the way we reconcile our personal perspectives with the rules that govern the world of time and space. As the magnificent liner glides down the river to the ocean its image gets smaller, but we do not then believe that it is becoming a mere toy in a bathtub. And though the moon sometimes seems to shine only for us, reappearing from behind the clouds and loyally following our elusive path, the knowledge that it remains fixed in its own orbit is never altogether forgotten.

Constancy helps us withstand the vicissitudes of fate and fortune. But sometimes fortune is too harsh for even the most courageous and firmly rooted. There are letdowns that are unbearable; a home swept away by fire or hurricane, forced retirement from a lifelong job, the desertion of a loved one, the stillborn baby, the death of a child or a parent. When disaster strikes, the absence of community that is typical of our alienating contemporary societies leaves us totally vulnerable and unprepared.

Our disenchantments with funeral arrangements and cemetery rituals, our inability to share our sorrows, our shame at admitting temporary helplessness and hopelessness, our cynicism toward any public display of caring or concern, our hurried, crowded lives that have no time or room for the unwelcome anxieties and letdowns that are essential aspects of our humanness—all these force us to lock up grief, to confront our personal crises as though we were all alone in the world, as though there were no one to turn to. Emotional constancy survives only in the contexts of partnership and community. When we are left alone to mourn our losses, then splitting takes over.

Even normal mourning involves a mild degree of splitting. Anyone we have profoundly loved has also been the target of our most violent thoughts and fantasies. With constancy we accept the idea that no human being is perfectly good or absolutely evil; we accept the imperfections of our loved ones and hold on to a sense of their goodness even when their personal devils torment us the most. We tolerate our ambivalence toward them and see them as whole human beings with both frailties and virtues. We do not cast out the part of our self that sometimes thinks wicked thoughts about the ones we love. We retain our wholeness and the wholeness of the loved and sometimes hated other. However, when a loved one dies, we can no longer tolerate the thought that sometimes we hated him and sometimes treated him with lack of concern or caring. Nor can we tolerate any vision of him as less than perfect. If the dead must be idealized, then who becomes the target of our hatred? We mourn by singing the praises of the dead and by hating ourselves a bit; traditionally we tear our hair, shred our clothes, turn away from pleasures, dress in somber clothes, weep with despair. And even when we spurn tradition, we often unconsciously adopt the mannerisms and foibles of the dead one—usually the very traits that tormented us the most while they were alive. By identifying with the dead we keep them alive inside us. We stave off the finality of death.

The guilt and self-recrimination of mourning are difficult to bear when we feel that we are all alone in the world. This is why tradition instructs us not to lock up our grief, not to mourn silently. We share our deep sadness with others, unashamedly displaying our tears, our sense of loss, our regrets that we did not behave better toward the loved one when he was still alive, our childish wishes for the loved one to return so that we now could do all the good for him that we neglected to do when he was here. By sharing these thoughts and feelings, our normal mourning subsides. We gradually stop punishing ourselves. We begin to remember the dead as they actually were. Soon afterward we can even bear the idea that sometimes they were hateful and that we hated them. The wholeness of the other and the wholeness of the self are restored.

Our normal propensity to idealize the dead and find another target for our anger is intensified when we are too fragile to bear guilt or profound grief. Then splitting takes over completely. When his parent dies, a young child has too fragile a sense of constancy to sustain the pain of guilt, so he manages his sadness and anger by inflicting all his hatreds on the surviving parent and remembering only the perfection of the parent who died.

An adult whose constancy is weak, an adult who cannot bear regret or guilt, might mourn the death of his mother much the way a child would. However, in the adult mourner splitting can sometimes become extreme. It can turn the self-hatred of guilt into a violent, impotent rage which gets focused outside the self. The man who cannot tolerate the guilt of mourning might then vent this rage on his wife, disparaging and denigrating her as though she embodied all the tyrannies he once knew in his mother. If his mother had tyrannized him by possessing his mind and body as though they were extensions of her own self, he will accuse his wife of having possessed his mind and body and robbed him of his selfhood. But impotent rage toward his wife is only half the job. He must also find a place to locate his mother's holiness—her ample breasts, her sumptuous lap, her comforting arms, her adorations of his mind and body. He finds a place in another woman, a woman ready to become the receptacle of his mother's virtues, a woman he can idealize with a passion equaled only by his savage hatred of his wife. Now his vilification of his wife can proceed safely. He has kept his mother alive, her wickedness in one place, her perfections in another. Finally he succeeds in transforming his wife into the monstrous mother he once dreaded. And the adoring/adored one does not survive the weight of his expectations for perfection: Her idealized image crumbles into nothingness as he begins to see her as the ordinary person she actually is. In the end, the world has been emptied of every shred of goodness and virtue. At last he is all alone, with the devils of his childhood locked inside him—which is the way self hatred gets expressed when splitting takes over the job of mourning the dead.

Constancy is the force that creates unity out of the disparate and often contradictory images of self and other. The part of the self that longs for merging oneness remains connected to the part of the self that stands alone and holds on to the right to possess one's own mind, body, thoughts, special treasures, fantasies and illusions. With splitting there is neither the ecstasy of oneness nor the exhilarated vitality of separateness that joins two down-to-earth people in partnerships of devotion, loyalty, playfulness, camaraderie, angry disappointment and grief. Splitting precludes the possibilities of whole human beings.

Those whose inner world is split into the all-good and the all-bad cannot move freely between oneness and separateness. They turn away from ordinary partnership. They furiously reject those who might act as though they had a right to a separate existence. A person whose deepest fear is that someone will discover the vulnerable child beneath his magnificent cloak of grandiosity cannot stand vulnerability and imperfection in his adoring/adored ones. He must continually reinflate his deflated image by sharing in someone else's power. He must shine in the glory of the perfect partner. When the glitter of his partner fades to reveal an in-the-flesh actual person, he will devalue her and cast her away. Sooner or later the world will turn its back on him for his shallowness, his lack of empathy or real concern for others, his ruthless manipulations, his desperate adorations. He will have been so successful in hiding his helplessness and vulnerability that no one will realize that he should be pitied and cared for. Ultimately fortune will deal him the very hand his quivering apprehensions have presaged. He is never filled up or held. He is indeed unloved and unlovable. But, most of all, the unspeakable fear that he is powerless and vulnerable is substantiated. He is not omnipotent; he cannot magically will the comings and goings of those to whom he clings with such desperate neediness.

At the peak of his early months of omnipotent, merging oneness, the infant is already beginning to become aware that the comings and goings of his mother are not entirely ruled by his appetites and excitements. From then on he is a gambler with the inevitabilities of separateness. His four-month-old mind—even though it is still a simple body-mind of sucking mouth, looking eyes, listening ears, turning head, reaching-out hands, stiffening muscles and inner rhythms of tension and relaxation—begins to reckon with fate. As powerless as he actually is, the baby who has the confidence of oneness and the courageous vitality of alert eyes and reaching-out hands finds a way to take charge of his destiny.

Though he doesn't know it, much of the infant's courage

comes to him through the changing dialogue he has begun to have with his mother. The merging bliss of oneness dialogue is joined by a dialogue that appreciates separateness. Yet the illusion of oneness is still maintained. Oneness love is the passive love of merging bodies, the blending of the tensions and relaxations of two bodies that become one. There is no need for words or conversation. This is just the right kind of dialogue for mother-infant oneness and for the beginnings of any love relationship. However, if the lovers do not go on to appreciate one another's separateness, love will stagnate. As the boundaries between the self and the other begin to build, lovers begin to have conversations with their eyes and fingertips, conversations that say, "You may go away but I will always be here when you return." "I know I can go away, and you will still be here when I return."

By four months the passive dialogue of molding bodies is supplemented by the active rhythms of mother-infant conversation. The mother has caught on to the idea that her baby adores the excitement of initiating and terminating his own conversations. As he waves his arms and kicks his legs with anticipation, the baby turns his face toward his mother's face. He gurgles and coos. His mother answers him by intuitively matching the pitch and tone of his sounds. Gradually their mutual excitement builds. Soon the two of them are "speaking" simultaneously. When the baby has had enough excitement he averts his gaze from his mother's face for a moment or two. Then, with complete confidence, he turns his face back to find his mother waiting and ready for more conversation. The baby gets the courageous idea that he can turn away when he chooses and return when he chooses without disrupting their conversation.

The patterning of simultaneous conversation is something like the famous mother-infant games of peek-a-boo and catch-me. In these games the baby toys with separateness without feeling endangered by abandonment. A baby is able to do this only after he has made an attachment to a mother he can count on. He can count on her face reappearing and her delighted look when his face reappears. He can depend on her to follow him when he challenges her to a catch-me game. He tosses away his toys with the confidence that they will be returned to him by a partner whose acts of going away and returning are a central focus of his existence. Nor is it an accident of fate that many babies invent their first treasured possession just around the time they brave the adventures of peek-a-boo, catch-me and tossing-away.

The constancy of the adult begins with a relatively helpless infant's attempts to engage the mysteries and ambiguities of a fate he dimly apprehends. The baby confronts these mysteries in the context of a human partnership that includes his parents' capacities for empathy, devotion, loyalty, camaraderie and their toleration of disappointment and grief. On the baby's side of the partnership there is no empathy or devotion, only a body-mind of exquisite sympathy, illusion, playfulness, urges for mastery and exploration, rage, cheerfulness, irritability, satiation, quivering apprehensions and fierce appetites to be filled up and held. The definitive letdown out of which his human emotions, moods and values will be born has yet to come.

The person whose existence has been impoverished by splitting goes on testing fate in much the same way that an infant tests his human partner. However, unlike the parent whom the infant can depend on to follow him in simultaneous conversation and catch-me—the mother or father whose adoring face will reappear when he flirts with the excitement of a peek-a-boo game—fate has no loyalty. The adult who dares not entrust himself to the arms of an ordinary human partner is like the disappointed child whose mother's face is always turned away, the humiliated child who looks up to see frowns instead of mirroring admiration. The adult gambler prefers the risk of an impersonal magical partner who might restore his lost omnipotence, to a human partner who might disappoint him. Fate tempts him with her spectacular promises. She lures him and then turns her back. So, whether he chooses the dice table, the heroin ecstasy, the alcoholic reverie, or the everlasting search for the all-perfect lover, such a person will sooner or later confirm his worst apprehensions. As the card turns he waits for Lady Luck to smile on him. Chances are her face will be turned away. Instead of recovering his lost omnipotence, he refinds vulnerability and humiliation.

Between the flirtations with separation and the final letdown, there is a brief period in the second birth when the infant does find the perfect partner for a perfect love affair. With his new partner, for a time the infant will forget about the enigmas of separateness and the sometimes disappointing features of his earthbound mother. And like his mother of oneness and his security blanket, his new partner will sustain his illusions of perfection. Only now the child will truly have reached a moment of self-perfection. Near the beginning of his second year the child will take his first upright walking-away steps. This momentous event usually occurs just as the child's body-mind has been able to conquer most of the mysteries of the sensate world of time and space —which is why he finds his new partner so enchanting. The toddler has a love affair with the world. The sensate world mirrors all the spectacular things the child imagines himself to be, just the way his mother's face did when it reappeared for simultaneous conversation and peek-a-boo.

In his love affair the child is an artist. Like the artist he soars above the everyday world; but also, like art, his glorious feats resonate with the sounds, colors, shapes and motions of the earth. In his exhilarated madness the child supposes he has created a world that holds him. And each day, the world confirms his acts of creation.

For the ordinary child it is a brief hour of madness and joy. For the artist it is a way of life. It is believed that

artists are born with gifts of attunement to the sensate world
and that they retain this unique attunement throughout life.
The artist's special vision reveals the patterned relationships
in the outer forms of the world. Where there are three dots
of color, he reacts to the rhythms and organization of a
triangle. The artist's sympathy dissolves the boundaries between the animate and the inanimate, the me world and
the not-me world. The nonhuman world is alive with human
intention. The intentions of human characters are revealed
through what they see, hear, touch, imagine. As the child's
love for the world temporarily allows him to forget his down-
to-earth attachment to his mother, the artist's act of creation is a love-gift that spreads over the world, temporarily
taking the place of ordinary human love. And perhaps it is
also true that in flights of creation artists hold in abeyance
the facts of vulnerability and aloneness in the world. We
often suppose that artists are impoverished in their personal
lives—that they are out of touch with the earthly emotions
of family and friends. Yet we also know that in their lofty
acts of creation they encompass the commonplace in all its
irreconcilable ambiguity. Artists hold a special mirror to our
daily passions and reflect the underlying mysteries and
enigmas of these passions.

*The azure-leaved, orange-flowered, three-cornered cur-
tain flows toward the touseled rectangle of white tablecloth,
blending with the bronze-red of the apples and the white-
ness of the cloth. A goblet, a bowl and a pitcher are a cen-
tered trio of uprightness amidst the absolute roundness of
the bronze-red apples. The unexpected presence of just one
tear-shaped, wine-red apple converts the blue-white triangle
of goblet, bowl and pitcher into a perfect rectangle. The
flowing lines and layered shapes of the* Nature Morte *are
animate, more sensuous than any actual apple or actual
goblet. Even so the lines become the apple we ate this*

*morning, the table we once imagined and then forgot about
until now.*

*Gabriel and his bronze-haired wife, Gretta, leave the
dance and annual feast given by his aunts. They return to
their lodgings; Gabriel longing for the distant music of their
past ecstasies, Gretta wrapped up in her memories of a
former love—memories awakened by the last song of the
party. She tells Gabriel of the love who died for love of her,
turns her back and falls asleep. Gabriel is alone. He thinks
about his wife's lost love and his eyes fill with tears. He
watches the silver snow outside the window and imagines
it falling on the hills, the waves, the churchyard, the head-
stones, the Universe, the living and the dead. And we weep
for Gabriel without knowing exactly why. Again and again
we listen to the rhythms of the waltzes and quadrilles, the
runs of the Academy piece, Gabriel's after-dinner speech,
the drinking toast of the "jolly gay fellows," the final song
about the wet dew and the dead babe. We re-view the
colors and shapes; the goose, the red and yellow jellies, the
Smyrna figs, the purple raisins, the red wine, the pudding
on a yellow dish, the blue and bronze of Gabriel's* Distant
Music, *the silver snow. And each time we understand one
more reason why we weep for the living—and the dead.*

We celebrate artists and adore them. We also envy them
their courage. And when the poet is merely lofty or merely
mundane then we are quick to declare the poet unfit for
adoration. What we celebrate in art is reconciliation; the
reconciliation of perfect harmonies with the rhythms and
shapes of daily existence.

This is why we celebrate the child's love affair as a true
act of creation. Although he soars, he mirrors for us the
perfect attunement with the sensate world that we once had

and then lost forever. We are enthralled by the child's discovery of all those sounds, colors, shapes and textures which we have long since relegated to the ordinary and unnoticed. We envy the child his perfection. We wish we still had his absolute security, his ability to embrace the world. But we also tremble for him as we tremble for the acrobat, the conqueror of Everest, the high-leaping dancer, the juggler, the jester, the actress in her passionate revelations, the poet's last line, the high-flying Icarus. And surely as now he soars the child will fall. This is the beginning of a cycle of exhilaration and letdown, of an impulse to fly above the world and a sudden need to be enclosed and earthbound, that is at the heart of an adult's life and spiritual contradictions. So we tremble for the child as we realize how rare are the moments of unfettered exhilaration, as we foresee the letdowns that life has in store.

Though we would wish to hold back time and let him go on forever with his love affair, the child's own mind will not permit the stay. In a few months his almost perfected body-mind will be joined by an imperfect, thinking, symbol-making mind that will wrench him out of the sensate paradise of infancy. He will sink from the elated near-ecstasy of his love affair to the blue-gray near-despair of his new beginnings.

In the coupling of his sensate mind with the images, ideas, words and fantasies of his thinking mind, the child will learn that his relationships with other people have a great deal to do with the vicissitudes of his appetites, excitements and bodily sensations. In this way the child will acquire the first emotions of human partnership. With these simple emotions to guide him, the child will carve out the first space on earth that belongs only to him. As he steps into this space, the child will begin to interpret the earth through the hues of the vast spectrum between ecstasy and despair.

The succeeding events of life may temporarily uncouple sensation and thought. However, the links between the body and the mind are never totally severed. It is true that all too frequently the frantic activity of our civilized mind alienates us from our bodies. Still, hormone secretions, heart poundings, synapse twitchings, dilations and contractions of blood vessels, contractions and expansions of muscles, brain waves of alertness and sleep, sensual excitations of skin, mouth and genitals, go right on silently influencing our thoughts and acts of creation. And when the forces of civilization wrench us from our biological roots, the body asserts its passions, making itself heard in migraines, ringing ears, back spasms, intestinal ulcers, wry necks, heart anginas, stiffening joints, viruses, eczemas, warts, tics, rages, irritability, impotence, tension, panic and quivering apprehensions.

The body will also assert its authority by promoting higher-level connections between sensation and thought. The human mind constantly transposes its mode of apprehending experience in concert with alterations in body organization.

The sixteen-month-old's thinking, symbol-making mind comes into existence in connection with a revolutionary change in the priorities of bodily sensation. Bladder, rectal and genital pressures become recognizable as distinct from other inner bodily sensations. As these pressures coordinate with the upright mastery of the child's muscular-skeletal system, the child's awareness of his body-self is sharpened. Thus the body boundaries of the self acquire more precise definition simultaneous with the child's growing capacity to image symbolically the difference between himself and others. Sensuality is transformed into eroticism as these new bodily pressures become linked to an emotional relationship with a not-me person who can be either adored or hated.

The hormonal and muscular-skeletal changes of adolescence are accompanied by changing modes of apprehending the world of time and space and by a reordering of previous emotional reconciliations. Initially the bodily and mental alterations of adolescence are disconnecting. Past, present and future are uncoupled in preparation for another new beginning. The adolescent mourns the lost emotional ties of his childhood; he rails against the disappointing empty present and longs for the all-perfect utopias of the future.

The strident muscular tensions of body growth, the incessantly changing appearance of his body, and the sudden onslaught of intense genital arousal temporarily sever the links between bodily sensation and emotional/intellectual relatedness to the world outside the skin, leaving the adolescent with the terrifying impression that his body boundaries are dissolving. Unable to be at home either in his body or in the world of practical, down-to-earth reality, the adolescent is cut loose from his moorings. He loses his bearings. His moods shift unpredictably from ecstasy and elation to despair and hopelessness. Though frightening and disorienting, these bodily changes and their accompanying mood fluctuations encourage the adolescent's new way of thinking about the world and organizing life experience.

In the transition from childhood to adulthood the human mind undergoes another revolution. Child thought is practical and concrete. Adolescent thought is formal and abstract. With the purity of formal logic, the adolescent will refind himself and forge a larger vision of what he might become. For a time he is able to structure a new world completely in his mind without ever needing to refer his ideas or hypotheses to the palpable or the real. As the real is preempted by the possible, the adolescent imagines possible worlds and possibilities of self previously beyond the range of his mind. In contrast to the disconnected chaos of his bodily sensations and the confusions of his personal relationships, the inner world the adolescent constructs is held together by ideal proportions, perfect arguments, ultimate reasons—the chastity of if-this/then-that propositions. Divorced from the carnal arousals of the body, the adolescent mind transforms lust into asceticism, unassuaged bodily appetites into religious ecstasies and the poetry of the soul. In its loathing for *Real-*

politik the mind of pure logic erects flawless political systems.

Alone, unfettered by considerations of practicality, sensation or emotion, the logical mind, grand as it might become, would never end corruption, reconcile longings for oneness and strivings for separateness, or comprehend the origins of loathing, longing or desire. We must assume that the adolescent mind periodically reconnects with the body, for in their rebellions and ecstasies adolescents make it clear enough that they rub against the grain of the adult world in order to refind their own edges and that they seek sensation and take risks in order to regain a semblance of their lost omnipotence. Which is not to say that it's all merely personal: The reforging of personal edges and personal risk-taking are what change the shape of the world.

The adolescent who exposes himself to the fractures and dislocations of personal reorganization steps into the adult world with a readiness to expand the boundaries of the real. Adolescents are often accused of fanatical and utopian politics. But by temporarily preferring the purity of his visionary reformations to the disappointing contradictions of the real world, the adolescent protects himself from madness and cynicism. From his visions new beginnings will emerge as once more possible perfection is wedded to the real.

We are held together by the unity of the mind and the body. When our mind works in concert with our body we feel whole and exhilarated. At birth we were taken from the physical unity of the womb and cast into limbo. Soon afterward we began our psychological birth. We began this second birth in unity—with our body-mind of molding oneness. But the other aspect of our infant body-mind was the stiffening-away of growth, the urge to explore the world outside the mother-infant orbit. At first we hesitated; we ventured forth and then checked back to home base. With our imperfect body-minds we pondered the comings and goings of our mother of home base. At last our body-mind was perfectly in tune with the sensate world of time and space. Oblivious to home base, we soared above the mundane earth. As our body-mind was joined by our new mind of thought and words and symbols, we lost this perfect attunement. We were once again in limbo, about to chart another beginning. We were thrown into the crisis of having to recognize our separateness from mother, and through this crisis we finally achieved our initial sense of separate selfhood.

Henceforth, each time we enlarged the boundaries of our self, we re-experienced the temporary limbo of suddenly not knowing who we were or who we might become. Yet as adults we continue to push out from our confining boundaries. We cut ourselves loose. We declare ourselves free of the safety of home base and inevitably we return. The cycle of breaking free and returning to base is one that we are engaged in as long as we are truly alive. What few of us have understood is that the choreography and rhythms of our personal cycles of breaking loose and returning were set in motion by the events of our second birth.

The infant begins his life in the new world by entering into a partnership with a mother whose mental life has been retuned by the bodily changes of pregnancy. These dramatic alterations in bodily experience are temporarily unsettling for a woman, but they invigorate her and shake her loose from her customary modes of acting in the world. The hormones of pregnancy will stimulate and reawaken a woman's memories of her own infancy and childhood. Though most of these memories are contained in fantasies which remain unconscious, they make themselves felt in an intensification of a woman's emotional attitudes of nourishing and protecting what is precious to her, preparing her to mother a vulnerable newborn whose appetites to be filled up and held are boundless. And though she will be an ordinary mother with an ordinary baby, she will hold her baby just well enough to give him the illusion that he has created his own heaven.

Chapter Two

The Beginnings

Birth to Six Weeks
(In Limbo)

The First Partnership Birth is the rupture of the state of biological oneness of mother and fetus. Mending the rupture is the major task of the mother-newborn couple. During the first month of human life mother and newborn must come to know each other in a manner that will replace the physical oneness of the womb with psychological oneness, a oneness that is as essential to life outside the womb as biological oneness was to life in the womb.

From the moment of birth until several weeks after, a newborn and his mother are joined neither in biological oneness nor in psychological oneness. The infant is in limbo —between two worlds, between two vastly different environments. His birth from the physical environment of the womb has taken place, but he is still only at the border of his new environment—the psychological environment that will bring out his innate humanity. In order for a newborn to take his first steps toward becoming human, the space between the two environments must be bridged by both members of the mother-newborn partnership. Yet the role that each will play and the equipment that each will bring to this complex task are vastly different.

The newborn brings only a physical self; the mother, a psychological self. It is not without import that an infant is ushered into the new world into the arms of a mother who has a psychological past consisting of fantasies, memories, a capacity to tolerate loving and hating, an understanding of the dimensions of the world of time and space, and a sense of herself as a person with a separate and unique identity. From the very beginning moments of her baby's life, a mother's psychological past will enhance her infant's slowly evolving sense of psychological selfhood.

The Mother's Part   After reassuring herself that all the baby's body parts are there, a mother relaxes into the first coming together. In this first coming together of mother and newborn, a kaleidoscope of fears, hopes, memories and illusions momentarily crystallize in the mother's mind. An impression concerning the nature of her newborn's destiny is triggered by the mother's scrutiny of her newborn's facial expressions and her experience of the newborn's first bodily movements.

A mother's first impression comes upon her unexpectedly, as though from outside herself, and she is usually convinced that something real about her baby is responsible for it. In fact a baby does bring his unique inherited tendencies and the in-the-womb experiences that belong only to him. His way of presenting himself to his first human partner is his alone. Yet how much of the first impression comes from the newborn and how much from the mother cannot be known. The mother's impression is shaped partly by her own conscious and unconscious fantasies and partly by the real characteristics of her baby.

The fantasies that underlie the mother's first impression will undergo elaboration with each new phase of the infant's discovery of self. They strike a chord in the mother-infant relationship that will resonate throughout the course of his psychological birth, profoundly influencing its outcome and resolutions. This chord is then embellished by the subsequent challenges and crises of life.

It is customary to regard fantasy as the great deceiver, the Pied Piper that seduces us away from the claims of reality. Our waking life seems to be dominated by looking out and reaching toward an actual world. However, there is scarcely a moment when fantasy is not influencing our manner of apprehending the actual. Far from being a symptom of human frailty, fantasy paints the world with the full spectrum of human vitality.

A mother's fantasies about her child will always influence and enrich her functioning as a mother, just as the fantasies of pregnancy helped to prepare her for mothering.

The Mother-to-be The impression called forth in the mother's mind by her first coming together with her newborn is but the observable tip of a massive iceberg. Beneath the surface lie the innumerable unconscious fantasies that have been stirred up by the hormonal and metabolic changes of pregnancy.

The strange and somewhat bizarre fantasies of pregnancy are so silent that much of the time a woman is but dimly aware of them. Occasionally they surface in her dreams and in her musing daydreams. These fantasies and the anxiety they often generate are not portents of danger. They are a normal part of a normal pregnancy. They help a mother to free herself from her more conventional patterns of thought and emotion. They encourage her to undergo the personality reorganization that will prepare her for mothering a newborn. The inner turmoil is temporarily disquieting, but it breaks down the rigidity of old patterns so that a woman may be more flexible with her baby.

Many people think of pregnancy as a condition that depletes a woman in order to satisfy the needs of the fetus growing inside her. This is not at all true. The metabolic and hormonal processes that support the life of the fetus serve to heighten the energies of the mother-to-be. In addition, they kindle the childhood memories and attitudes that will facilitate the woman's psychological move into motherhood.

The hormonal alterations of pregnancy are the somatic link between the mother's early childhood attitudes and the psychological experience of pregnancy. Although each trimester of pregnancy makes its specific contribution to personality reorganization, in general pregnancy represents a prolongation of the lutein phase of the menstrual cycle. Lutein, often called progesterone, prepares the uterus for the fetus and maintains the pregnancy. Lutein predominates in the first and second trimesters, but shortly before the birth estrogen secretions rise—activating the uterine contractions of birth and preparing the mother to let go and deliver her baby into the world outside her body. In contrast to estrogen, the hormone that facilitates the outer-directed attitudes associated with copulation and delivery, lutein promotes a readiness for conception, inner-directed feelings, and the receptive and retentive attitudes that are reminiscent of the mother's early childhood attitudes of receiving and holding-on.

Receptiveness is a person's openness and availability, her willingness to receive what the world has to offer. In the earliest months of her life, a woman felt an inner goodness and wholeness as she was held and nurtured by her own mother. At that time inner goodness was equated with psychological oneness—the unity of the self that comes from being adequately nourished and protected. An infant who is held will trustingly open his arms to reach out to the world. When a woman revives in herself this early attitude, she opens her arms to receive the baby into the new world— just as she opened herself to receiving him into her womb.

The holding-on, or retentive, attitude belongs primarily to a later phase of the woman's childhood. It belongs to the

time when she began to become aware of her separateness
from her mother. At that time the conflict between wanting
to continue to hold on to the mother and, simultaneously,
wanting to hold on to what belongs to the self was at its peak.
This conflict represents the definitive crisis of becoming a
separate self. Goodness is equated with possession of what
belongs to the self—including rightful ownership of the
body. Now the woman holds the baby in her womb. After
he is born she will be a presence that holds her baby well
enough to let him possess what rightfully belongs to him.
The holding environment she will create will provide enough
security so that the baby will be free to explore the new
world on his own without feeling that he is neglected or
abandoned.

A pregnant woman's attitudes of receptiveness and holding-on prepare her to restore a sense of oneness between
herself and the newborn after he has left the physical oneness of the womb. Also accompanying the lutein-dominated
phases of pregnancy is an inner-directed feeling state, often
referred to as vegetating, in which the mother-to-be focuses
her energies on her body and on the fetus growing inside
her. Vegetating can be a friendly sensation of nourishing,
receiving and holding on to the fetus or a frightening experience of decay and disintegration. A woman whose sense of
self is linked exclusively to "higher level" cultural and intellectual attainment is often frightened by the implications
of vegetating. She becomes overly organized and self-
sufficient, rigidly defending herself from giving in to the
attitudes that might reorganize her personality. She may end
up continuing to be a tightly organized, efficient and capable
mother, but she will have missed an opportunity to enrich
her life destiny. When a woman can permit herself to take
full advantage of the vegetative turning-inward normal to
pregnancy, she also comes to discover that her self-centered-
ness stimulates hopeful fantasies about her child-to-be. Many

women work until the day the baby is born and still allow themselves to drink in the inward-turning, fantasy-enriching experience of pregnancy.

The initial fatigue and other discomforting reactions to the hormonal changes of pregnancy decrease after the third month. Gradually the normal turning-inward is complemented by an expansive opening out to the world. The pregnant woman's expansiveness is much more than the obvious expanding of her physical body. It is a psychological expansiveness that expresses her growing feelings of hopefulness. Motherhood holds out the possibility of re-creation and promise, and a new baby represents an opportunity for change for the better. The hormonal and metabolic accompaniments of pregnancy support these feelings of hopefulness and energy expansion.

The reorganization of personality that pregnancy encourages often brings out unforeseen, previously quiescent aspects of a woman's self. At moments the inner push toward personality reorganization can be terrifying. Change entails risk. It always raises the potential for inner conflict. We do not expect then that pregnancy will be totally idyllic, vegetative and peaceful. At times the hopeful, self-centered mood of elation prevails. At other times, insecurity, depression and anxious stirrings become prominent.

The mother-to-be of our generation is at risk. She is often too much on her own, locked into herself by strident self-sufficiency. She has often denied herself the affection and nurturant holding of husband, family and friends which is essential to her well-being. Real deprivations, whether of love, financial security, friendship or proper diet, interfere with the state of well-being of a pregnant woman. And with such deprivation, hope attentuates. The anxiety and occasional depression that normally accompany the changes of pregnancy are then heightened and last longer. A sense of frustration and resentment takes hold. The more deprived a woman feels, the more she comes to imagine herself as incapable of gratifying her baby-to-be. The final step in this sequence of deprivation, hopelessness and resentment about one's ability to fulfill a mothering role is the full turning of hostility toward the self and the fetus, which is part of the self.

This self-hatred transforms the content of a woman's pregnancy fantasies. Hopefulness is transformed into ideas that the body is harboring a monster, a wild animal that methodically and maliciously drains away the energies and life-blood of the self. Doubtless every pregnant woman goes through moments of panic when such hostile ideas overwhelm her hopefulness. Actually, these "Rosemary's Baby" fantasies are very common at one or another time during pregnancy.

Deprivation and resentment inevitably open the door to the monsters and hated aspects of the self that are usually kept locked up. Since the fetus is so much a part of the mother's body, it can easily come to stand for many aspects of the mother's self-image—particularly aspects that she usually keeps hidden in the deeper recesses of her mind. The fetus can represent the unwanted self as well as the cherished self.

Women do not find it easy to talk about pregnancy fantasies, and those fantasies in which the fetus becomes a terrifying monster are pushed out of awareness as swiftly as possible. Whatever trace they leave in the mind is experienced as a rushing tide of unpleasant emotion. Anxiety, depression, hopelessness and panic usually follow these awakenings of the unloved self.

Most likely to remain in a woman's awareness are those thoughts having to do with the fetus's resemblance to the happier aspects of the self and to the cherished aspects of the prospective father. She muses about the child's possible relations to herself and her husband. So even before birth the baby-to-be has been an angel and a monster. And it already has been given a tentative role in the triangle of mother-father-child.

The Father-to-be Husbands sometimes share in the hopeful thoughts about the baby-to-be and its possible role in the constellation of the family. A man who can permit himself to fantasize about his unborn child is demonstrating his love for the baby and for his wife. By sharing their hopes, husband and wife deepen the bond between them. Not surprisingly, a man tends to resent the times of pregnancy when his wife gets depressed and anxious. Such emotions in a wife are taken as an affront to a man's virility. They diminish the power he experiences from his projection of himself in the role of protector and provider. Ironically, anxiety in a pregnant woman may temporarily sever or weaken the love bond that usually makes a husband want to support his wife. During these times of her emotional disequilibrium, "just when she needs him most," a husband may be alienated from his pregnant wife. He also comes to resent his unborn child.

A prospective father has a hard time being part of the experience of pregnancy. He is estranged from the emotions and fantasies that are so much a part of the pregnancy experience for a woman. The reasons for this estrangement are partly biological but largely cultural and social.

On the biological side, fathers-to-be do not experience the hormonal and metabolic changes that establish the bond of oneness between mother and fetus. Prospective fathers are not pushed to self-reorganization by alterations in hormones and metabolism. Nor are they directly challenged by the bodily and emotional changes that define the natural course of a pregnancy. They are not linked to the fetus in the actual biological way. A prospective father's only possible source of contact with the fetus is through the emotional links provided by his own dreams of the future and by his emotional knowledge of what it means to be a baby or a mother.

The sharper the distinction a culture makes between masculine and feminine roles, the more a prospective father will be alienated from his tender, nurturant impulses. He therefore will find himself unable to empathize with his wife's emotions during pregnancy. Moreover, when manhood is severely defined as total independence and self-sufficiency, a man is denied his right to his childlike strivings. Consequently he has difficulty being close to his own children.

A man's fatherliness is enriched as much by his acceptance of his feminine and childlike strivings as it is by his memories of tender closeness with his own father. A man who has been able to accept tenderness from his father is able later in life to be tender with his own children. When a man becomes a father it is particularly important for him to regain emotional contact with his history of once having been a child and a son to a mother and a father.

A man's earliest experiences of being received and held by a mother in a nurturing environment can be reflected in the way he feels about nurturing others only if he allows himself to revive such early nurturing experiences and permits himself occasionally to be dependent. Many men who have been well-nurtured in early childhood cannot revive the memories and emotions associated with good mothering, because in our culture the values associated with masculinity require that male children renounce their ties to the mother and reject dependency and neediness. And while it is true that men (and women) who remain absolutely dependent will stay immature and therefore incapable of nurturing a baby, an all-out total renunciation of dependence and neediness also squelches the possibilities for nurturant behavior. Many fathers are so out of touch with memories of neediness that they find it impossible to empathize with neediness in others. They resent being needed and resent those who are in need. Independence and self-sufficiency help a man to be a good provider for a family, but if they make him uncomfortable with his wife's occasional neediness during pregnancy, he may not be able to empathize with the neediness of his newborn.

The absolute dependence of the fetus and his wife's self-absorption during pregnancy may well awaken intense competitive strivings in a man. He feels deprived of his wife's customary attention and thinks of the fetus as a greedy robber. With these thoughts come resentment of the pregnancy, and similarly, the eventual image of the fetus as a monster.

Nevertheless, a man who can trust the tide of memories and fantasies of his own childhood will have an opportunity to redistribute the balance between dependence and independence, personal neediness and the capacity to nurture others. And his capacity to empathize with his wife and newborn will be enhanced.

After the birth of the baby, men are often deprived of the emotionally resonating experiences that would establish the bond between themselves and the newborn. It is not unusual for fathers to feel alienated from mother and baby for several months—sometimes for years. When a father has the chance to see his baby being born or simply to hold his baby right after birth, his hopeful fantasies surface with no trouble at all. He becomes part of his baby's life right from the beginning.

The Newborn's Part   The newborn has no past and therefore no psychology. He has no fantasies, no good self or bad self, no angels or monsters inside him, no love or hate—only moments of feeling physically vulnerable and let down and moments of feeling physically whole and held together.

"The baby is being a baby for the first time." Yet he comes with a biological readiness that will allow him to make the most of what the world offers him.

There are two parts to a newborn's biological readiness. One part consists of his unique inherited potentials. Such potentials are what make the newborn different from all other human beings on the face of the earth—hair color, blood type, temperament, the range and quality of intelligence, the age at which puberty will begin, whether or not one will become bald, the general outlines of a physical body with unique strengths and weaknesses.

The other part is the result of the evolution of the human species. This the newborn shares with all other humans— crying, sucking, smiling, becoming wary of strangers at around eight months, creeping before walking, acquiring a thinking mind in the second year of life, an irresistible urge to explore the world, being able to adapt to a changing environment, an intense need for human attachment and dialogue.

From his parents the newborn inherited the unique and the shared characteristics, and all of these will subsequently be modified and augmented by the environment he is born into. To the extent that his environment is human, a newborn will acquire humanness. To the extent that the environment favors his uniqueness, he will fulfill his unique potentials.

Different environments foster particular kinds of intelligence, favor certain temperaments and body types, affect the age of puberty, sustain fantasies about the meaning of femininity or masculinity, determine the balance between wariness and the need to explore the unknown, respond differently to crying, sucking, creeping away, thinking with a thinking mind.

There is no known human environment that will permit a newborn to realize the entire range of his unique possibilities. Some aspects of his uniqueness will remain unexpressed and silent. Environments that encourage personality reorganization during times of life crisis will awaken more of these silent aspects of personal uniqueness. But most human environments facilitate the expression of those characteristics that the newborn shares with the rest of humanity. In this regard all newborns will have somewhat similar experiences in the new world. What is important to realize is that the self that is "me and nobody else" has as much to do with features common to all human beings as with characteristics that are unique and personal.

The Evolutionary Preparedness of the Newborn   A baby is born with numerous features that have been designed by nature to insure survival during the first weeks and months of life. The characteristics and behavior patterns that come from evolutionary inheritance tend to stand out at crucial turning points in the life cycle. Some of these behavior patterns are no longer essential for individual survival, but they may still have enormous significance for the survival of the species. Much of the psychology of the human infant is built around his evolutionary inheritance.

Three of these inborn results of evolution are particularly pertinent to the emotional survival of the newborn. They are the stimulus barrier of his otherwise immature nervous system, the actual physical appearance of newbornness, and the smiling response.

The Barrier   The newborn's out-of-the-womb environment is a terrain of unpredictable and unfamiliar sights, sounds, odors, temperatures and movements. Only a few stimuli, such as the rocking motion of the mother's body and the mother's heartbeat, are vaguely familiar. In general, the newborn's surroundings consist of unorganized (because the newborn has yet to learn how to organize) and fragmented stimuli. If the infant's nervous system were not protected, his first weeks in his new environment would be experienced as an onslaught of intolerably intense stimulation. Fortunately, the inborn equipment of a newborn features a nervous system that is relatively impervious to outer stimulation. This relative imperviousness is called a *stimulus barrier*.

In the first weeks of life, the baby is capable of shutting out disturbing sights and sounds. Almost immediately after birth the newborn is capable of selecting which stimuli he will attend to and which he will shut out. He seems to be able to get used to low-level stimulation and learn to tolerate it. But he avoids high-intensity stimulation; in fact, many of his reflexes which will soon disappear are designed to help him shut out sights and sounds that are too disturbing. Ideally, no more reaches the newborn from outside than he can manage. The nervous-system barrier then is like a semipermeable membrane. The barrier is more effective in some babies than in others. It may be too permeable in some and not permeable enough in others. But in most newborns it is just right.

As the weeks go on, the infant's adjustment to his new world becomes somewhat less than perfect. The barrier becomes much more permeable. The infant's sensory awareness of the world around him is increasing at a rapid rate, but his ability to organize and act with his muscles to take in these sensations is lagging. Because his motor actions are not as developed as his sensory equipment, a four-week-old infant has but a limited ability to manage all the new impressions that are suddenly impinging on him. Furthermore, the little discharge movements that had previously allowed the newborn to rid himself of disagreeable and disturbing inner tensions—the startles, mouthings, twitchings and discharge smiles—are also decreasing in effectiveness. Inner tensions begin to mount as the infant's capacity for alertness to the outside world outpaces his motor ability to manage the sights, sounds, odors and movements that are arousing his senses. Most infants become irritable and fussy during their fourth to twelfth week of life. Some are fussy all day and others only intermittently. Even the quiet, placid baby becomes somewhat fussy during this period. Some babies develop the notorious three-month colic around this time—an indication of the tension they are experiencing.

Up until now, the stimulus barrier has made life in the limbo between physical oneness and psychological oneness tolerable. Psychological oneness between mother and infant will go on to become, so to speak, a psychological barrier analogous to the physical stimulus barrier. From four weeks until the infant is more capable of regulating his own intake of stimulation the mother must do it for him. Her presence and her empathy replace the nervous-system barrier. The more a mother has gotten to know her baby in the beginning four weeks of his life, the easier it will be for her to help her baby feel safe even though the physical barrier has dwindled away.

It is not remote to suppose that an infant's evolutionary inheritance would include some features to insure that a mother-infant attachment bond would have been formed by the time the stimulus barrier disappears.

The Appeal of Helplessness   The need of an infant for a mother is clear enough. The beginnings also include a mother's need for a baby to mother.

A mother's history and her current psychological readiness for mothering are good enough insurance that she will nurture and protect her baby. At the time she gives birth, her psychological need for the baby is already as intense as the baby's physical need for her. Nevertheless, a newborn human does have some inborn characteristics that stimulate his mother to want to mother, to care for him and become attached to him in a specifically human way. These characteristics facilitate and educate the receptive, holding-on attitudes that the mother acquired during pregnancy. In the main, these characteristics are best described as the innate appeal of the infant's helpless physical appearance and immature body movement.

The best cure for the normal letdown and physical fatigue of a new mother is the stimulation that comes from mothering a helpless-looking infant. Naturally, such a cure depends on the emotional and physical support of the mother's environment. An emotionally or physically starved mother is too depleted to feed and care for a needy newborn. It is well-known that a nutritionally starved pregnant woman of the ghettos of our modern world is likely to have a newborn who is unable to make appeals that would facilitate mothering. The mother loses her capacity for attachment, and the newborn fails to thrive. If undernourished, neither member of the partnership can educate the other.

Usually a newborn is able to educate his mother. The mottled skin of the newborn, his hairless body, unfocused eyes and uncoordinated body movements give him a helpless and vulnerable look. His vulnerable appearance makes a mother want to hold him and care for him. Many of the newborn's facial expressions and body motions stimulate body adjustments on the mother's part and increase fondling and body contact between her and the infant. Their bodies become attuned to one another. If a father doesn't get a chance to hold his baby soon and often after birth, he will find the wrinkled, limp, thrashing of his baby unappealing and funny looking. He will be bewildered at his wife's quick responsiveness to the newborn's "sweet appeal."

Another important aspect of the newborn's appeal are the fat pads on the inner surface of his mouth. These fat pads augment the newborn's ability to suck. In addition they are part of the innate appeal of newbornness. They are responsible for the "cute" fat-cheeked look we commonly associate with immaturity and babyhood. Cartoonists and artists take advantage of this association by exaggerating the fat-cheeked look when they wish to designate innocence, vulnerability and immaturity.

In many other animal species the odor, sounds, skin color and touch of the newborn also facilitate mothering. In mammals particularly, the immature, helpless look of the young corresponds directly to the young animal's real helplessness and dependency. For instance, the immature coat color of certain infant monkeys becomes increasingly adult-looking in direct correspondence to the monkey's increasing ability to engage in coordinated independent locomotion. In the human the gradual loss of that appealing fat-cheeked look is one sign of the ending of babyhood and the attainment of independence and mastery of the physical world. The mastery of upright locomotion makes the human child *look* independent. But in contrast to the infant monkey, the human infant must go one step further before he is truly capable of independence. He must go on to achieve psychological as well as physical independence from his mother. He will keep some of his fat-cheeked look until he does.

The Infant Smile   Of all the appeals made to a mother, the infant's smile is probably the one that gives her the most pleasure. It bolsters her confidence in mothering and makes her feel needed in a special way.

Smiling is a universal human gesture. There are many varieties of smiles: shy smiles, love smiles, pleasure smiles, mean smiles, surprise smiles, broad smiles—false smiles. In all societies the smile is an indication of the bond between one human being and another. Most often, it is an affirmation of human attachment—a greeting, a way of saying welcome or we belong together. But it also can signify the termination of existing bonds and attachments—the smile before dying or slaughtering an enemy.

By tracing the natural history of the smile during the first weeks and months of human life we are able to chart the infant's initial steps in moving from an exclusively physical state of being to a state of psychological being. The early development of the smile tells how a universal expressive movement begins to acquire its psychological meaning.

In the beginning the baby is not smiling in special recognition of his mother. But he seems to be, because her voice and her touch are the most effective stimuli to his smile. The baby's growing ability to be roused into smiling during the early weeks of life is important in strengthening the bond between mother and child. Even the blind child will smile though he has never seen a smile. Blind infants seem to be trying to focus their eyes in the direction of the mother's eyes as they smile, though they have never seen the mother's eyes. Eye-to-eye contact and smiling are inborn responses that speak of our human preparedness to become attached to other human beings.

The smile of the first week has no psychological meaning. It is a simple discharge of physical tension. Like all other discharge movements present at birth—such as startles, twitches, mouthings, sobbings, erections and taking in air—smiling is the baby's response to physical conditions within the body. Moreover, there is no way to rouse the one-week-old to smile by presenting him with excitations from outside. He will usually smile just as he closes his eyes or lapses into drowsiness or light sleep. He will never smile while in his brief states of near-wakefulness. The focus of the one-week-old is inward. The outside world barely touches him. When he smiles he is merely ridding himself of inner tension and his smile is a brief grimace.

As early as the second week of life, a high-pitched human voice effectively rouses an infant's smiling. Gentle, rhythmic rocking also sometimes does the trick. It is beginning to be possible for the outside world to reach the infant. The two-week-old smile is not just a grimace. It looks different from a simple discharge smile. The eyes wrinkle and the baby's mouth gets wider. The two-week-old has his eyes open when he smiles in response to outside stimulation, but his eyes are glassy, drooping and unfocused, giving his face a drunken, somewhat vapid appearance. People who already love the baby find his drunken smile appealing and amusing.

Although the outside world is reaching the infant, his major preoccupation is still with his innards, and the discharge smile is still much more prominent than these occasional droopy-eyed wakeful smiles. The stimulation from within the newborn's body is a constant source of tension which must be discharged.

By the third week the first truly alert, open-eyed smiles make their appearance. While awake with a focused bright-eyed look, the infant smiles more frequently, particularly when he hears the sound of a human voice. The movement of a nodding face can also produce smiling. The combination of nodding head and human voice elicits smiling more effectively than either of these stimuli alone. Inner sensations still demand most of the infant's attention, but he is definitely showing an increased capacity for alert attention to the outer environment.

The gradual move away from inward preoccupation to outer awareness steadily continues. At around the fourth to sixth week of human life several new signs of increased interest in the outer world begin to appear. The smiles are now accompanied by other responses that mark them as specifically human. For one thing, the smile of the four-week-old lets us know that what is happening in the outer world can once in a while take precedence over events happening inside the body. A baby will interrupt his feeding, stop sucking, and smile when he hears the human voice, particularly his mother's voice. It is as though the four-week-old cannot refrain from smiling when he hears the human voice. The peremptory nature of the human voice is enough to make the infant temporarily forget the urgency of his feeding appetite. Sometimes he will interrupt a bout of crying or fussing when he hears his mother's voice.

Around this time the infant begins to respond to the human voice with a human voice of his own. Previously, most of the sounds heard from the baby were cries, whimpers, sighs, yawns, grunts, moans and groans. Now he gurgles and coos in response to the human voice and he smiles. These gurgling and cooing sounds are believed to be the beginnings of human verbal communication.

Surprise smiling is another new kind of smiling. By staring, a baby of five weeks can put himself into a hypnotic trance or state of fascination. If something moves suddenly before his eyes while he is in this state, the infant momentarily startles. Then he smiles with surprise as though he were ridding himself of the tension of this unexpected event. In this respect, the surprise smile is a relative of the discharge smile, but because it is in response to an outside event it also partakes of outer responsiveness.

At five weeks, inner discharge smiles are still prominent, especially when the infant is drowsy and just about to fall into a light sleep—that is, when the infant is *almost* asleep. The surprise smile seems to occur when the infant is *almost* awake. Hypnotic fascination and drowsiness are both states of consciousness in the border region between sleeping and waking. In a state of fascination we are not entirely alert and we can easily be taken by surprise.

The infant surprise smile, which is primarily a discharge smile, is the earliest forerunner of the later surprise smile, which is a psychological smile. The fact that a human being often smiles when frightened or taken by surprise is another reminder of how early physical expressive movements survive to acquire complex psychological meanings. It reminds us also that fear and pleasure are sometimes closely related.

Being frightened is not always without enjoyment. Our fascination with ghost stories and tales of adventure partakes of this delightful mixture of fear and pleasure. Infancy games such as catch-me and peek-a-boo, which make their appearance around the eighth month of life, also have this mixture of danger and pleasure. We can either run away from something that takes us by surprise, or we can approach it. Usually, if we are not too frightened, we do a little of each. The surprise smile of the five-week-old is somewhere between an approach and a distancing—a compromise that relieves the tension created by uncertainty.

Near the end of her infant's second month of life, a mother begins to notice a significant change in his way of relating to her. Whereas previously the baby seemed to look right through her, now the baby looks at her as though he really recognizes her face. She discovers that she can play games with him and that when she "talks" to him, he answers back.

Just around the time of these observations, there is another milestone in the history of the infant smile. His smile is no longer a perfunctory smile at anything humanlike. The baby appears to be looking for something—and he will not smile until he finds it. The most important thing about this smile is that it is voluntarily and actively produced by the infant. From the beginning it is most often something specifically human that rouses the infant's attention and smiles. Contours and edges often capture his attention and hold it. But nothing can make a baby smile or gurgle and coo quite so readily as something human. Nothing can hold his bright-eyed attention for quite so long. Now before smiling the infant carefully searches the face—first the contour of the hairline, then the mouth, and finally the eyes. The moment the baby's eyes meet the eyes of the mother, he smiles. And he will only smile after having made eye-to-eye contact. It is as though the baby had been searching for something he knew would be there. He seems to smile out of recognition. This smile of eye-to-eye recognition is not consistent or reliable until the end of the third month of life, but the first indications of it appear just when a mother is getting the sense that she is really communicating with her infant in a mutual dialogue.

Eye-to-eye contact is an important component of human communication. What we do with our eyes becomes a measure of how friendly or close we feel toward another human being—turning the eyes away, averting the gaze, looking directly in the eyes, or closing the eyes altogether in order to maintain a state of intense intimacy. When smiles are accompanied by eye-to-eye contact we feel more certain of their friendly intent—unless such a smile comes from a total stranger, and then we might wonder at the presumption of his eye-to-eye familiarity. A smile accompanied by gaze aversion can be alluring; it signals friendly intent but hesitancy to approach.

Eye-to-eye contact is soon to become a precondition of infant smiling. The search for eye-to-eye contact is one more indication of the human infant's appetite for human communication.

Variations and Uniqueness Many of the features of the evolutionary inheritance of the newborn are expressions of his appetite for mutual dialogue with a mothering person. The dialogue serves as much to insure the survival of the newborn as it does the survival of the species. Inherent in the earliest mother-infant dialogue are the potentials for all later erotic, verbal and cultural dialogue between one human adult and another. However, this earliest dialogue does not always go smoothly. In societies where newborns are similar to one another, mother-infant couples are more likely to have similar early dialogues.

In some parts of the world newborns are more like one another than in other parts. In any given society, the degree of variation among newborns is largely a function of the degree to which the adults of that society have been permitted to procreate with "outsiders." Since traditional societies have provided few opportunities for marrying and procreating with outsiders, uniformity in genetic inheritance is the rule. Moreover, the cultural standards of such societies generally support the physical and temperamental qualities that its members are born with. Because of the similar diets and temperaments of their mothers, the in-the-womb experiences of these newborns are also likely to have been similar, thus assuring further their similarity at birth.

In the Zinacanteco society of the Chiapas Highlands of Mexico, for example, the difference between one newborn and another is slight. From birth almost all babies exhibit smooth body movements that are virtually free of the startles and twitches commonly observed in Caucasian babies. Newborns are quiet but extremely alert to the sights and sounds of their new world. Very soon after birth, the Zinacanteco infant is swaddled and wrapped up on his mother's body with his face almost completely covered. For approximately five months he is carried in his mother's serape all day. At night he sleeps by her side. At the slightest sign of hunger, the infant is nursed—he hardly ever has to cry. A Zinacanteco mother's actions seem deliberately designed to keep the baby quiet. Arousal and alert attention to the outside world are discouraged.

Zinacanteco children tend to be much like their parents and also like the other adults and children they will encounter in their lifetime. As they grow older, one child may become known for his grace, another for the swiftness of his comprehension of bird migration, and still another for his wit. However, seen in the perspective of the full range of possible human variation, the extent and magnitude of variation between one Zinacanteco and another is comparatively small. Even from one generation to the next there is little change. The rules for generational transaction between mother and child, father and child, child and grandparent have been the same since the history of these people began.

Traditional societies are immensely different from ours. In our modern societies, traditions sometimes change so rapidly they scarcely deserve the appellation "tradition." In addition, because the history of nontraditional societies includes a high degree of outmating, there is considerable genetic variation between one newborn and another. Cultural and biological forces conspire to obscure the commonalities of life experience. At the same time, modern societies place a high value on uniqueness and personal striving. Differences and individuality are subtly and often directly encouraged.

The newborn of a modern society enters the world with inherited characteristics that mark him as different from other newborns. Although not all his differences will become evident right at the beginning of his life, some are apparent immediately, and these will play a vital role in the earliest unfolding of the mother-infant relationship.

How much a baby cries, how easily he can be soothed and comforted, how much he enjoys body contact, how clearly he demonstrates whether he is awake or drowsy, how much he engages in quiet, alert exploration of his environment, how much stimulation he requires, how soon he becomes visually alert, how easily he comforts himself, and how much inner discomfort he experiences and tolerates are some of the characteristics that may vary from one newborn to another. Such inherited differences will affect the kind of mothering the newborn receives.

Cultures vary in their attitudes toward infant crying and the ways in which they soothe and comfort. As with the Zinacanteco, in many traditional societies a baby's crying is discouraged. Mothers carry their babies constantly and they feed them the moment they sense the body stirrings that signify hunger. One theory has it that in the early history of mankind a baby's cry would attract predatory animals, so the baby was carried constantly and fed frequently to quiet and protect him. Because it could summon dangerous animals, a baby's cry was an occasion of terror to the entire group. Even now, in our modern world, we still react with some anxiety to the sound of a baby's cry. The most tolerant move quickly to put an end to it. Consciously our efforts are to soothe the crying baby. Part of our reaction, however, must be a remnant of the primitive fear that crying will bring danger to the baby and to ourselves.

In modern societies babies are usually cached away in carriages and cribs, which disconnects the mother from her infant's body signals. Crying therefore becomes the baby's most effective signal for bringing him into contact with his mother. A baby who cries a lot may not be perceived as a "good" baby, but chances are he will usually get more attention from his mother and have more body-comforting experiences with her than a good baby who rarely cries.

Some babies are easily soothed and will not cry for quite some time after having been soothed. Others are difficult to soothe, and when they are soothed it is temporary—they may cry again in three or four minutes. An easily soothed baby gives a mother the comfortable feeling that she is an effective mother, a good mother. An inconsolable baby, on the other hand, can devastate even the most competent mother. She is certain that it is her failure as a mother—that she is a bad mother.

A few fortunate newborns are able to comfort themselves. They make numerous tension-reducing mouthing and sucking movements in their "sleep" and they may also be inordinately skillful at getting their fingers to the mouth for sucking. Because these babies are likely to cry infrequently and sleep long, they make fewer appeals to the mother than less self-sufficient babies. They do not avail themselves as readily of a mother's need to comfort and nurture. A mother might feel rejected by such a baby.

From the beginning, some babies seem to crave visual exploration of their environment more than bodily contact or human interchange. A mother who has fantasized that she will have a cuddly, body-molding baby feels unwanted by the baby whose body continually stiffens into alertness so he can look around at the world.

In contrast, an overly intellectual mother who might have been warmed into sensual responsiveness by a cuddly, attachment-seeking baby will feel less uneasy when confronted by a noncuddly, exploration-minded baby. The fact is that such noncuddly babies also need human communication and body contact experiences even though they may require somewhat less than other babies. A mother's body and presence still serve as the essential beacon of orientation for a baby's explorations of the nonhuman environment.

Some noncuddly babies are left on their own too much,

which later may result in scattered, disoriented explorations of the world. Or, an exploration-minded baby might grow up to become an intellectual (like his mother), but he will have missed the sensual body-contact experiences that amplify and enrich knowledge about the world. Later on in life, such a person does not have the cushion of the basic form of self-confidence—feeling good about the body. Adorations of the mind preempt the exhilarations of sensuality.

Since the newborn of the modern world is not constantly carried and soothed by the rocking motions of his mother's body, his family is often preoccupied with the patterning of his sleep-wake cycle. Popular mythology has it that a baby sleeps twenty of the twenty-four hours of the day. Actually, in the beginning the baby is neither fully awake nor fully asleep.

The characteristic state of wakefulness, when it does occur, is alert inactivity. The baby lies very still, quietly taking in the sights and sounds that present themselves to him. Occasionally he turns his head to follow an object that has caught his attention. Only after three weeks or so does a baby become fully alert, but even then the periods of full awakening are brief.

Most of the time the infant drifts from one state of half-consciousness to another, propelled largely by the need to rid himself of inner tension. He tends to be drowsy just after feeding and just after a period of alertness. Drowsiness then blends almost imperceptibly into irregular light sleep.

Babies differ in the ease with which they can be roused into alertness. Some become immediately alert and attentive when they hear their mother's voice. A mother finds that she can easily rouse such a baby by talking to him and handling him. Such babies are more attentive to the mother's face. They smile more and they are generally more responsive to the outside world.

The clarity of the waking state also varies from one newborn to another. Some indicate distinctly whether they are drowsy, lightly asleep, or visually alert. In other newborns these states are blurred and indistinct. The latter newborns are confusing to their mothers.

Obviously there are few rules for "good" mothering that are suitable for all newborns. Adding to a modern mother's perplexity is the problem of how to accommodate her baby's more apparent attributes—say, quietness—and at the same time to encourage his less apparent appetites and qualities, such as silent longings for rhythmical rocking and body contact.

These earliest differences among newborns do not have any *direct* or *specific* influence on later personality traits. Only in the most general way is it sometimes said that an irritable, frequently crying baby will go on to become an active, high-strung, alert child and that the quiet baby will grow into an even-tempered, hard-to-ruffle child. A newborn's preference for visual exploration over body closeness can become a predisposition to being more masterful with things than with people. Nevertheless, most of these early variations among newborns are best thought of as variations in the reaction to being newborn.

This is not to imply that such variations are completely without effect on later development. The actual effect of these earliest differences has to do with the differences they make in the tone and quality of the mother-infant relationship. This depends heavily on a mother's awareness of the differences, on her real reaction to them, on her attitudes toward them, her previous expectations, the degree and strength of her self-esteen, and the support she receives from her husband and others in her environment.

Ultimately, variations among newborns become relevant to the extent that they make it easier or harder for a mother to understand and care for her baby. They can and do influence how close a mother feels to her baby and how good she feels about herself as a mother. A mother's thoughts about the meaning of frequent crying, easy soothing, loving to be fully awake and alert can play a major part in determining her baby's later personality. A mother can begin to superimpose on these characteristics the adult qualities of goodness or badness, compliance or stubbornness, intelligence or stupidity, happiness or misery. A newborn's inherited characteristics can only acquire such psychological meanings if someone in the infant's environment is interpreting them that way.

During this time of her baby's life, a mother's sense of her own self-worth is subject to much fluctuation. The first weeks of life can accentuate either new confidence and hopefulness or her vulnerability and helplessness. The more conscious she is of her fantasy interpretations of her baby's ordinary uniqueness, the more she allows herself to experience them, the easier it will be for her to hold together through the complex emotions that are stirred up by mothering a vulnerable and helpless newborn.

The modern mother—particularly if this is her first baby and she has been raised in the enclosed nuclear family typical of modern industrial societies—is often not well prepared to understand the needs of a newborn even though she has undergone psychological reorganization during pregnancy. Although evolution has provided her with a helpless-looking, fat-cheeked baby meant to evoke mothering responses, the vulnerable, constantly crying, always hungry, never sleeping newborn can also terrify a mother and awaken deep anxieties about her capacity for mothering.

In contrast to mothers in traditional societies, the modern mother is not prepared to wrap her newborn to her body in a dashica or serape or to sleep with her baby or to fall into the mood of maternal preoccupation that goes along with constant carrying and feeding. Furthermore, it is more difficult for her to share experiences with other mothers since maternal styles and newborn temperaments are so variable.

Most modern mothers actually enter a state of profound

shock when they realize that caring for a newborn means that one day and night will blend into the next day and night. Like her infant, she is neither fully awake nor fully asleep. She drifts from one day to the next, "accomplishing nothing" and falling apart from fatigue. The disruption of her ordinary adult sleep cycle, a disruption which may go on for several weeks, is bound to awaken her rage and make her resentful of her newborn. A mother is shattered by these unwelcome, unforeseen emotions and also by her own neediness and longings to be taken care of. Such daily attrition of her sense of self-sufficiency makes a mother doubt that she will ever be good enough to care for her baby.

Because a modern mother often calculates her worth in terms of how well she can manage on her own, she feels let down and disappointed in herself and her baby as she discovers how much she needs the assistance and holding of her family and friends. In competition with some imaginary perfect mother, she continues to try to do it all alone—and then she feels as if she's drowning. She wonders, "Why didn't anyone tell me it would be like this?" She recollects the pains of childbirth, when she also felt as if she was drowning and she raged, "No one ever told me!"

In a month or so, just about the time the stimulus barrier wanes, the newborn will become more mutually responsive to his mother. His gestures will be easier to read, he smiles in response to his mother's voice and he seeks eye-to-eye contact with her. His sleep-wake cycle, although still not at all predictable, is somewhat more distinct. On the mother's side, the emotional reorganization stimulated by the hormones of pregnancy continues after birth. Lutein is the hormone that promotes lactation and it goes on stimulating the receptive and retentive attitudes that help a mother to identify and empathize with her baby.

So, notwithstanding the variability of newborn behavior, the frequent mismatching in temperament between mother and child, and the modern mother's unpreparedness for maternal preoccupation, the routines of daily life will have provided numerous opportunities for creating a climate of intimacy between mother and infant. Even with all her uncertainties about feeding and holding, the mother will be able to assist her baby in his movements out of the inward focus of limbo and into the dialogue that will establish his humanness.

The First Dialogue Through a prolonged and extensive interaction with his mother during the first weeks of life, the newborn gradually becomes part of his mother's psychological environment. The newborn and his mother spend many hours together, involved with each other, focusing attention on each other, getting to know each other. The behaviors of one serve as subtle cues for the other. They begin to communicate in a specifically human way in a mutual dialogue.

The first dialogue of the human being has no words. It takes place in the coming together of the newborn's body with the body of his mother, and it includes the times when they move apart.

When the baby enters the new world, he has a language —the inborn gestures and potentials that give him a readiness to reach out, to discover the world, and eventually to create his own knowledge about the world. But he needs an interpreter who can make what he is ready to receive sensible and real. The specific qualifications of the interpreter are a knowledge of the history and dimensions of the new world, and an emotional availability that enables her to come to understand the needs of a helpless newborn who must nonetheless eventually travel the vast distances of the new world on his own. Because she has a psychological past, a mother has special knowledge of the vastness and complexity of the actual new world, and she also has a special understanding of the smallness of the world that can be made real to a newborn baby. A mother's emotional availability has been partially assured by the preparations of pregnancy. However, emotional availability also means being able to modify interpretations according to the baby's changing requirements for closeness to her and distance from her. In this the mother must be educated by the baby. When she translates the outer world to the baby, a mother must also come to understand the language that the baby brings with him.

The first dialogue then has to do with the way the mother interprets and receives the inborn physical gestures of her baby, and with the way she holds the baby and the way she puts him down. As the baby grows and develops, his dialogues will extend in ever-widening circles. The space of the first dialogue is an enclosed, compressed inner space, like the space at the core of the atom. The energy of the first dialogue is intense like the energy at the center of the atom.

In their first coming together, both mother and baby are energized by the gestures and bodily movements of the other. The energies of the enclosed space of the first dialogue orient the newborn after his rupture from the innermost space of the womb. A mother feels replenished, filled up and completed by the energies of her new baby. The better she gets to know her new baby, the better able a mother is to make the world real for him. The better the baby gets to know his mother, the better prepared he is for psychological oneness with her.

Each interpretation of his movements, gestures and sounds, each event that reaches him from the outer world in a sensible and meaningful way, gives the baby the feeling of having a mother who knows what it's like to be a baby for the first time.

Chapter Three

Oneness

Four Weeks to Five Months
(The Lap Baby)

From the time he is four weeks old until the end of his fifth month, the infant will undergo the two fundamental metamorphoses that endow him with his essential humanity. This period of babyhood is called "oneness" because in the first of these transformations the baby will be liberated from his preoccupation with events inside his body by an illusion that he is at one with events in the outer world.

As he leaves limbo and enters into oneness, the baby has no way of knowing that the events which bring him serenity and the feeling of wholeness emanate from a mothering person. Every now and then he is dimly aware that pleasure and bliss come to him most often in the presence of a special touch, voice and body movement. In his illusion, however, the infant supposes that touch, voice and body to be his own.* Merging, molding, serenity, harmony, wholeness,

---

* I have emphasized that the infant mind until fifteen or eighteen months is a body-mind. All subsequent references to such thought processes as supposing, recognizing, conjecturing, imagining, pondering, generalizing, Hegelian resolutions, are meant to be understood as produced by a body-mind. With the appearance of symbolic representational intelligence (described in the conclusion of Chapter Five and in Chapter Six) the body-mind is joined by the thinking mind, bringing about a different order of self-awareness and thought.

bliss and perfection are the dominant motifs of the infant's first metamorphosis. As these motifs are elaborated they build toward one of the pinnacle attainments of a human life—the infant's special attachment to his mother. This special attachment constitutes the infant's second metamorphosis. The attachment bond between an infant and his mother will give him rein to discover his place in the world.

The bond to his mother issues from the infant's recognition that her presence is somehow implicated in his profoundest pleasures and his impressions of boundless perfection and well-being. He discovers the importance of discerning the details of her comings and goings, her facial expressions, and her way of talking, playing and feeding. His longings for his mother begin to carry as much weight as his appetites for satisfaction and pleasure.

When the five-month-old is ready to move out of the shared orbit of mother-infant oneness he will take with him his two fundamental acquisitions—a relatedness which binds him to the commonplace details of life *and* a capacity to re-create the illusions of perfect harmony and bliss. Oneness describes how the infant acquires these two sources of his humanity. How he learns to reconcile the contradictions between them is the story of his second birth.

Holding   The first hundred times a baby receives the breast in his mouth he comes to it with fierce energies that spread across the surface of his skin and through the inner walls of his body. These energies drive the baby with an urgency to be filled up. At birth the baby does not know what a breast is, but he does know to turn his head and mouth toward it, and he knows how to hold on to the nipple and suck. Each time he is allowed to take the breast in a way that makes good use of his inborn knowledge of head-turning, holding on and sucking, the baby has an experience of harmony and well-being. Being understood in this way is what we mean by "being held."

"Holding" is everything that happens to an infant which sustains him and produces wholeness and integration. When the environment of a baby fits itself to the baby's inborn energies, gestures and movements, the environment holds the baby. When the nipple is pushed into his mouth without regard for his urges, or when the breast is too far away for him to turn toward it and reach it, the baby has the experience of being let down and falling to bits.

For a human baby there is no environment without a mother. In the first weeks of life he is but fleetingly aware of the events that constitute her presence—a rocking motion, eyes that gaze into his, a nipple in the mouth, a caress on the surface of his body. Each of these holds the baby. The way a mother acts in the world to make it safe, harmonious and interesting for her baby can convert any environment into a holding environment. She doesn't always have to hold her baby in her arms or cuddle him or walk with him in order for him to have the experience of being held. Putting a baby down when he needs to be alone is also holding.

In her manner of holding her baby a mother also brings the possibility of illusion into his life. To begin with, the baby's energies for reaching out and grabbing on to the world are diffuse and vague. But within a few weeks these energies become focused.

With his gestures and body movements the baby demonstrates his urge to find objects and boundaries in the outside world that correspond to the knowledge he brought with him. While lying on his stomach in the center of his bassinet, the baby pushes his legs and arms until the top of his head comes to rest at a border of the bassinet. When he is in his mother's arms, he strains, squirms and grunts until his body molds perfectly into the contours of her body. Turning his head, he reaches and searches with his mouth until his mouth circles the nipple. When he is alert, he scans the world until his eyes light on two eyes and he smiles.

At first the baby's only knowledge is in his excitements

and gestures. He has no sense of what he is searching for until his movements bring him into contact with something that matches up and harmonizes with his searching body. The baby is a conjurer who creates magic without comprehending exactly what its outcome will be: the nipple meets his searching mouth; his body fits into a yielding softness that smells and feels like his own body; the top of his head comes to rest against a boundary. The baby has the illusion that he has created the nipple, his mother's body, the edge of his world. When a baby's environment holds him, he begins to have the illusion that his excitements and gestures have created the world.

By holding her baby, a mother gives him an illusion of harmony and safety. Yet she is not deluding the baby or leading him away from the world of reality. Everything the baby creates when he is held is there to be created. He can only conjure what actually exists. All that need happen is that what exists be made available to the baby in a way that makes sense to him. A mother introduces only what is manageable for her baby, and she keeps out what will not make sense. Thus the baby can have the illusion that the world he discovers is in harmony with his excitements. What the mother introduces to the baby is real enough, but she allows him the temporary illusion that he is at one with the universe and with her holding presence. A baby who has been held will have the sense that life indeed once was perfect.

The Mother's Presence   By the time the baby is two months old he is becoming more aware of his mother's presence. Before this he couldn't tell the difference between his own spitting out, defecating, urinating, startling, sneezing and mouthing and his mother's efforts to rid him of tension and discomfort. He drifted from drowsiness to alertness with only the barest ability to absorb the stimuli that impinged from outside. As his mother interpreted the world, she gave the baby the illusion of being at one with her and with the meanings she rendered. An abundance of these near-perfect interpretations holds the baby together and begins to anchor him to the world of reality. He gets the sense that his mother's presence satisfies him and keeps him whole. Every time she rocks him, feeds him, cuddles him, speaks to him, the baby's interest in her increases. He begins to discover that her smell has something to do with getting filled up inside. His body is more relaxed when she walks around with him, when she helps his mouth to reach the breast. The baby begins then to associate safety and wholeness with the presence of his mother. The need for her touch and look becomes as powerful as the baby's need for food.

A feeding is no longer complete without a look in her eyes or a fingering of some part of her body or clothes. When his eyes make contact with hers, he begins to coo and gurgle. Getting drowsy and falling off to sleep is nicest when his body is molded into the body of his mother. The rocking motions of her body as she walks with him and gently rubs his back after a good feed make the meal seem especially satisfying.

By two months the baby has become aware that he is held together and protected from tension and excitement by these special events that go on outside the walls of his own body. This new awareness constitutes a quantum leap into humanness. The two-month-old does not absorb the momentous significance of his new awareness all at once. He now only vaguely senses that the most significant feature of these outside events is a presence with odors, touches, heartbeat and body movements that are in harmony with his own bodily states. The match between the infant's gestures and his mother's holding presence is good enough to sustain the infant's illusion that he and the mother are one. He is still not fully aware that her presence is different from all the other humanlike aspects of his surroundings.

The two-month-old is still dominated by physical need.

He doesn't much care where his pleasures and gratifications are coming from. Anyone will do, so long as he is comforted and soothed. Nevertheless, when he is bright-eyed and alert even a two-month-old can discriminate the differences among mother, father and stranger. Within ten seconds of sighting his mother's face or hearing her voice, the baby gets excited, his face lights up with a smile, and he gurgles and coos. His father's presence also makes a baby come to attention and get excited. He gazes in his father's eyes, but he doesn't smile so quickly as with mother and there is much less gurgling and cooing. As for the stranger, no matter how much he tries to act like the mother or father he simply can't get the baby to respond in quite the same way. Eventually after staring for a while the baby may smile at the new person, but he is less enthusiastic and his smile is tentative. At two months the baby recognizes his mother, but he does not yet demonstrate the active intense preference for her that he will at five months. The significance of her presence is just dawning on him.

By three months the infant is less caught up in cycles of inner tension and relief. He has been lured out of his preoccupation with his insides by the humanness of his mother's presence and the special dialogue he has with her. The pleasure and excited delight that pervade his body when he is in her presence afford his first taste of confidence in the world. Now even when tense or uncomfortable or excited by his appetites the baby is able to anticipate her smell, touch, look, comforting presence. His body fills up with pleasurable anticipation. He can wait. He confidently expects that help will come. Arousal and excitement are no longer such frightening events.

Day by day he becomes more alert and attentive to the actual happenings in his environment. In moments of quiet aloneness, waiting for mother, looking at the faces of strangers, studying his hands, sucking his fingers, fingering his bottle, the baby is commencing to sort out and classify the world into me and not-me, inside and outside, human and nonhuman, mother and not-mother.

In the beginning the baby is bound to his mother's presence by virtue of his physical excitements and appetites. By three months he is already bound to her by his psychological desire for human dialogue. The dialogue the baby has with his mother is more intense and satisfying than any other human dialogue. The fear of loss of dialogue with his mother will become more central in the baby's life than his fear of hunger or inner tension.

Mutual Cueing and Empathy   How does a mother learn to hold her baby? This question worries a mother, particularly if she is being an actual mother for the first time—not a playhouse mother with a doll that can be carried upside down by its feet and thrown under the couch for a day or two and emerge none the worse for it all. Having an actual baby is less awesome than it might seem at first, once a mother realizes that the matter doesn't rest entirely in her hands. In contrast to a doll or a fantasy baby, an actual baby is able to educate his mother if she gives him half a chance. A mother learns how to hold a baby by tuning in to what he is ready to teach her. Baby and mother educate each other with mutual cueing.

A baby has a repertoire of grunts, sighs, coos, postures, droopy-eyed looks, alert looks, finger grasps, head turnings and mouthings and a set of cries and fretting sounds that give a mother some idea of how she should hold him and interpret the world to him. A mother has a psychological past, a fantasy life, memories of childhood and an appetite for holding her baby, all of which ready her to understand what the baby is trying to tell her. She then moves her body in a way that makes the baby feel understood. If she doesn't get it quite right at first, the baby is able to shift his posture or grunt in a slightly different way until she gets the point.

The word "oneness" evokes an image of bliss where nothing exists but mother and baby gazing fondly into each other's eyes, the baby cradled perfectly and the mother absorbed in her beatific state of motherhood. Actually the beatific moments are rare. A mother is usually so occupied with diapering, rocking, feeding, bathing and wondering what her baby is crying about that on some days the moments never come at all. Most of the mutual cueing between a mother and her baby goes on when they are so busily engaged with the commonplace affairs of early babyhood that the mother doesn't realize that she is studying her baby. Whenever a mother picks up her baby for a feeding or a diapering she is reading his cues. Each feeding affords her fresh opportunity to study her baby's hand movements, while he studies her body and clothing with his fingers. Sometimes the sight of the opening and closing stroking gestures of her baby's fingers makes a mother want to put her own finger into her baby's grasp. She may lift his fingers to her mouth to kiss them or rub them against her lips. When her baby sighs or turns his head away from her breast, his mother lets him rest from the feeding. The baby gets the message that it's all right to stop for a while because the breast will still be there when he is ready to turn back. The baby catches on to his mother's gestures and silences, and moves his body so that she knows when to cradle him closer and when to give him room to kick his feet and stretch himself.

Crying is another kind of baby cueing. Although considerably more forceful and much harder to ignore, crying is nonetheless as subtle in its various shades of intention as finger movements and body posturing. When a baby cries, his mother listens to the cry wondering whether it is a hungry cry, a need-to-be-rocked cry, or perhaps the piercing cry of tension which says that incomprehensible sounds, sights and movements from the outside world are impinging on the baby's wholeness. Maybe it is a tension cry that comes from a gas bubble or unusually strong rumblings of digestion? Other cries are not true cries but fretting sounds that will stop after a few minutes even when the mother does nothing at all.

At first, cries are as puzzling as everything else about the baby. Very often a mother simply can't comprehend what the baby wants and she says so to the baby: "Why do you keep crying?" "What is it you want me to do?" "Please tell me what you want." There are days when nothing satisfies the baby, not even his feedings and rockings. In the long run, although a beginning mother may not believe it, a baby can tolerate not being understood so long as the general background of his life holds him every now and then in a way that conveys understanding. Babies have a way of flourishing in a human environment and adapting to the ordinary vagaries of their less-than-perfect human mothers.

Some babies are easier to read than others. Usually the more alike they are in temperament the easier it will be for a mother to read her baby's cues and the easier it will be for the baby to comprehend the gestures of his mother. There are exceptions. A highly excitable, hyperresponsive baby does best with a mother who is able to be especially calm. When an overly excitable baby has a mother who is as excitable as he is, the partnership will run into stormy weather.

One characteristic of an excitable mother is her disbelief in partnership. She takes on the full burden of making her baby grow, as though the baby had no life or energies of his own. She has the idea that she can bring a baby into existence by filling it up with herself. An excited mother tends to respond in exactly the same way to all her baby's needs —always feeding, always rocking and bouncing, constantly talking, constantly picking up and putting down in a manner that has no rhyme or reason. Being unable to locate the baby's distress as coming from the baby, the excited mother interprets his cries as a plea for more stimulation.

Early in life no baby has any way of knowing where his

distress is coming from. When a mother's readings are right enough, the baby begins to apprehend the source of his distress. Then his postures and gestures and crying sounds become distinct and focused. The excitable baby has more than the usual difficulty in locating the source of his distress, so his cueing remains vague for a longer time. It is harder for such a baby to educate his mother, and particularly so when she is as high-strung and tense as he is. Yet when there is a balance between the stimulation he needs and the restful quiet of oneness, even an excitable baby can eventually get the idea that he is being held and understood. The moments of harmony and wholeness will stay with him just as they do with any other baby. Having to work harder at being understood sometimes makes excited babies quite competent at getting what they want out of life.

A baby can usually educate his mother, but a mother brings something to the partnership that a baby won't acquire until much later in life. A mother has empathy for her baby. And though a baby may be exquisitely sympathetic to his mother's body movements and heartbeat, her tensions and relaxations, and her moods of sadness and peace, he cannot empathize with her. Mutual cueing is for the baby to be understood—a baby is not expected to understand a mother. Empathy is sympathy plus understanding.

Empathy is commonly thought to be a sacred and mysterious quality of the human mind, and the depth of a mother's empathy for her baby sometimes appears particularly incredible. At the sound of her baby's hunger cry a mother's breasts fill with milk and the milk flows uncontrollably until the baby stops crying. A scarcely audible alteration in her baby's breathing rouses a mother from deep sleep. Because there is a connection between how the mother's body reacts and what in fact her baby might need, such phenomena fall in the range of empathic responsiveness.

More frequently, however, a mother's empathy originates in judgment and reason. Although she responds intuitively, without conscious reasoning, her actions with her baby are guided by her knowledge of what it means to be a baby. If all a mother could do was sympathize with her baby, she wouldn't be much use to him.

Mothers, of course, do sympathize. When her baby cries, a mother's eyes may fill with tears. Her stomach may contract painfully at the sight of his arching contortions as he attempts to rid himself of digestive tensions. The affinity between mother and baby allows her to enter into his emotional and physical states and make them her own. But sympathy alone doesn't put things right.

In sympathy the boundaries between one person and another dissolve. The sympathy of a two- or three-month-old baby, whose boundaries have not yet been formed, is boundless—which is why he shares so totally in his mother's moods. However, if a mother is to be effective in bringing the world to her baby she must have one face turned to reality. She has to have her wits about her.

A mother's empathy has two sides: the side that takes in what her baby is conveying, and the side that meets his message with a sensible interpretation of the world. Empathy makes it possible for a mother to respond *effectively* to her baby's cues.

Nevertheless, a baby soon learns that some of his cues are not responded to at all and that in fact some are responded to in a manner that lets him down. A mother's empathy does not endow her with perfect understanding—which is all to the good. While it is important for a baby to have the temporary illusion of a boundless universe that conforms perfectly to his needs, minute accretions of less-than-perfect understanding stimulate and nourish the baby's appetites for growth and change.

In the first months of life, a mother's love for her baby is unconditional. She does what she does without expecting her baby to appreciate her or return her love. Nor does she actively try to disillusion him. Her unconditional love *and* her less-than-perfect understanding prepare the baby for his inevitable disenchantment.

Choreography—Molding and Stiffening   As the infant undergoes his second birth, his changing needs for emotional closeness and distance will be reflected in his manner of approaching his mother and pushing himself away from her. In earliest infancy the choreography is confined to the mother's lap, but the energies that inform the baby's body movements are no less intense than they will be when he slides off his mother's lap and creeps off into wider circles of space.

Between two and five months an infant cannot take steps toward or away from his mother. Nor can he creep away. He can barely sit up unless someone props him on a pillow or puts him in an infant seat. But he can posture his body, lift his head, turn his head away, follow events with his eyes, touch, grasp, smell and listen. The limp, thrashing, uncoordinated body gestures of the first month of life have been replaced by movements with direction and intentionality. The movements and postures also have emotional and psychological meaning. As early as two months, the posturing of an infant's body expresses his sensations of oneness —and also the sensations of separateness.

Molding is the prototypical posture of the lap baby. The baby curves his body and expands it, especially in the chest and stomach regions, until its contours fit perfectly with the contours of the body of his mother. At two months the infant does not feel the contours and edges of either his body or his mother's. The fit, as far as the infant is concerned, is so perfect that all boundaries melt away. It is as though he and his mother are merged—the being of one dissolved into the being of the other.

The odor, vibrations, body noises and movements of the mother become the odor, vibrations, body noises and felt movements of the baby. He imagines that the sensations and rhythms of his mother are coming from inside his own body. Since the molding posture minimizes the edges between a baby and his mother, he easily picks up the positive and negative mood changes of his mother. When she is content and confident, the baby is permeated with the bliss of her unconditional goodness. In their unity, mother and baby move together within a magic orbit that keeps out all that might disturb the baby's bodily peace. The tensions on the inside of the baby's body are converted into pleasurably alternating rhythms of gentle tension and quiet relaxation. These inner rhythms are the core of the body-self of a human infant, furnishing his body with its harmony and wholeness.

The walls of the body have two skin surfaces—one, which we commonly call "skin," that faces outward to the world, and one that faces inward, forming the lining of the inside of the body and the alimentary canal of mouth, throat, esophagus, stomach and intestine. The mouth region, combining as it does both skin surfaces, is nature's first bridge between inner and outer worlds. Information comes to an infant from the stirrings on the inside of his body and from the sensations that flow inside when he sucks, smells and touches. Thus his first experiences of the new world are indistinguishable from the sensations and rhythms that emanate from "inside." What is outside blends in with the rhythms of heartbeat, stomach contractions, eliminative urges and swallowing. "Gut" knowledge rules the infant's perceptions and sustains the illusion of oneness.

In the first two or three months the lap baby molds to his mother—her arms, stomach, thighs and chest—surveying the world from the vantage point of the blending of their bodies. Peaceful tension-relaxation rhythms, eyes looking into eyes, the mother's heartbeat, the feel of the nipple, sucking motions, the lap that merges with the baby's back, neck and buttocks, all blend into a single perception which could as well mean "breast" as it could "sucking and swallowing." Whatever is not perceived in this fashion is an interruption of the bliss of oneness.

But if nothing were ever to disturb the peace, the second birth could not begin. The world outside the mother-infant orbit could not become known. The mother would never be comprehended as a person in her own right and the baby would not form the other part of his body-self—the rind, or outer boundaries of his body.

The baby discovers the rind of his body by *stiffening*. Hunger, cold, digestive problems, too much light, too much noise, sudden movements disturb oneness, producing tension inside and on the surface of the baby's body. He uncurls from the molding posture and thrusts his arms and legs outward from the center of his body. His body stiffens. His head is thrown backward and he arches his body away from the body of the person holding him.

On those occasions when a mother is in a bad mood or feeling tense about herself or her baby, the baby reacts as though her tensions were coming from inside his own body. He automatically stiffens. Stiffening his body is the baby's natural way of pushing out tension. Although the baby imagines he is escaping from sensations inside, stiffening also succeeds in removing him from the unpleasantness that comes to him from the outside world. Spitting, sneezing and coughing are kinds of stiffening. On some days the baby may spit up the food that his mother gives him, pushing out the tensions of too much noise, too much mother, or funny-tasting milk.

Molding is the curve inward and toward others. Stiffening propels outward. But it is not merely an escape device—it also releases the body and brings it into an altered mode of relatedness to the world. A baby's bright-eyed alert look means that he is relatively free from tensions, yet his alertness is always accompanied by a slight stiffening of his body. Stiffening goes along with outward-directed alertness, looking and listening, reaching and grasping. When looking is combined with touching with the hands, another bridge is constructed between the inside world and the outside world. Stiffening also marks out the rims of the body surface, pressing the baby to rub against the events that happen outside the walls of his body.

Toward the end of his fourth month the baby is still a lap baby, but his attitude and posture are considerably more alert. He often perches upright at the edge of his mother's lap, balancing his body with his own back and neck muscles —his mother's hands and fingertips providing unobtrusive support. Once in a while he stems his legs, stiffening them against the lap of his mother, leaning his body away from hers. That way the baby gets a firmer look at his mother's face and he senses the edges between her body and his. As he perches and pushes away, he stimulates his muscles and the outer surface of his body. By now the baby has had numerous experiences that have contributed to the awakening of his outer-body surface: being bathed and dried, rubbed and caressed, dressed and undressed, patted and walked about. Now even when he molds, the blurring of one body with the other is less total. The pressure of his mother's body against his own tones up edges of his body. A spark of surface tension keeps the edges of his body permanently alive and energized. Molding and stiffening soon become more a matter of degree than two sharply differentiated body postures.

Thus by the time he is five months old the baby is somewhat aware of the boundaries of his body, but only at special times and still only vaguely. He scarcely perceives that his feet and hands belong to the same body. They have a way of sometimes "disappearing" and the baby forgets all about them. Inside and outside sensations are often indistinguishable. Nevertheless, the baby has achieved his rudimentary knowledge of the two sources of his body-self. He now has a core experience of a body-self derived from the pleasantly alternating rhythms of tension and relaxation associated with safety and holding. Similarly, stiffening alertness, the pressures of his mother's body against his, being alone to study his fingers, being bathed and caressed make up the baby's first lessons in boundaries and edges. The five-month-old is a very definite someone—a self with harmonious rhythms and safety inside, and alertness and edges facing out to the new world.

The Baby's Mind—Sucking, Grasping and Looking   A baby can educate himself. When a mother leaves him alone in his bassinet, she communicates to her baby that he is not abandoned. She does not overwhelm him with radio noises, rattles, mobiles, toys and music boxes. She places within the reach of his eyes and hands the few objects he is able to take in on his own. What a baby finds out on his own, lying in his crib, cannot be taught him by anyone else. The knowledge he acquires supplements the lessons he learns lying in his mother's lap.

The basic subject matter of an infant's self-taught lessons is his body—what his body can do, how the various parts of his body fit together and act together, and finally the effects his body has on the world. For the first twelve months of life the only mind a baby has is a body-mind. With it he examines, imagines, explores, ponders, studies, supposes, conjectures, conjures, classifies and generalizes, even though he has no words, thoughts, or definite images to call on. The baby's first order of business, then, is to find out a few things about the workings of his body-mind.

Initially, from his second to fourth month, the baby's mind consists largely of kicking, hand-waving, listening, touching, smelling and, most eminently, sucking, grasping and looking. During this time, toys serve exclusively to excite and perpetuate the sensations and movements that constitute the baby's mind. The two-month-old grasps for the sake of grasping. He kicks for kicking's sake. He couldn't care less about what happens to the objects he holds in his hands. The fact that the rattle he grasps makes a sound is of no moment. It's grand and serious enough just to grasp and shake.

A baby's hands will become his most important tool for manipulating the world, but before he can use his hands effectively he has to find out what hands are. A newborn waves his hands about. He touches. He grasps. But it all happens quite by accident and his hands go to no particular place. An infant's hands can't get where they want to go unless they are guided. At the start of life only the baby's mouth can guide his hands to any definite place, and not surprisingly, the place is the mouth—nowhere else. A few fortunate babies can get their fists to their mouths for sucking in a matter of days, but most babies can't do this reliably until their second or third month. Although the baby doesn't learn much about the world in the act of getting his fingers to his mouth, the working relationship between the hand and the mouth teaches him a valuable lesson in what hands are all about. The baby imagines his hands by sucking his fingers, fist, or thumb. Sucking energizes the baby's hands. At the same time, the sucking movements generate vitality and sensations on the inner surfaces of the baby's body.

At birth a baby can suck. He can also grasp. So, early on in life he also studies his hands by grasping whatever chance brings within range—a rattle, a blanket corner, his father's shirt, his mother's finger. A few weeks after learning to get his fist to his mouth, the baby discovers that things he grasps can also be brought to his mouth for sucking. Likewise, he begins to suppose that he is able to grasp whatever he happens to be sucking. If the baby grasps his blanket, he is likely to bring it to his mouth for sucking. Grasping stimulates sucking and sucking makes the baby want to grasp. The working relationship between hand and mouth has moved up a notch.

The baby now also responds to the sound of his own voice

by listening, and the act of listening in itself can activate the baby's cooing and gurgling. The sensations and movements that make up a baby's mind are being put together by these circular activities of sucking and grasping, listening and vocalizing. For a while all the baby does is repeat the circles over and over again. It's quite enough.

Although this is a good enough curriculum for a two- or three-month-old, it doesn't give the baby the power to act as an agent who moves the outside world and controls its happenings. A baby will not achieve the status of manipulator and controller of his hands until his eyes are sufficiently educated to guide the hands where the baby desires them to go. So long as the mouth remains in charge of things, the baby's hands will not go very far. In contrast, his eyes will inform the baby about the existence of events and objects that are some distance from his body. When eyes and hands get to work together, then a baby will *reach out* to the world.

At around two months a baby begins to follow the movements of his hands with his eyes, but he can't ever get them to stay in view. The baby's hands cease to exist the moment they disappear from view; they appear and disappear unpredictably. At this stage of life, the baby's mouth is still much cleverer than his eyes. The baby's mouth usually seems to know where the baby's hands are. And the hands know how to find their way to the mouth.

From the perspective of the two- or three-month-old, the hands he sucks, the hands he looks at and the hands he grasps with are three different sets of hands. Nevertheless, his hands are fascinating; hand watching, hand grasping and finger sucking are the favored lessons of an infant lying alone in his bassinet. At around four months there is a subtle shift in the baby's attention. He indicates a strong desire to hold and grasp the objects that present themselves to his eyes. Because of his intense interest in his hands, he is bound one day to see his hand near the rattle he desires to grasp.

If it is within reach the baby may even stretch his fingers and find himself grasping a rattle.

Thus he begins to watch his fingers on his blanket as they rub, scratch and fondle it. As he brings the blanket corner to his mouth for sucking, he suddenly halts. He stares at his fingers on the blanket. He forgets all about sucking the blanket. How is the baby able to interrupt his habitual circuit of grasping and sucking? The act of looking is what immobilizes his hands. Looking holds the hands in place, preventing them from falling away into nonexistence or going automatically to the mouth. By holding his gaze the baby is keeping contact with the outside world—the world has less of a chance of slipping away.

The five-month-old can turn his head and hold on to a moving object with his eyes. The baby can hold on to his hands with his eyes. He can control hand movement with his eyes. He still isn't able to reach too far for what he wants to grasp, but the baby's eyes have acquired the ability to lead the hands where the baby wants them to go.

The outside world now comes under the control of the baby's mind. The baby gets his first inkling that his body can make things happen. In his first manipulations of the outside world, the baby will consider his mouth, hands and eyes to be the prime movers.

Now the baby can remember his hands when they disappear from view. He has a continuing sense of where they are. The hands he looks at, sucks on, shakes, grasps with and pulls with are the same set of hands. So now the baby is interested in the various effects that hands produce in the world.

A mother usually puts a rattle in her baby's crib in a place where the baby's hand is apt to come across it. At first when the baby isn't touching the rattle or grasping it, it doesn't exist; his body doesn't remember where it is. At five months, the baby's eyes remind the baby of the rattle's whereabouts.

The baby grasps the rattle in his hands. He shakes his hands. The rattle makes a sound. The baby brings the rattle before his eyes in order to examine the connection between the shaking movement of his hands and the sound coming from the rattle. He supposes that shaking hands produce sound. For a few days he shakes everything he lays his hands on. He looks at his shaking hands, listening for the sound of a rattle. Some shaking things make sounds and some do not. But for a time the baby persists in the notion that shaking a part of his body will produce sound. He shakes his head as though that would make the sound that comes from a rattle. Once in a while the baby is able to bring the rattle to his mouth. The soft rubber surfaces of the rattle soothe the baby's gums, lips and the inside of his mouth. But the rattle is unresponsive and ungiving; not at all like the soft, molding, pleasant-smelling body of his mother. Nor does the rattle taste like his own fist and fingers or produce gentle rhythms inside his body the way his fingers do. This is another way a baby gets to suppose what a rattle is. And what it is not.

In and around the baby's world are objects that he can touch and look at. Not all can be put to the baby's mouth. Some, like the wicker sides of his bassinet, make scratching sounds when the baby runs his fingers across them. Listening to the scratching sounds might make the baby feel like cooing, or he might shake his hands to keep up the sound of scratching. He soon finds out that only scratching makes scratching sounds.

Moving objects hold a special fascination for a baby. Movement is associated with humanness. At times the movements out in the world momentarily confirm the baby's impression that movement and humanness go together. Mobiles or leaves on a tree have a way of falling into facelike configurations as they waft in the breeze. The baby then smiles with mistaken but happy recognition. He coos, talking to the leaves. But something is amiss. The leaves stop moving before the baby is ready for them to stop. And the leaves don't make sounds back at him. Leaves and mobiles suddenly move again and set up patterns that are strange to the baby. He may still smile but now the baby is surprised and his smile is a surprise smile. The novelty of the situation commands the baby's interest but he is confused and puzzled. His mother knows just when to move and when to be still. Her eyes don't disappear. Her face doesn't get jumbled that way and neither does the face of his father or the other faces that occasionally parade around the room. Furthermore, the baby can hold his mother's gaze by simply gazing back at her. She can be counted on to know the right moment to answer the baby's cooing.

Unfamiliar experiences with nonhuman moving objects alter the baby's expectations of the world. Certain moving objects reciprocate and respond as though to confirm the movements of the baby. Some parts of the world empathize with the energies of a baby and some seem not to. The difference between animate and inanimate has presented itself to the baby's mind. Sometimes the baby can have a dialogue with moving things. At other times the dialogue falls apart. In order to investigate this problem further, a baby needs time to be alone and time to be in his mother's lap.

Having a Conversation For the first two months the dialogue between a baby and his mother is a dialogue of quiet gesture. After baby and mother have gotten to know each other, interactions between them become comfortably ritualized. They depend on each other and on the several dialogues that make up the baby's day—the feeding dialogue, the bathing dialogue, the diapering dialogue, the carrying and rocking dialogue. When feeding her baby, the mother holds him near her breast and waits until the baby's posture, fingers, mouth and lips signal that he is ready to hold the breast and suck. A baby may feed in a leisurely way or fast and furiously if that's his style. His eyes are sometimes

closed. When his eyes open he finds his mother's eyes looking into his. Mother and infant gaze at each other. Other
babies might stare at the breast and finger it. Once in a while
the baby interrupts his meal and gurgles and smiles. His
mother answers. The baby relaxes into the peace of the
predictable feeding dialogue. The dialogue stays with him
when he's all alone.

When mother and baby are looking into each other's eyes
they are having a conversation. They are satisfied merely
gazing and occasionally touching fingers. By the time he is
three months old, however, a baby indicates his desire to
have more stimulating and exciting dialogues. At this age
the baby's mind has begun to acquire active ways of shutting
out the sights and sounds that might make him irritable or
worried. He is building up his own stimulus barrier. Therefore he is not so dependent on his mother for protection
from excitation. During the day the baby is more frequently
alert and bright-eyed, and at night his sleep is deeper and
longer. Cycles of feeding, sleeping and waking, night and
day, are more distinctly organized and "scheduled." When
the baby is awake, his energies flow outward in a search for
interesting challenges. Every so often he kicks his feet and
gurgles in readiness for a bout of stimulating conversation.

A mother understands what her baby is asking for when
his body poses an invitation for something more than mere
finger-touching and eye-gazing. The baby's new kind of
playfulness is an experiment—a method of confirming his
increasing sense that he is becoming capable of managing
his excitement. But not everybody is invited to the party.
Only those who understand the rules can come. In order to
have a conversation with a three-month-old it is essential to
have a sense of what excitement means to a baby. A baby's
idea of conversation is different from the usual adult variety.

Eye-to-eye contact is permitted for starting adult conversations, but after a few seconds the intimacy becomes
embarrassing. The speaker glances away and back in the

course of the conversation, and finally he punctuates the end of his statement by returning his gaze to the listener's eyes as though to say, "It's your turn now." With their eyes, the participants in an adult conversation mark off an alternating pattern of speaking and then listening. Eye movements support the rules for polite everyday conversation. Lovers, quarrelers, and mothers and babies sometimes have different ways of going about a conversation. Their conversations are more exciting and out of the ordinary.

Lovers and quarrelers hover on the brink of annihilating one another with their passions. Lovers hold each other with their eyes, speaking the identical words at the identical moment; they do not mark off their separate boundaries by alternations of listening and then speaking. They turn their eyes away and then return their gaze, trusting that the sympathy of their synchronous longings will once again bring them together in merging oneness. And repeatedly the lovers risk the melting of boundaries. Though they merge and speak as one, they continue to exist as two separate individuals.

Quarrelers test the extent of their hatred by raging as one. They come together in mutual acrimony. They look past each other and through each other. Their eyes rage, they shout simultaneously, the vilifications of one drowning out the denigrations of the other. Though they speak as one, they must make sure of their boundaries and separateness. In this way quarrelers assert their power and invulnerability. Many couples will only chance the coming together of love after risking the savageries of mutual malevolence. For them the merging ardors of love are more frightening and shameful than the boundary-setting furies of hatred.

A mother isn't ashamed of the ardors of eye-to-eye contact or love-talking with her infant child. Her high-pitched voice and elongated vowel sounds are just like infant sounds. As she speaks to her baby, a mother's facial expression becomes an exaggeration of humanness. She stretches her mouth wide, raises her brows, and opens her eyes as far as possible. Frequently she brings her face very close to the baby's face, holding her exaggerated expression and gazing into her baby's eyes for an unusually long time.

Merely by staring into her eyes in an inviting way, a baby can get his mother to speak to him. When that doesn't work, kicking his feet and smiling will certainly do the trick. The first few conversations, the baby just listens and smiles delightedly, and when he's had enough he simply turns his gaze away.

By the end of the third month the baby embellishes his end of the conversation. He gurgles and coos in response to his mother's baby talk. At first mother and baby politely alternate the roles of speaker and listener. But the more fun they have, the more the arousal of their conversation builds. When they finally really let go, they are so perfectly in tune that they speak simultaneously. Once the enthusiasm has built to this peak, the partners scarcely ever bother to wait and take turns. A mother keeps up the pace until she senses her baby's satisfaction and willingness to terminate. The baby is then left with the impression of having generated his own excitement and managed it all quite nicely.

The high arousal, exaggeration and heated simultaneity of mother-infant conversation reflect the power of the emotions that bind them to each other. Whenever conversations are steamed up by powerful emotions—patriotism, mourning, religion, battle—human beings tend to speak in unison, most often to dissolve the barriers between one person and another, occasionally to make sure the boundaries are still there.

A baby's excited conversations with his mother are spawned out of their basic dialogue—the dialogue of gestures that convey wholeness and safety. The baby is finding out that when he turns his crude and formless excitements in the direction of his mother, he is able to convert them into the meaningful dialogues of adoration and aggression.

A baby learns a great many lessons lying alone in his crib, but some matters can only become comprehensible in the context of dialogue and conversation.

The Real Madonna Many mothers find the molding closeness typical of oneness to be the most gratifying experience of motherhood. They virtually bloom in the climate of intimacy and preoccupied mutual attunement that comes from being at one with the baby. Reading her baby's subtle, wordless cues through her own empathic gestures is an experience that such a mother would like to prolong. It is not unusual for mothers who thrive on oneness to suppose they are superfluous when their baby is more emphatic and lucid. "Now that he doesn't need me, I wish he would grow up." "I used to be able to understand him perfectly. He never had a chance to be unhappy. Now he keeps pushing me away and I don't understand him at all."

For other mothers the baby's total neediness and dependency during the time of oneness can be bewildering and frightening. The style of these mothers is usually better suited to the later phases of motherhood. They look forward to the time when the baby is independent and clearer about what it is he wants and needs. All the feeding, bathing, burping, rocking and holding are chores which bring fatigue and frustration rather than pleasure. The mother may feel guilty because she doesn't "follow the books" and truly delight in cuddling her baby and holding him close. Not infrequently she discovers that other people, perhaps the father or grandmother, are much better at soothing and comforting the baby. She becomes discouraged and wonders about her adequacy as a mother.

All mothers, even those who derive their greatest rewards from these earliest months of the baby's life, have moments of resentment about having to devote so much of their energy to the physical care of this helpless and needy creature. It is a common experience for a mother to be angry with her baby when he cries and frets all day, awakens her constantly during the night, and spits up milk on her body and clothes. The powerful bodily needs of the baby are an assault on the bodily and mental integrity of the mother.

Yet a mother survives the absolute dependence of her infant. She comes through the first five months of motherhood as a whole person. But whether or not she is aware of it, the mother has been through an emotional upheaval. Her resources and confidence have been put to a trial—a trial which is all too often made more severe by a mother's severity with herself and her unrealistic expectations of self-perfection. A mother need not match up with her infant's illusions of perfection in order for the infant to thrive and be whole. A mother survives best when she allows herself the imperfections of an ordinary mother.

In the course of becoming an ordinary devoted mother, a woman is deprived of the gratifications and certainties that other mortals take for granted. Gone is the beat of ordinary time, vanished the rims and surfaces of ordinary space and the familiar roots that held her to the earth. A mother wonders who she has become and whether she will ever again be the same as she was before her baby was born. In the beginning weeks, night blended into day like a hall of mirrors reflecting a remorseless succession of feedings and holdings, diaperings and bathings. The baby has treated her body as if it were his. He has sucked out what he needed and thrown away the husk without so much as a sign of gratitude. The aura of soured milk, diaper smell and baby powder envelops the body of the mother.

At last the day arrives when time begins to order itself into a recognizable pattern of predictable startings and endings. On that magical day the baby plays alone after a feeding, enjoys a hug and a walk-about and contentedly goes off for his nap. The "routine," the "schedule" has finally come. For mother there is time for a shower, a private thought, a look into a favorite book, a nap. However, the next week, some-times as soon as the next day, the baby becomes irritable again, dissatisfied and ungratifiable. The anticipated naps do not take place—not for baby, not for mother. Feedings terminate in howling complaints.

Some days are better, but some are awful. After the most miserable morning, mother and baby somehow make it for a walk to the park. On the way the baby gives his most angelic smile to the chuckling stranger who peers into the carriage. "What an affectionate, sweet baby," says the stranger. The mother's throat becomes a lump of anger. She is in no mood to respond good-humoredly to the well-inten-tioned comment on her baby's disposition. *How little you know*, she thinks. *Behind that smile is the soul of a devil.*

A mother survives. Most of all, she survives her hatred for her baby. A mother who has been held as a baby is able to endure her hatred because she knows that she will not vent her anger on her baby or destroy him. She is the victor be-cause she does not convert her angry thoughts and emotions into actions that would abuse or hurt her baby. When they return from the park she feeds her baby and holds him. They may have a conversation or game together. She continues to soothe him when he cries, though she may feel like crying herself. Typically, a mother does not appreciate the full ex-tent of her victory. Her anger terrifies her even though it brought not a shred of harm to her baby and she went right on being an ordinary devoted mother.

It is easiest for a mother to retain a sense of her own goodness when her baby is thriving and content. Her baby's misery arouses despair and anger. She conceives of her anger as a distortion, a blemish on the picture of ideal motherhood. She is certain she is the only mother who ever had murder-ous, dreadful thoughts about her baby.

Every time a baby's misery leads a mother to suppose that she has failed him, it stirs up memories of the failures of her own babyhood and childhood. Accordingly, her despair and bewilderment are compounded. She imagines she has failed in two directions: as the mother of her baby, as the baby of her own mother. By envisioning herself as a bad, frustrating mother she unconsciously revives an image of herself as the bad, frustrating infant of her mother. Perhaps she imagines she was a greedy baby who drained away all her mother's goodness, or a sick, feeble baby who never gave her mother satisfaction. It is likely she also imagines that she had a mother who always failed and disappointed her. These silent, barely recognized memories and fantasies eat into the confidence of a mother. But, since nobody ever had a perfect mother and nobody ever achieves perfect babyhood, such awesome fantasies are actually predictable and ordinary.

During these trying months a mother often needs some special holding for herself. She also wishes for someone else to hold the baby for a time. At these moments most fathers and grandparents can take over holding the baby very nicely. They are likely to be calmer, and the baby thrives. Nothing restores a mother's confidence quite so well as the sight of her thriving baby. Every now and then a mother needs to get away from her baby to get her bearings and collect her wits.

Sentimentality, defiant self-sufficiency, false pride and fearful denial of her ordinary anger will prevent a mother from asking for the help and comforting she should have. Ordinary anger is then all too easily converted into bitterness and uncontrollable rage.

The five-month-old has no anger or hatred. His love is still the amorphous, shared perfection of his mother's goodness. From the baby's point of view he is an angel baby held in the sumptuous lap of a saintly Madonna. The primitive form of love he experiences is based on his need to be held together and manage his excitements. The bits and fragments of his life are held together by his mother. When he is satisfied and thriving, he supposes that he partakes of the goodness of his mother. When he is trembling with excited hungers, he possibly imagines himself to be an attacking devourer. Badness for an infant is in his dread of attacking too fiercely, falling forever, and falling to bits. Nevertheless, the baby who has formed even this most primitive love attachment learns that his excitement doesn't destroy and that the wholeness of his being is always restored. He finds out that he is not annihilated by his tensions and excitements.

So the angel-Madonna image is not a lie. The illusion of shared goodness is a necessary precondition for the eventual comprehension of badness and hatred. As the baby comes to recognize that he does not share in the magical perfection of his mother's goodness, he will realize that he sometimes hates her and that she is not always there to make him feel whole and good. He will then bear the idea that love is not perfect. And he will also learn to locate his goodness within himself. Then he will have the possibility of becoming an adult who can measure the extent of his anger and aggression.

Illusions hold the fabric of human life together. Through illusion the crude energies of human nature are shaped into culturally viable forms of love and hate. Sentimentality and pollyannaish denial of evil are the subterfuges which trivialize human emotions. In contrast illusions are not frauds. Only when they are used to screen out the possibility of the demonic do the icons of angels and Madonnas lie.

For her baby who temporarily thrives on the illusion of goodness and perfection, the ordinary devoted mother is a saint. As for herself, the mother of a young infant soon wants the boundaries of her being restored. She has been able to risk falling apart and the excited sensuality of becoming one with her baby. But, in an ordinary way, she wants to sleep when she is tired, to eat an unhurried, un-interrupted meal, to shower her body, to read a book, to plant flowers, to make love and be held.

Separation Begins At about four or five months, just around the time that a mother experiences the need for the firm edges of her own boundaries, her baby begins to act in ways that help her to be comfortable about becoming a person again in her own right. A baby's special smile to his mother at the peak of oneness is the signal that the second birth is about to begin. This smile is altogether different from the two-month-old's automatic smile of recognition. The two-month-old was responding to the familiarity of his mother's brand of humanness. His being merged with the humanness of her voice, smell, body movement and heartbeat. Little by little this primary bond of oneness has been augmented by the specific dialogue the baby has with his mother.

At five months the baby's smile of recognition is accompanied by concentrated looking and careful study of his mother's body and clothing. His eyes and head turn to follow her movements in and out of the room. He *actively* holds his body at attention to listen for her voice and watch for her appearance. Now the baby does more than merely recognize the difference between his mother and others. He *actively* keeps track of her comings and goings. The baby is actively longing for his mother—which means that his first human memories are being put together.

The baby now has a specific attachment to a specific mother. He will play out the drama of becoming a separate and unique self with this *one* human partner and with no other person. His father plays a significant role in the drama, but until separateness is achieved the father's part is confined to a subplot that enriches and fills out the basic mother-infant relationship.

Many other people may have become familiar to the

infant by the time he is five months old. He might smile in almost the same way to his father, grandmother or sister as he smiles to his mother. Yet nothing he will experience with them will be so commanding or intense as the bond the baby has with his mother. He will not be so disappointed with others or love them or hate them with quite as much passion. Their loss or disappearance will not bring the child to the edge of despair.

The special relationship the infant shares with his mother must be flexible enough to include love for others. It must be strong enough to bear the strain of the child's struggles to become a self. Above all, the specific attachment to the mother must hold together when the awful fact of separateness finally dawns on the child. At each step of the way, whenever his mother disappoints him or the world frustrates his efforts to conquer it, the child will long to restore the primary bliss of oneness, when the harmony inside him was like being an angel baby in the lap of a Madonna.

Chapter Four

Beginning Separation and Early Conquests

Four Months to Eleven Months
(Reaching Out and Creeping Away)

The Invisible Bond   Nobody has to tell a baby when to begin to separate. The aliveness that girds the baby's muscles and impels him to look with his eyes and grasp with his fingers comes from inside the baby. With his attachment bond secured, he can begin to explore the world outside the mother-infant orbit of oneness. Like a seedling, a baby requires only the right kind of soil and nourishment. Then the energy of his growth processes will be able to do the job of pushing him into the world. The same growth processes ensure that the baby knows just how to reach out to the world and drink it in.

What makes a baby a good deal more complicated than a flower, which has its blossoming neatly settled and arranged right in the seed, is the baby's natural tendency to uproot himself and take off. Whereas a flower stops growing once it is torn from the soil, a human baby flourishes only when he can gratify his urges to uproot and get moving.

A baby's soil is his attachment to his mother. This is another way of saying that an infant's physical growth is nourished and given direction by psychological forces. During the period of oneness we could watch the attachment bond being formed in the molding and stiffening postures of the baby and the holding gestures of the mother. Likewise, as he gradually separates, some approximation of a baby's changing comprehension of the bond will be evident in his movements through the space that surrounds his mother. But for the most part the psychological forces that give a baby his human vitality are as invisible as the energies that empower him to grow and expand. The bond represents the starting point of the baby's psychological birth.

To the five-month-old, the notion that either he or his mother exists without the other is inconceivable. It is not that a five-month-old is selfish or possessive. He simply has no way of envisioning himself without simultaneously conjuring some aspect of his mother—her touch, her holding arms, her smell, her eyes, the nipple in his mouth, her presence in the world. The second birth is dominated by the psychological changes that will make it possible for the infant conjurer eventually to comprehend that his mother is a separate human being. Fortunately a baby's awareness of the disappointing and frightening fact of his separateness will not come to him until his memory, judgment and body movements are more reliable and certain.

Like cosmic rays and atomic particles, which are also invisible, the bond between mother and baby makes itself known by the effects it produces. The bond is powerful enough to pull the baby back to safety as he wanders across the thresholds of the world. The baby's confidence and courage inform us that the bond is also flexible enough to let the baby wander. Although the mother's breast no longer flows with milk at the sound of her baby's cry, she can look at him from across a room and apprehend whether he needs to be picked up, smiled at, or left alone. Although the mother now comes and goes in her own orbit as the baby does in his, their separate orbits are polarized by the energies of the bond. The bond is like a magnetic force which attracts a baby to his mother and a mother to her baby. It is a field of emotional relatedness through which others may pass without ever being touched. However, anyone who understands what it is like to be a baby or a mother is able to see it. A mother and a baby electrify each other with a look or a silence. While talking to a friend, a mother may shift her position in her chair. The baby, playing on a mat in another corner of the room, looks up as though to make sure she is still there. As he confirms her presence, he smiles. His smile catches his mother's eye. Without dropping a beat of her conversation the mother smiles back and says, "Hi! there."

The field of emotional relatedness which constitutes the invisible bond keeps the attraction between a mother and her baby alive, bringing them together when the baby is in a state of need and allowing them to part when the baby has restored his wholeness. In this way a baby is able to grow into his own being, while playing alone in the presence of his mother.

Babies know when to start separating. A baby's inborn appetite for human relatedness is strong enough to restrain his natural growth urges, especially when he hasn't gotten the kind of nourishment he needs. A baby whose mother has been depressed, overtired, or otherwise emotionally unavailable for holding and dialogue may delay his first moves into separateness. He keeps on trying to mold and keeps his attention turned away from the world outside the mother-infant orbit, until he gets the relatedness that will establish and sustain the invisible bond. On the other hand, some babies start to separate unusually early, particularly those whose mothers had no belief in the baby's urges to grow and grab on to the world. Such mothers act as though the entire responsibility of shaping a baby belonged to them. Their continuously intrusive excitability may often prompt a baby to move into separateness as quickly as possible.

Such babies seem to prefer strangers, and as early as three months they stiffen against the entrapment of oneness, looking eagerly to the other-than-mother world.

Most often by the time a baby is four months old he has acquired the psychological energies that will regulate the energies of his growth processes. Together, both sources of energy contribute to the power and flexibility of the invisible bond.

The Mother of Separation   A mother views the bond between herself and her baby from the wide end of the telescope. The bond is the most focused part of her life, but it does not constitute her entire vision of existence. There are moments when she concentrates all her emotional energy on creating a holding environment for her baby. However, her world is infinitely vaster than her baby's compact world, and she can imagine an existence for herself that has nothing to do with the existence of her baby. The baby is not in her mind constantly, but when she wishes, a mother can image her baby's face and body. She can even picture the details of the room he might be in and imagine exactly what he is doing. Her heart may ache and she may worry when separated from her baby, but a mother knows that before too long she will be back with him. A four-month-old baby has no way of confirming his mother's existence when she is away from him. So he relies on magic to make himself safe. He imagines his mother as an extension of himself.

How the vague possibility of separation from mother at four months becomes a more or less firm reality toward the end of the second year of life is the dominant thread of the tapestry of the second birth.

The other thread is the energies and sequences of the infant's inborn growth processes. The way a baby reacts to reaching out, sitting up, creeping, standing and walking will reveal just how far he has come in his second birth and what it means to him. The two threads are inextricably enmeshed. Neither has human meaning without the other. There would be no need for a second birth if the infant's total neediness and appetite for human attachment had not bound him into oneness with his mother in the first place. Correspondingly, the second birth would not take place if the infant's urges to grow and expand were not pushing him out of the orbit of oneness.

The world is beckoning. The infant reaches his arms out to touch it. He stretches his body away from the body of his mother. He perches at the edge of her lap. When she holds him, his leg and arm muscles push his body up so that he can be sure to have a good view of the world over her shoulder. His arms press against his mother's chest and his head inclines away from her face for a more distant perspective on her. The baby studies his mother's face with deep concentration as though he had never seen it before.

The face he examines is not the face of the mother of oneness. The mother of separation is "out there" in the world—a mother-in-the-flesh who lives outside the bounds of the baby's body, alongside the other things that are out there. Yet she stands out against the background of all other faces, voices, sounds, sights and movements. Her face, her body and her presence light up the contours and corners of the rest of the "out-there" world.

Without an attachment to a mother, a child cannot locate himself in the world. Creeping and walking proceed in a vacuum. The child is cast adrift without orientation or direction. Distance is meaningless to a young child unless it is distance from someone with whom he has a dialogue. Deprived of the beacon of a mother's presence, a child has no place to return to, no way to imagine how far or where to creep or walk. There is no exhilaration or joy in moving the body. Instead the child falls and bumps into the objects of the out-there world in a desperate attempt to locate the edges of his body and the boundaries of his world. Later, words may be spoken, but they cannot be used for dialogue and conversation.

The mother of separation comes and goes in her own orbit. The five-month-old now has to reckon with her comings and goings as he begins to move in his orbit. As he pushes away from her he must be able to find her again and come back to her. Reaching out is irresistible. But it worries the baby too. He is not sure what to do with all his energy and excitement. Will it carry him so far that he will lose his mother? Will he lose his direction in the world? And what has happened to the mother of oneness?

The mother of oneness stays with the baby as a reminder of well-being, satisfaction, relaxation, confidence and goodness. The baby who can revive and hold on to these reminders knows where he is in the world. He trusts the world's novelty and finds it curious and interesting—not altogether strange or threatening. Such a baby does not have to worry too much about the location and existence of his actual mother. His confidence includes the idea that his actual mother—the mother-in-the-flesh—will stay put. She will be his beacon of orientation, his anchor of safety. She will not cast him adrift or abandon him.

While the mother of separation does not stay put in one place, she does make sure that her comings and goings are not mysterious. Her movements are predictable and reliable. She is never gone so far or so long from her baby that he imagines he has lost her forever.

The mother of separation creates a world that stimulates her baby's curiosity. She is in tune with the excitement of exploring, searching, stretching and reaching. When she notes her baby's interest in a toy, she places it far enough away to help him stretch but close enough for him to reach. When his eyes are entranced by a new toy or when he is bending all his efforts toward creeping away, she doesn't grab the baby up and redirect his attention to herself. She is near enough for him to come to her or call her when he needs her. She lets the baby play alone in her presence so that he can undergo the psychological birth that will endow him with his personal uniqueness.

Choreography—Creeping, Home Base, Checking Back, Refueling Several months before he will creep across the room and out the door a baby begins to inch his body to the edge of his mother's lap. His body is eager to slide down and onto the floor, but at five months his mind cannot encompass the full sweep of lap-to-floor movement. He perches and inches until his mother catches on. She helps the baby down and places him on his stomach so he can play alone at her feet.

The baby plays alone by reaching out to touch with his hands. His eyes are telling his hands where to go. The vision of hands going to a definite place in the world stimulates the rest of the baby's body to entertain the idea of reaching. Reaching out is the basic step of creeping away.

To bridge the interval between reaching and creeping, each baby will invent his personal solo improvisations: reaching up, rolling over from stomach to back, reaching again and returning the stomach to the floor; rolling over from stomach to back, sitting up and bending over; reaching with both hands and sliding chest and stomach and knees forward in a belly crawl; rolling over onto the back and hitching the back forward; lying on an arched belly and propelling the body forward or sideways or backward; rolling over and over straight across the room; swiveling in place on an arched belly; sitting up, holding on to a chair, and pulling the body to a stand; reaching up to a sit and just practicing sitting without ever rolling over or swiveling on the belly.

The two-kneed, palms-on-the-floor, stomach-and-chest-off-the-floor posture that readies the baby's body for the two-kneed, palms-on-the-floor, stomach-and-chest-off-the-floor, rocking-forward, reaching-out motion called "creeping" may be arrived at after several weeks of rolling over and belly crawling, or after several months. Having gotten to the basic posture, the baby still must puzzle a bit about how to shift his weight and alternate his arms and legs. For a few days or weeks the baby practices getting up on his knees, rocking back and forth and contemplating the next move. Most babies decide on the convention of right-knee/right-palm, then left-knee/left-palm alternation. A few leapfrog forward —both hands and then both knees. Others lift their knees off the floor and bear-walk, alternating right toes and palm, left toes and palm.

Nobody had to show the baby how to creep. His body-mind figured out which hand came first and the alternating (or nonalternating) reaching movements of hand and knee. A thinking word-mind is stymied by the problem of creeping. The baby's father or mother would struggle to order the phrases to describe the palm-knee alternations, but get them down on their knees and they'll know how to creep almost as perfectly as a baby.

During the interlude between reaching out and creeping away, the rhythms of self-negotiated rolling over, rocking, belly crawling and sitting up augment the harmonious rhythms inside the baby's body. Mouth, hands and eyes get linked up with the newly demarcated parts of the body-self—knees, stomach, chest, arms, elbows and palms. Now, between knee and palm is a girding aliveness that conjectures a relationship between neck muscles, chest muscles, back muscles and stomach muscles. The lively improvisations of the expanding body-self solidify the baby's experience of his individual existence. But the baby has mixed feelings. When he first begins to creep, the advantages of roaming freely and using the body all the way are often outweighed by nagging uncertainties. For the moment, the creeping baby's exhilarated mood is toned down by circumspection. Sitting up and creeping away tweek the baby with unwelcome reminders of separateness. So the baby hesitates.

The spirit of exploration steamed the baby to slide off his mother's lap and onto the floor. Now that he can creep he certainly isn't about to waste his time in the narrow confines of lapdom. Nevertheless, with all his artful abandon, the baby is seldom unmindful of the whereabouts of his mother's lap. Lap is a baby's home base.

The invisible bond that gives the baby rein to discover his place in the world also brings the creeping baby back to home base. Home base is his reference point. As his creeping is just about to carry him over a threshold into another room, the baby halts abruptly. He peers over his shoulder. With his eyes and a circumspect tilt of his body, he checks back, orienting himself to his mother's position in space. Once more his body turns toward the inviting prospect of the uncharted room ahead of him. He raises one palm and brings one knee forward as though to move on. Instead he continues to waver on the brink. Again he checks back. Will he go ahead or turn back? The question hangs in the air. If the baby should now decide against further exploration, he will almost surely scramble back to mother. As he touches home base he leans his body toward his mother, hinting for a gesture that will confirm the constancy of their bond—a pat on the head, a loving look, a brief snuggle, or a peacefully molding feed on the mother's lap.

In these ways a baby recharges himself. He refuels on the loving energies that flow to him from his mother. Then he's off for another foray of adventure and exploration. But not necessarily through that doorway.

After a day or two of wavering and returning to home base for refueling, the baby checks back for a last look—and through the doorway he goes. He disappears into the next room with all sorts of courage tucked inside him: the energies of love, confidence in his mother's presence, the exhilaration of body mastery, and a space/action memory of the actual location of home base. Within seconds the beaming face of the conquering hero reappears. Now an admiring look from mother is all the refueling he needs. And he patters off—this time for a longer journey.

The rein of the invisible bond slackens. The baby disappears more often and for longer periods of time. However, there is no mistaking his attachment. No matter how far he goes, every so often he checks back with home base. Should he check back and discover an empty chair where he expected to find a mother, the baby is crestfallen.

Some babies never roam too far from home base. They sit at their mothers' feet, contentedly mastering the small circle of toys that lie within arm's reach. Even these babies periodically check back to the mother's face for a look of confirmation and reassurance.

Many babies do not bother actually to touch base for emotional refueling. They get all they need from a loving look. Being looked at with admiration and appreciation charges up a baby's body. The sheer delight of it will cause him to wriggle and squirm, kick his feet, slide on his belly and gurgle. Admiring looks put edges on the baby's body. They also stir up delicious rhythms inside the baby. These looks give him confidence in his body-self and courage to creep across thresholds.

Refueling is essential to the well-being of a newly separating baby. The baby is constantly being lured by the world. His body grows with such urgency that the baby *must* practice his creeping. He *must* peer into the unknown. His horizons *must* expand. It's a lot for a baby to contend with when he's still not too sure where his body begins and ends, when he's just begun to separate into his own being. He isn't ready to let go completely. Moreover, once in a while all this belly crawling and creeping doesn't put the baby together. It exhausts him. He almost falls apart. With a bit of refueling he puts himself together again.

The intoxication of conquering new horizons is expressed

in the bouncy spontaneity of the baby's creeping style. When the baby checks back to home base for some refueling, he lets us know that he isn't all that intoxicated.

What about a baby whose mother is withdrawn, depressed, or just "not there" to charge him up with emotional energy? Such a baby might cling to his mother's foot, or hug the pillows of his mother's favorite chair, or find a cozy corner to retire to, or insistently clamber onto the mother's lap to assume a molding posture. Another child might sit before a mirror, rocking on his haunches, gazing intently at the face he finds reflected there. He gives up caring whether anyone comes or anyone goes. Eventually he might even forget about adventures or creeping away.

"No" and "Don't"—Doing and Being Done To Several months before he learns to creep away, when he's just beginning to separate, the single most commanding feature of the infant's world is his mother. Her face is the main focus of the baby's scrutiny. The baby inspects with his eyes as his fingers roam his mother's cheeks and lips. He sticks his fingers between her lips, half-expecting her to suck on them or kiss them. Settling in for a feed, the baby will occasionally feed his mother by poking a few of his fingers into her mouth.

As his mother carries him around, he grabs on to her hair and gives a good hard tug. Although the five-month-old is pretty efficient at grabbing hold and tugging, he doesn't always know how to let go. So he keeps on tugging away until his mother loosens his grip. The mother's eyeglasses and necklace also come in for some wild tugging and pulling. Once in a while the baby pokes his fingers into his mother's eyes, nose or ears. He bites and pinches her shoulder and delightedly slaps at his mother's face with his fingers.

In his inspections of his mother's body the infant handles her with tender feeding gestures and also with the excited muscular aggression that comes from the urgency of having to pull, scratch, poke, tug and grasp. And even though the bright-eyed, attentive look is often replaced by dreamy-eyed reverie, the baby is absorbed in what he is doing. He's taking things in but waiting a while to try to make sense of it all.

The baby continues to relish the satisfying rhythms and hand sensations that come from finger-sucking. And he's enormously intent on putting everything he grasps into his mouth. Into his mouth go his mother's fingers, her necklace, her shirt, her hair. Now the baby doesn't only suck. At seven months he has a tooth or two, so he bites and chews.

A mother responds with different sorts of body movements and attitudes when the baby feeds her his fingers, when he tugs at her hair, when he chews on her shoulder, when he pinches her hand, when he yanks off her eyeglasses.

During oneness, a mother's body gestures were designed to boost her baby's illusions. The holding environment she created confirmed her baby's body movements and excitements. All in all, whenever possible, she said yes to the baby. Yes-saying endowed the baby with self-confidence. He learned to trust the world outside his own skin.

Because the affirmations of the first dialogue also bound the baby to the familiar and valued presence of his mother-in-the-flesh, the baby has the possibility of comprehending the new dialogue of separation. He will go along with the messages his mother communicates even though he can't fully appreciate what they're all about. The new dialogue between a baby and his mother has some very definite do's and don'ts and a number of no's.

Do's are communicated to the baby by the altogether spontaneous way his mother's body moves toward him when she appreciates his gestures, what he's doing. She confirms her baby's feeding gesture by leaning her body forward and taking a sip or two of the fingers he has poked into her mouth. Don'ts are conveyed as she pulls her body away when the baby bites and pinches. By the time he's nine or ten months old the baby will have gotten the idea that it's acceptable to bite his rubber and wooden toys but not his mother. He may playfully experiment with this idea for a while longer, but he's gotten the gist. He may also by that time have arrived at the notion that some of his grabbing and poking is permissible, while other expressions of his reaching out to the world are not.

A baby counts on his mother to let him know about these matters. Perhaps even a tiny four-week-old infant sometimes has terrible apprehensions when he attacks his mother's breast with his fierce feeding energies. So, although a baby can't altogether absorb the implications of his mother's first do's and don'ts, he's grateful to know something about the different ways he's supposed to express his excitements and energies.

The baby is a driven creature. Above all, he must give vent to his urges to examine the world and move his body through space. He has to grab, pinch, tear, pull, scratch, bite, chew; creep under tables, between chairs, through doorways; pull himself up on bookcases and the sides of his playpen. It makes sense to the baby to do these things because these are the actions that confirm his belief in himself as a master of his own mind and body. The older he gets, the more he resists having things done to him; the more he wants to do and act all on his own.

At six months the baby prefers to be fed by his mother or father rather than by anybody else. He can have a pleasant eye-to-eye conversation with them while he's downing his meal. They put the spoon in his mouth in just the right way. He can depend on them to allow him to rest between swallows. They appreciate his special tendencies to munch slowly or grab the food in fast and furiously.

Nevertheless, by the time he is eight or nine months old a baby is usually impatient with spoons and the whole business of *being* fed. He might even like to feed himself with a spoon, but he still can't manage this feat. So spoons become perfectly fine for throwing and banging, but they are also impediments that stand in the way of the baby's urge to handle the food that goes into his mouth. Eating a meal doesn't make sense any more unless the baby can tear his toast, smash his bananas, and poke his fingers into his vegetables and cereal. He very often also likes to feed his parents a bit of the meal. This gives him the satisfaction of knowing that he can do to others what they once did for him. Furthermore, his parents' acceptance tells the baby that they appreciate his feeding gesture. The baby thinks his way of handling his food is wonderful, and he wants to be admired for it. When he's fiercely hungry a baby may even permit his mother's or father's efficient way of getting the food into his mouth with a spoon. Still, the baby is likely to put his hand on the spoon and help it along so that he can have the experience of feeding himself.

Some mothers and fathers resolve the bedlam of the meal table by holding the baby's hands and getting the business of spooning food into his mouth over with as quickly as possible. It makes sense to an eight- or nine-month-old to feel his mother's body move away from his when he bites her. He finds it totally mystifying when he is prevented from smashing his food and when he has spoons thrust in his mouth. This sort of no-saying makes the baby hate his food and dread mealtimes. He will fight back as best he can by turning his head away from the attacking spoon or by solemnly holding each spoonful in his mouth without swallowing. Sometimes he shakes his head from side to side and finally brings the dreadful situation to a conclusion by spitting the whole mess out.

A baby can give up eating solids altogether. He begins to think of his natural way of exploring the world and eating a meal as emotionally tinged acts of aggression. Such ideas, vague and unformed as they must be in the mind of a nine-month-old, are bound to mute his appetites. Each time a baby loses an opportunity to turn his appetites and excitements into something comprehensible, he loses confidence in himself.

After a while a baby is no longer content to be the passive recipient of food and arbitrary no-saying. The growth energies that urged him to separate also fill him up with aggressive energy. Originally the aggression has nothing to do with hating or anger. It is there to transform the baby from a passive-being-fed, molding-being-held infant into an active doer, a master, a conqueror of the universe, a body in charge of picking up what he wants to hold between his fingers, throwing away what he regards as superfluous, and retrieving what he wants to come back.

Rage A baby uses his aggressive energies to piece the world together. But it certainly doesn't always look that way. In piecing together, the baby sometimes tears and smashes. He bangs spoons and casts away his toys. He also pushes his mother away and turns his head from her offerings of food. And he won't be still for a diapering unless he's suitably entertained. The baby often doesn't make too convincing a show of the peaceful intentions behind his aggressive way of handling the world. His actions have all the earmarks of rejection, stubbornness, destructiveness and plain disobedience. The baby doesn't have quite these ideas in mind. In all likelihood, though, he is conjecturing a *bit* of destruction when he tears a box of tissues to ribbons. That's why he counts on his parents to keep his tearing and smashing in proportion. He studies his mother's face and body movements in order to comprehend the shape of his aggression. But his mind can't comprehend when her face and reprimanding voice interpret his actions as willfully destructive.

There are occasions when a baby can get really violent. Even then he probably doesn't have any actual destruction in mind. Being put into the crib just as the rest of the household is coming alive with the excitement of guests arriving; being swooped up for a bath when the concept of putting one block on top of another consumes the baby's mind; being told no to the fourth cup of water just when the baby was counting on a few more reappearances of his father's face; being dressed for an outing to the store just when the baby had readied himself to curl up with a bottle and have a quiet reverie—these ordinary and necessary don'ts are part of the routine happenings of a baby's day. Some days the baby can handle them with equanimity. On other days he's shattered.

Then the don'ts remind the baby of being done to—of having lost control over what will happen to him and what won't happen to him. Thus the baby loses both the confidence of oneness and the courage of a conquering hero. This double-edged blow to his self-esteem leaves him bereft. His vulnerability and helplessness are exposed. Deprived of the confidence and courage that held him together, the baby is reminded of the attacking fierceness and the falling to bits of his beginning weeks in the new world. The world he has so painstakingly pieced together has been torn asunder.

To an eight-month-old, who lives in the moment, who has but a limited conception of time, there is no way of supposing that things will ever be whole again. The fragmented, disappointing world that confronts him with an intolerable don't is disappointing forever.

However, the baby doesn't just give up and sleep the whole problem off. He protests. While his manner of expressing his wish that the wholeness of his world be restored is unreasonable and a little mad, he is revealing his hopefulness, his wish to make things better. He rages against the world. His rage is a storm of diffuse, undefined feeling that might destroy the world—himself and his mother and father along with all the rest.

The baby's cry becomes an ear-piercing scream, a howl of anguish. He kicks and shakes the bars of his crib with unmistakable fury. He bites and pinches—himself, his mother, his pillow. He turns red in the face, blue in the face. Some babies rage so furiously that they lose their breath and faint. Others may shred their clothes and smash their heads against the wall. Babies urinate and defecate and vomit as though to rid themselves of the anguish inside them.

It is an awesome sight, enough to scare the wits out of an ordinary person. It's particularly easy for a mother and a father to panic and get caught up in the baby's passionate rage. They wonder what terrible thing they've done. In their adoration of the baby they anguish with his anguish. Or the wildness of the baby awakens the wild monsters inside the parents. They begin to shake the crib and rant and rave at the baby.

So long as they go on sympathizing with the baby, the parents will be no use to him at all. Once they gather up their wits, they will be able to understand that behind the baby's rage is a vague wish to make life whole again. Then they can help the baby to recover. Their empathy will be communicated to the baby.

Even at the height of his protest a baby can still take in the sound of a calming, yes-saying voice assuring him that "everything will be all right." Before him stand two intact parents who have not fallen apart or been destroyed by the violence coming from the baby—which is all the baby wants to know, that things will change for the better and get whole again. As the eye of the hurricane passes, the baby calms down and peeks out at the world. He regains contact with his body and notes that all the parts are still there and connected with one another. His screams and howls turn into ordinary cries, then whimpering and sobbing. The baby is ready to be picked up and washed up from the ravages he has wrought. The baby's storm was a vague hope that things could be better. And something good came of it after all.

This doesn't spoil a baby. Empathy of this sort gives him hope. It helps him regain his confidence and courage and come to terms with the limits of his excitements and energies. The baby of eight or nine months doesn't calculate "If I rage then I'll get what I want." He doesn't begin to suppose that rage is a way of really changing the world. His rage derives from the panicky sense of ceasing to exist. The main thing is for the baby to get his existence reconfirmed after the rage passes away. The parents' empathic manner of helping him put himself together again shows him the difference between raging passions and actual harm or destruction. In this way he takes in the idea that his occasional passions won't actually destroy. Thus when a little boy becomes a father he will be able to endure his occasional hatred for his own baby. He'll go right on being an ordinary devoted father even when his baby's irritability and misery drive him to the brink of madness. On the other hand, a baby who goes through life thinking he can never change the things that may go sour on him gives up hoping. When his own baby is miserable he may fall into abject hopelessness. He might even vent his hatred and do real harm.

A baby gets to feel safe about testing out his excitements when he knows his parents will be there to hold him together. That's what parents are for. He gets to know that his parents go on loving him and that he won't really harm them. His passionate adorations and rages won't swallow them up. It's part of the basic dialogue between a baby and his parents for them to translate the baby's explosions into comprehensible ordinary human emotions like hope and anger and courage to go on when adversity strikes.

Alternative Dialogues—The Stranger A mother's presence is the bedrock of a baby's existence. Their dialogue goes deep into the time when her humanness endowed him with safety and harmony inside and brave edges facing outward to the new world. When this first basic dialogue has been good enough, the baby is inspirited with a willingness to reach out for alternative dialogues.

A baby has had a father right from the beginning. His father soothed him and fed him and bathed him and diapered him. The father held the baby in his arms and paced him through many a night. Father and baby played games and had conversations. The baby has been aware of his father's presence in the world all along. Often it was his father's calming voice and arms that soothed the baby's tensions away. There may have been long stretches of time when the father was much better than the mother at holding the baby. The baby noted his presence and measured the differences between his father's presence and the presence of his mother. Fathers represent another way of looking at life—the possibility of an alternative dialogue.

For the first years of life mother and baby play dangerously on the margin between oneness and separateness. The balance between mutual envelopment and moving apart is delicate. A father's presence in their world keeps a mother and a baby in touch with the fact of their separateness. The baby trusts the dialogue with his father even though it's different from the dialogue he's had with his mother. He learns that dialogue with a mothering presence isn't all there is to life.

Fathers have a special excitement about them that babies find intriguing. At this time in his life an infant counts on his mother for rootedness and anchoring. He can count on his father to be just different enough from a mother. Fathers embody a delicious mixture of familiarity and novelty. They are novel without being strange or frightening. Needless to say, if a mother doesn't trust her husband and is desperate to possess the baby all for herself, the baby will regard his father as a frightening stranger and dread being left alone with him.

With his father the baby gets an opportunity to be careless—to experiment with danger. Fathers tend to ignore the well-plotted routines that mothers set up to ensure the baby's safety and wholeness—much to a mother's despair when she returns home after a relaxing day of her own to a cranky, overly tired, overly hungry, falling-apart baby. Nonetheless, while she was gone father and baby probably had a good time of it, romping with abandon and scotching the schedules.

When a mother is going to be away for more than a day or an evening a father usually uncovers his hidden talents for anchored mothering. He is able then to follow the strategically mapped-out routines, often inventing a few of his own that might even be better for the baby. But on an everyday basis he's at his best when he acts like a father. It makes sense to a young infant when his father acts like a father and his mother goes on acting like a mother.

Later on in childhood, after baby and mother have worked out the dilemmas of separateness and the baby has a better idea of his own selfhood, it will be meaningful and enriching to know a mother who isn't all rootedness and homey routines and a father who might be mostly a tender holding presence. But right now, at the beginning of the baby's complicated second birth, the differences between a mother and a father help him to piece the world together and to clarify the meaning of differences.

Other people—grandparents, sisters and brothers, the mother's best friend, the next-door neighbor—get to be familiar to the baby. If the mother communicates her trust in these people, the baby will regard them as delicious novelties. Anybody the mother trusts whom the baby sees often enough partakes a bit of the presence of the mother. With each new person the baby tries to work out a mode of familiar dialogue he can count on. What worries an eight-month-old is being invited to take part in a dialogue that is totally strange and unpredictable. Strange dialogues awaken the possibility that the baby might run away with himself. All babies are stirred up by novelty. Just as their minds are roused by the sight of an open doorway, so they are attracted to new people. Yet they hesitate on thresholds and they are wary of new dialogue. A baby is most likely to balance his wariness of strangers with courage when he is ensconced in the safety of his mother's lap. From the vantage of the lap a baby might spontaneously reach out to a stranger. He might play the game of reaching out to the stranger and then retreating back to his mother's arms, chortling with the delight of his extraordinary bravery.

Another baby might be still more daring. Tentatively, he might creep toward the stranger. His journey is circuitous and halting. But as long as the meeting place is but a few feet from home base he manages the intrigue of encounter very nicely. Arriving within a well-considered range of the stranger, the baby inspects for a moment the toy that the stranger offers him. Then with all speed he creeps straight back to the familiar territory of home base. From there the baby stares at the stranger in sober wonderment. However, he is ever mindful to keep his eyes averted from the eyes of the stranger. If eyes should meet, the encounter is over. Eye-to-eye contact is much more than the baby counted on. It signifies an exciting intimacy to which strangers are not entitled.

In the presence of their mother or father some babies even allow themselves to be held in the arms of a stranger. They explore the stranger's clothing, pen, jewelry. After a while such a baby might run his fingers over the stranger's face as though to determine whether this fascinating creature weren't smuggling in forbidden merchandise under the familiar guise of nose, cheekbone, eyes and lips. Having completed the serious work of his customs inspection, the baby sails back into the snug harbor of his parent's arms. He looks in his mother's eyes and his face lights up with the joy of reunion. So while this baby was not reckless or uninhibited when faced with the problem of strangeness, he didn't turn away from it either. He confronted strangeness and sized it up in his mind.

For other eight-month-olds the sight of a stranger in the

room is more than they are prepared to deal with. If such a baby is fortunate enough to be seated on his mother's lap when the stranger makes her approach, he will turn away and quietly cling to the security of lapdom. However, if this kind of baby happens to be all alone on the floor or riding along in the solitary confines of his carriage when the stranger presents herself to him, he will flutter like a fledgling bird that has fallen from its nest. With a cry of distress, he searches desperately for his mother. He stretches his arms toward her beseechingly, begging to be picked up and saved from the menace of strangeness. He buries his head in his mother's neck and shoulders, sobbing or heaving a huge sigh of relief. Those who witness this not altogether uncommon reaction to strangers will remark the obvious: "That baby is afraid of strangers."

In fact he is afraid of himself. The stranger reminds him of terrible things: of his vulnerability, of being done to, of his separateness from mother, and most of all, of unpredictability. The baby doesn't know what he would do or how he would act with the stranger. The baby who panics at the approach of a stranger doesn't trust himself.

Between wonderment and panic is a wide range of possible reactions to strangers. But all babies are wary. As soon as a baby has a special attachment to a special mother, the sight of a strange face will sober him. By the time he is seven or eight months old, the baby's sobriety is heightened with at least a tinge of worry. Even the bravest of explorers will eventually slide into the safety of home base. Wariness of strangers works two ways, the more obvious being the flight of the baby *away* from the stranger. The path of flight, however, is not without direction or orientation. It is *toward* someone the baby can count on.

Some variant of wariness occurs in almost all human babies soon after they have become attached to one person and just before they are ready to creep away into the unknown. Hesitating on the threshold is basic to the choreography of early conquests. It was written in long before the baby made his appearance in the world.

About one million years ago, in the early morning of human evolution, the innumerable specific details that strike the balances between attachment and the urge to expand into new territory began to work themselves into the sinews of the human mind. Those humans who survived the harshness of the Pleistocene long enough to produce new life passed these details on to future generations. Wariness of strangers, then, is as much a part of the baby's preparedness for psychological birth as is his appetite for human dialogue, the appeal of his smile and fat-cheeked helplessness, his ability to guide his hands with his eyes, and his urge to creep away.

The room across the threshold is not a vast uncharted jungle looming with predatory animals. The stranger in the park is not a dangerous enemy who will snatch the baby away and separate him forever from the familiar safety of mother's lap. Yet the apprehensive wariness of the twentieth-century baby echoes back to the Pleistocene, when such matters were of real concern. At that time the baby's actual survival depended on his having made an attachment he could count on before his body was animated by the urge to reach beyond the confines of his mother's lap.

The immanent dangers of jungles and enemy tribesmen no longer plague the daily existence of most human babies. But the humanness of the human baby continues to be shaped by the balance between the safety of familiar dialogue and home base, and the urge to wander into the unknown. Occasionally a genetic accident or a total failure of environmental holding will cast a baby adrift without the anchor of home base. He clings to everyone or no one. He roams the world aimlessly, filled with unfathomable dreads and apprehensions.

Between the awful devastations of these accidents of nature and nurture and the ordinary human attachment are the infinite human variations that make one person a cowardly,

clinging homebody, another a reckless adventurer who never
settles down to one love or one home base, another a self-
sufficient Narcissus whose apprehensions keep him fixed on
his own mirror image. But most of us are just cowardly enough
to hesitate and get our bearings before we set off into new
territory; we keep on valuing the old familiar faces while
daring the excitement of fresh dialogues; we love ourselves
just well enough to trust that others will care for us, too.

Peek-a-boo   A five-month-old can't do much when he sees
his mother disappear through a doorway. His map of the
world doesn't mark the possibility of other rooms. Perhaps
the doorway is the edge of the world? Nevertheless, when
the baby has confidence in himself he is able to take these
disappearing acts in his stride. The presence of his mother
is all around him, so he doesn't worry. Also, the voice and
footsteps and water running and windows opening are inti-
mations of the continued existence of mother—somewhere.

On many a day the baby is particularly pleased with himself; he's nicely filled up from a good meal and some exciting
conversation, and he's had a few good ideas about the way
the mobile on his crib jumps up and down and swivels around
every time he kicks his feet on the side of the crib. To a five-
or six-month-old the action of the mobile and the action of his
kicking feet are continuous. The baby is able to keep the
spectacle of mobile swiveling before his eyes because he
imagines that his kicking feet have the power to create swiveling mobiles. Such notions give the baby confidence in his
mind. He feels powerful.

Much of the time, however, the five-month-old is powerless.
Puzzling things happen to him and he can't do much about
them. He can't follow his mother through that doorway. He
can't remember her face until it reappears before his eyes.
On top of that, on the days when the baby doesn't have confidence in himself, he gets tense inside from reminders of his
mother's separateness.

A mother doesn't know her baby thinks this way. Even if she did, there wouldn't be much she could or should do about her separateness and occasional disappearances. However, when her baby is around five months old, a mother adds to her repertoire of dialogue and conversation the game of peek-a-boo. Peek-a-boo puts some brave thoughts in her baby's mind concerning this whole business of disappearing and reappearing. The game also includes an idea or two that builds up the baby's confidence in himself.

This is how it goes: As the mother's face disappears behind her hands, the inside of the baby's body flutters. The fluttering is reminiscent of the awful tensions of being let down and falling apart. Though they hint of disaster, the baby gambles with his fluttering tensions. The mother's face reappears. Instead of falling apart, the baby relaxes. The baby flirted with the enigma of disappearing and reappearing. And he found harmony at the core of his body-self.

"Peek-a-boo, I see you," says mother just at the moment when her baby's body relaxes at the sight of her reappearing face. The mother's trilling voice and the animated look in her eyes are telling the baby, "What a beautiful baby you are. How wonderful you are. How happy I am to see you." The baby looks back into his mother's eyes. Mirrored there are all the spectacular and powerful things he sometimes imagines himself to be. A baby gets to know what he is by what is mirrored in the faces of those who look at him. The mirroring admiration of the peek-a-boo game is a caress that paints proud edges on the baby's body. With relaxed harmony inside and proud edges outside, no wonder babies love to flirt with the fate of the peek-a-boo game.

Does the baby suppose that he keeps the spectacle of his mother's disappearing and reappearing going by his madcap squirming and chortling laughter? Are his mother's actions merely a logical continuation of the action of his body, like the mobile that swivels around every time he kicks his feet? Or is this earliest version of peek-a-boo another experience of being done to? The fact is that at five months the baby is a passive spectator. He lies there *reacting* while his mother does all the acting. But the baby doesn't see it quite that way. He doesn't feel done to as he sometimes does when his mother really disappears.

When a baby's body is outlined with pride, it's almost impossible for him to suppose that he is being done to or that unforeseen events could really happen to him. And isn't it halfway to the truth to speculate that kicking feet keep mobiles moving and that chortling appreciation makes faces appear and disappear? From the five-month-old's point of view, peek-a-boo is a happy rhythm of acting and reacting, being done to and doing, appearing and disappearing, tension and relaxation.

At around the time the baby gets fed up with having things done to him, he invents his own variants of peek-a-boo. Though modeled on the disappearing-reappearing act of his mother, the baby's version has a couple of new twists. By nine or ten months the baby has gotten it into his head that maybe he's a pretty capable fellow and that he can take an active part in his own destiny. He can creep after his mother when she disappears into the next room. He refinds her after he creeps over the threshold. When a stranger appears in the doorway the baby can hide behind his fingers and make the stranger disappear. If a toy rolls behind a pillow the baby can have the active intention of finding the toy and lead his body to push away the pillow and reach for it. He can comfort himself with his special blanket or humming sound. He holds his own bottle. He feeds himself. And he gets passionately enraged without destroying the world.

These matters have not been settled once and for all. Not by a long shot. So the baby flirts with the possibilities of comings and goings, running away and being found again.

In his version of the peek-a-boo game, the baby is caught up with the question of how the world responds to *his* disappearances and reappearances. He is restless. He is not satisfied being the passive spectator of somebody else's enchanting disappearing acts. He puts a blanket over his head. "Where's the baby?" his mother inquires with mock-concern. Still no baby. "Where could he be?" "Where is that baby?" He's not to be found. The ten-month-old has a braver conception of peek-a-boo than his mother did. When he was a passive lap baby, her "I see you" reappearances were timed to provide quick relief for her baby's fluttering tensions. Now that he's in charge the baby prolongs the tension. At last he pulls the blanket away from his face, squealing at the look of relief on his mother's face. "Oh, there he is!"

The ten-month-old likes the predictable rhythms of "Where's the baby? There he is." Nevertheless, he's not content with stereotyped performances. Sometimes he prolongs the tension and sometimes he bobs up right away. He has a number of methods for varying his disappearances. A parent never knows when he's going to walk in on a disappearing act. The baby hears his father's footsteps at the doorway. The baby buries his head in the mattress of his crib. He lies there, fluttering and giggling. He supposes he's hidden even though his giggles give him away. His father searches in drawers and under tables, inquiring as to the whereabouts of the baby. The baby peeks out with the devil in his eyes, awaiting the magical "There he is" before he bounces up and bursts out laughing.

Next morning the baby is concentrating on averting his head from the last spoonfuls of cereal. It comes to him that his no-saying about the cereal and his disappearing acts have something in common. So he forgets about the cereal and disappears. From the tilt of her baby's turned-away head and his mischievous grin the mother gets the idea that her baby is gone. When he turns his head back to her, she's so delighted that she almost forgets about.the cereal too.

The baby is quite right of course. No-saying and disappearing acts do belong in the same category. Both assert the fact of his separateness and also his need to do and not be done to. A baby is always contending with the facts of his separateness and being done to. He often wishes he could lean back into the perfect harmonies of molding. But his mind is bursting with the excitement of being his own master—of deciding to go some place in the world and being able to go there. So even though he creates a lot of problems for himself, the baby reckons with the knowledge that he will continue to disappear over thresholds and stiffen himself against being swallowed up in the passive yes-saying of oneness.

Because the invisible bond pulls the baby back to safety as well as letting him wander, the baby is able to contend with the contradictions between yes-saying harmony and no-saying disappearing acts. With innocent ingenuity, the baby's body-mind comes up with Hegelian resolutions. His inventions of peek-a-boo are a remarkable synthesis of moving away and coming together again. The question is, "If I disappear or wander away or turn my head away from the spoon, will someone still be happy to find me again?" The baby tests this question by playing peek-a-boo and other games of chance.

Catch-me   "Catch me," invite the baby's dancing eyes, up-raised palm, knees on the floor, ready-to-burst-ahead body. Without a moment's hesitation, the mother assumes the posture of a catcher: head thrust forward, body leaning toward the baby, arms half outstretched, knees bent and feet ready to pursue. As though to reassure her baby that she's not truly a catcher of babies, the open-mouthed half-threat on the mother's face turns into a smile. Slowly and rhythmically she recites the familiar phrase, "I'm going to catch you." The baby laughs and off he goes.

Footsteps pounding behind him sound like an enormous and extraordinarily fleet catcher of babies. Yet, heavily threatening as they are, the footsteps never catch up with the creeping of the baby. The baby can't believe his luck. He stops in his tracks, sits up, and checks back to see if his mother is still in hot pursuit. The mother stops too, momentarily halting her pursuit. "I'm going to catch you." Quivering with excitement, the baby creeps on. He moves ahead so wildly now that he occasionally flattens out and falls on his face. Yet he keeps on going, checking back now and then until the race is won. The finish line is wherever the baby decides he's had enough. At last, as always, he wins the race. With a triumphant laugh, the baby turns back to his mother. He stretches his arms out so he can be swooped up and cuddled by the menacing catcher of babies.

Although it's all in fun, the initial performances of catch-me resonate with uncertainties. The role of the mother is slightly ambiguous. Is she the keeper of safety who follows her dashing-away baby into the wild in order to snatch him up at the last minute and save him? Or is she a catcher-of-babies from whom the baby must flee with all his might? When the baby checks back to see "if his mother is still in hot pursuit" he is checking to determine two things. "Is my mother still following me?" "Is that my mother or a strange catcher of babies?"

A baby's wariness of strangers and the quivering anxiety of his first games of catch-me usually coincide in time. The ritualized format of the game will soon resolve into the pleasant tension/relaxation cycle of running away and being followed. But at its inception catch-me is a little frightening for the baby. "Am I masterful enough to escape from a catcher?" "Will my mother follow wherever I go?"

Beneath these two awesome uncertainties lurks yet another danger. For the moment this one remains obscure. It hides in wait for the time when the baby has come to value his separate identity as the most treasured aspect of his being. When he is around eighteen months, catch-me games will bespeak the baby's concern, "If I assert my selfhood and claim my body as my own, might I once more be swooped up into the being-done-to, nonbeing void of oneness by a catcher of babies?" The menace of catch-me is real enough.

In some parts of the world the catch-me game is played differently. The Zhun/twasi Bushmen are a hunter-gatherer people who make their home in the arid semideserts of north-western Botswana. The Zhun/twasi, or "real people," are nomads. They roam in bands of thirty or so and settle into small villages where each nuclear family has its own temporary grass shelter. The Zhun/twasi forage the Botswana land for fruit and hunt for game, as their ancestors did during the Pleistocene. In Botswana the predations of leopards and hyenas are a fact of everyday life.

Zhun/twa parents do not wait for the baby to invite them to play catch-me. When the Zhun/twa baby is seven or eight months old he begins to creep away from his mother's side. He uses her as a home base from which he ventures forth to explore the world. When an unfamiliar face comes too close, the infant reaches toward his mother's lap, where he retreats to cling and to nurse until the stranger goes away. Around this time the mother invites her baby to a catch-me game.

As the baby plays a few feet from her side, the mother stands up and calls to him. He turns to look at her face. Slowly then the mother begins to run away from her baby. She makes certain the baby is following, and then she runs ahead without looking back. She listens for the sounds of a baby catching up. Suddenly the mother whirls around. On her face is a terrifying look. From her lips comes a frightening sound. The baby laughs uncertainly. He turns and flees. At that juncture the mother gives chase. The baby checks back to see if his mother is following. In a minute or two the mother calls to the baby, announcing that now she will be running away. The baby shifts directions and starts to creep after his mother. Mother and baby repeat the cycle of following and fleeing several times. Usually the game ends when the baby manages to catch up to the mother and cling to her before she has had the opportunity to turn around and become an object of alarm. It's all in fun and there is much smiling and laughing. Whether he catches up or not, the baby is allowed to cling to his mother when the game is over.

Until he's ready to creep or walk, a Zhun/twa baby is indulged with almost total yes-saying. From the moment he's born he goes everywhere with his mother, carried upright on her hip in a sling, constantly rocked by her walking and berry-gathering motions. He has free access to her breast at all times. He doesn't even have to cry; the anticipation in his rate of breathing, the slight fret sound, the gurgle or waking-up body movements are sufficient notice of his need to be fed. A Zhun/twa baby will continue to nurse pretty much whenever he wishes until his mother has another baby. Usually that happens when he's four. But it could happen anytime between 18 months and six years.

The Zhun/twa catch-me game is a dramatic preparation for separation and the end of unequivocal yes-saying. When the baby begins to creep, the mother continues to nurse him, but she is not so totally in tune with his subtle body gestures. The baby must come to her to get what he wants. And he is more and more pushed into the small childhood society of his tribal group. The mother chases the baby away, but she does so with certain provisos. She fully expects that the baby's bond to her will be powerful enough to induce him to follow her once again when she calls to him. Later his survival will depend on his following her example and the example of his father by a scrupulous imitation of the gestures of gathering fruit and beating animals.

The Zhun/twa version of following, fleeing, chasing and catching is somewhat different from the indoor variety of catch-me, but the underlying elements of catch-me are much the same as with most human babies and their parents. The game does not begin until there is an attachment between a baby and an adult that the baby can count on; the vitality of the game depends on a baby who has a notion of home base; it is an announcement of forthcoming separation; it is made up of love, laughter, quivering excitement and menace.

Tossing-away   Tossing-away is yet another game of chance that prepares a baby's mind for the manifold complexities of the meaning of separateness. While the baby's peek-a-boo and catch-me games are frequently said to be modeled on an earlier adult version, throwing and tossing away are decidedly pure inventions of the baby's mind. Parents would just as soon babies didn't spend so much time dropping toys from playpens, cribs, baby-tenders and highchairs.

The baby expects that what he drops or tosses away will soon be picked up and returned to him by his parents. From the baby's point of view the best thing about tossing away toys is having a willing partner who retrieves. In addition, the baby is carrying out an experiment. In its simplest form the experiment sets out to substantiate the baby's beginning supposition that "Whatever goes away comes back."

At five months the baby couldn't do much when his mother disappeared through doorways. Moreover, his map of the world was limited to what he could see in his grasp and the nearby spectacles he created when he kicked his feet against the sides of his crib. Lifting up a toy that exists in nearby body-space and following its course into distant space expands the borders of the baby's world. So when he tosses away, the ten-month-old is also playing around with the concept of space. And as with all his games of chance, the holding on and letting go of tossing-away replicate some problems that confront the baby in his everyday relationships with his mother—among them the opposition between his need to hold on to home base and his urge to let go and become his own master, and also the here/not-here patterning of his mother's disappearing acts. Like peek-a-boo and catch-me, tossing-away provides the baby with opportunities to master the idea of separation. It also offers the element of no-saying.

Such games of chance involve the pleasure of dialogue with other human beings. They have an orderly rhythm of now-here, now-not-here. In them is an assertion of a me that acts in harmony with a not-me partner. And, like some other mother-infant games of this period of life—such as "so-big," in which the baby estimates his growth by raising his hands high above his head, or the sensuous body-play of patty-cake, in which the baby has belly and chest "rolled and patted and marked with a T"—these games of chance make their contribution to the outlining of body edges and the confident relaxation rhythms at the core of the baby's being.

Illusion—The Security Blanket The ten-month-old is learning how to take charge of his own destiny. But at best his thoughts on conquering the mysteries of selfhood and separation are wonderful child's play. Every so often the baby is faced with the painful realization that his mind is really not up to facing the contradictions of separateness.

He awakens raring to go, with his body set to tackle the weighty agenda of the day. But, amid the pleasures of dialogue, creeping over thresholds, banging spoons and playing games of chance, the unfathomable insinuates itself into the baby's life: a yes-saying mother who reminds him of wholeness; a no-saying mother who reminds him of being done to, but who also sponsors his urge to reach out; raging passions that don't match up with longings to be held and looked at with admiration; a me world and a not-me world; a not-me world with readable human intentions and a not-me world of inanimate objects that work according to their own rules of time, space and motion; a not-me world of familiar dialogue and a not-me world that threatens with uncertainty; an inner urgency of growth that encourages the baby to suppose that he can be a conqueror and an outer reality that often conspires to betray this lofty notion; a mother who appears and disappears independent of the baby's longings and appetites.

The baby could retreat to his mother's lap and forget the whole thing. Often he does. But as soon as his energies are restored he braves forth once more. The baby could simply fall asleep. And sometimes he does. But now the contradictions of his ordinary life sometimes follow him in tension dreams of falling down, being let down, falling apart. Besides, a baby has trouble falling asleep in the midst of the excitement of reaching out. Now he must be eased into sleep by lullabies and pacifiers. Somewhat like an adult, he must cross a bridge from wakefulness into deep sleep.

There is a corner of the world where bridges are crossed and contradictions are held at bay. The baby creates a resting place for himself in the half-awake, half-asleep realm of illusion. He invents the idea of a security blanket.

The realm of illusion is not new to the baby. In the early months of oneness, the baby was held in a manner that allowed the energies and excitements inside him to find a resting place. He was granted the temporary illusion of a world "out there" that matched up perfectly with his appetite to conjure it. In his second birth, the baby will become a three-year-old who has some real ways of managing his excitements. Then his energies will fit with the actual contours of the human world. Right now, at ten months, he's between real managing and total helplessness. But he hasn't forgotten how to conjure or what to conjure.

Just before the baby began to separate, he was able to suck his thumb or hook his thumb onto his pacifier while caressing the side of his nose and his cheeks with his other fingers. As he nursed, his fingertips would stroke his mother's breast or her clothing. The warm softness of her body and clothing would caress the outside of his body. Soon the diaper on his mother's shoulder or the blanket that wrapped the nursing baby became an integral part of the total experience of warmth, softness, sucking sensations, the smell of the baby's body, the smell of the mother's clothing and body. Now and then cooing sounds of *mmum-mmum* or *gaa-gaa* accompanied the caressing softness outside and the sucking rhythms inside.

In time the blanket or its silky corner or the diaper or the *mmum-mmum* sounds became invested with the illusion of oneness, in which "peaceful tension-relaxation rhythms, eyes looking into eyes, the mother's heartbeat" built toward the single experience of mother-baby.

So now as he is being reminded of the contradictions of separateness, the baby holds on to a reminder of oneness. He keeps in touch with the illusion of his own perfection and the time when such things as differences between inside and outside and me and not-me did not exist. The reminder could be a cooing sound, a stroking gesture, or a rocking motion. Usually the reminder takes the form of a blanket or diaper which can be stroked, cooed to, or held while rocking or sucking a thumb or pacifier.

A mother in the flesh is perfectly fine as a home base that orients a baby's reaching and creeping. And as a not-me person, she makes an ideal partner for dialogue and games of chance. She's also good at helping a baby to comprehend the difference between natural aggression and destruction. Her sumptuous lap and her admiring looks restore the baby's emotional energies. Though she embodies these marvelous and necessary things, a mother in the flesh is also an all too present reminder of contradictions and of being done to. For a resting place from contradictions the baby wants the mother of oneness—a mother he can control absolutely. He wants a mother he can imagine to be part of himself.

As the baby presses the security blanket to his cheeks and nose it caresses him. It smells of the sweetness of a yes-saying mother and also of smells that belong to the baby. The blanket's molding softness is like the time when he and mother were one. The blanket exists "out there" in the inanimate world of rattles, bottles, pillows and mobiles. Yet it is alive with reminiscences of human dialogue. Further-more, the baby can scratch, pinch, rub and slap his blanket around without a no or a don't or any possibility of real destruction. The blanket withstands the baby's passionate excitements and it never lets him down. It's always there when he longs for it.

A security blanket is the one thing a baby can always fall back on, which is why he panics when it can't be found or when the mother-baby smells are washed out of it. The blanket belongs absolutely to the baby. Furthermore, he does not expect or desire that others will share in its magic. His mother or father may admire it or give it a new name or pack it up in a suitcase as if it were an ordinary blanket, but only the baby can invest it with aliveness. The blanket is the baby's first personal possession. Nobody gave it to him. He invented it.

When the baby becomes an adult he may be able to understand his inner life—his fantasies and excitements. He will then know that his inner life goes on existing while he goes on reaching out to the actual world. He won't let his inner life lead him astray, but neither will he act as though it did not count. Most often he will be able to tell which experience comes from inside and which from outside.

When the baby becomes a parent his inner life will enrich and vitalize the actual relationship he has with his baby. To some extent his fantasies will shape his baby's destiny. However, as an ordinary devoted parent he will not expect his baby in the flesh—who came into the world with his own energies and unique propensities—to match up with his fantasy baby. He won't confuse what he wants with what his senses and mind tell him actually exists. But as expert as he may become at managing the contingencies of everyday life, or as wisely as he may sum up the meaning of his fantasy existence, there will be many moments and even long stretches of time when he will once again need the resting place of illusion.

Illusion is not the same as fantasy. Illusion is the realm between the fantasies and excitements of the inner life and the contingencies of actual babies and actual mothers and fathers in the flesh. Later on, without the resting place of illusion, no human being would survive the strain of everyday confrontations between loving and hating, animate life and inanimate life, the me world and the not-me world, the yes-saying world and the no-saying world, the familiar world and the strange world.

So whenever the strain of uniting inner life with outer reality becomes too great, most human beings will act to bring back the illusion of psychological wholeness. From the time he invents his first security blanket or humming sound or stroking gesture or rocking motion, the human being reserves a part of his existence for the re-creation of an intermediate world of illusion in which me and not-me can once again be united. Poetry and special personal possessions are the creations of that intermediate world.

When someone asks us to share his intermediate world without taking into account the possibilities of our own intermediate world, we do not say he is a poet. We call him a madman. Similarly, when we meet a man who tells us that the illusory dreams which temporarily endow ordinary life with the sweetness of absolute beauty and virtue are but signs of human weakness, we say that he is bitter and disillusioned. We call him a cynic.

The baby who once in a while prefers the illusion of his security blanket to the actual presence of his mother is neither madman nor cynic—he's on his way to making metaphors.

The Baby's Mind—The Visionary Gleam A baby's mind has a direction of its own. It is energized to expand by looking eyes and moving hands, shoulders, stomach, knee, chest and toes. Short of tying the baby up, nobody could stop the baby's hands from going where his eyes direct them.

Yet the baby's mind does not become a mere machine of moving parts. From the beginning his mind was made human by his parents' holding presence and by the stamp of the social order that governs his small corner of the world. In a predictable way then, the baby's mind journeys along the unique lines that have been laid down by the human world in which he lives. It becomes a mind that goes here and not there. It cruises like a sailboat or a gunboat. By the time the baby is eight months old, the geometry of his mind is psychologically lawful. His mind hesitates on thresholds and measures the radius of its kingdom from the fixed center point of the mother's lap.

With each new turn of his mind the baby comes to value the world in a different way and to know himself as a different self. At first the world and what the baby could do were the same. Gradually the baby came to value the world for its own sake. The idea of valuing the world for its own sake first struck the baby when he began to take note of the special details of his mother's eyes, mouth, ears and voice. He began to get the impression that parts of her body existed outside the walls of his own body and that her eyes and voice were different from any other eyes and voice. By attending to the comings and goings of this especially valued person, the baby also got his first inkling of the rules that govern disappearing objects.

Soon the baby's mind was shaken loose from the narrow perspective of touching fingers, reaching hands and looking eyes. The rest of his body caught on to the notion of reaching. His eight-month-old mind reached his whole body over thresholds. Then he reached his body back to the fixed point of home base.

By ten months, the baby doesn't even need his eyes to tell him where to reach. He is able to find a toy that is out of his line of vision. Without using his eyes at all, he can conjecture the toy's position in space with the rest of his body. He simply reaches behind him and picks up the toy. In general, the kingdom of his mind extends to distant and hidden places; those objects that are not immediately present to the baby's eyes or held in his hands can be located in pockets, behind pillows, under couches and through doorways. His mind isn't up to the thought, "If I can't find my bear it might be behind the couch." But when the ten-month-old sees a couch, his body remembers that lost toys sometimes end up behind couches. When his father goes away the baby can't conjure his face, but the sound of a key turning in the lock makes the baby's face light up with anticipation. The face that appears a few seconds later is likely to be just the one the baby expected to see. Similarly, the baby can't evoke a picture of his mother's face when she isn't there, yet he recognizes immediately that the stranger is "not mother."

A ten-month-old has a much better perspective on himself and on how to fit his mind to the world around him than he did five months earlier, when he first began to separate. He is able to sort out the rules and dimensions that enable him to value the world for its own sake. He handles the world with hypotheses. When he sees a new toy, he doesn't immediately start to shake it or bang it. He hesitates, examining its up surfaces and its down surfaces. He decides which toys are for opening and closing and which for banging or for rolling or for shaking. He recognizes that his bottle has a nipple end and a bottle end that are different. If he wants to suck he knows to turn the nipple end toward his mouth. The bottle looks larger when the baby brings it up close to his eyes and smaller when he holds it at arm's length. Yet his eyes and his hands tell him it's the same bottle. His hands work in tandem. One hand does this, the other hand that. A noisemaker is for picking up with one hand and shaking with the other hand. Time has a before and an after. Grasping the toy that had been hiding behind the pillow comes after the before of pushing the pillow away.

The world is imposing its rules on the baby's mind, shaping what the mind can become and what it cannot become.

Each time the baby learns something new he takes in the rules according to the spirit of what his mind can already do. But his mind alters and improves itself according to the real possibilities of larger and smaller, before and after, front and back, inside and outside, now it's here and now it's not here—all the conditions that come from the out-there world of immediate time and space. The baby's mind is bettering itself by leaps and bounds. A problem remains. With a body-mind, a baby can't appreciate that the rules come from "out there."

A body-mind values only those qualities of the world that are immediately apparent to its senses and body movements. Such a mind can turn a bottle so the nipple end faces the baby's mouth, but it has no way of speculating that "turning" or "upness" or "downness" exist in their own right. His mind cannot represent the image of turning, even though his body knows just how to turn a bottle around. Since the body-mind is so intimately in tune with the sensate world in which it acts, the baby has no way of knowing that the rules that govern this world emanate from outside the walls of his body.

In many respects the ten-month-old is a more practical, down-to-earth fellow than he was at five months. Before acting, he hesitates, worries, considers and turns things over to examine their surfaces. He no longer imagines that the objects of reality are mere extensions of his actions and senses. He's stopped believing he can conjure a nipple merely by turning his head and opening his mouth to suck. On the other hand, part of him is still a conjurer. The energies that produced the baby's original urge to turn to the nipple and to reach out are still burning fiercely. The visionary gleam has not faded.

As in his earliest weeks in the new world, the visionary gleam of the ten-month-old comes from the direction and energy of his growing and expanding body. He now weighs about three times as much as he did at birth, and he is eight or nine inches taller. Never again will he grow so much in such a short span of time. He can't stop giving in to the energies of growing. From his first reaching out, sliding off a lap, standing and creeping, the baby has been swept away by the irresistible currents that will now convert him from a horizontal floor baby to a vertical upright toddler.

At ten months the baby is obsessed with verticality. Short of tying him down, he can't be stopped from standing up. He stands in his sleep. He practices it in his dreams. Now he holds on to table edges and helping hands. In a few months he will let go and take off on his own.

When that fateful day arrives, the baby will get the final proof of the absolute omnipotence of his body-mind. Yes, the world has its rules. But this world of rules has a ruler who knows all about before and after and here and not here. Admiring eyes and clapping hands will corroborate the triumphant glow and happy flutterings of the toddler's magnificent upright body.

By ten months the baby had become a clever reckoner with time, space and dimension. He was a cautious adventurer who checked his maps and perfected them before taking off. But the better he got at reaching out and reaching up, the more he got to suppose he knew it all. When he finally gets to stand alone on his own two feet, the baby will have reached himself right out of the original paradise of oneness.

However, no sooner will he wrench himself free of the deceptions of one paradise than he will go on to create a new deception. His uprightness has located him in the center of the grandest deception of all. Having a mother at the center of his kingdom restrained the baby's mind with worries and hesitation. Once he is at the center, the baby uproots and runs away with himself.

Chapter Five

"The Love Affair with the World"

Ten Months to Eighteen Months
(The Upright Baby)

Practicing and Using the Body All-Out   The baby is standing on his own two feet and walking away. By the time an infant has learned to walk away, he usually has mastered most of the dilemmas of relating his body to the physical world of time and space. Walking is a celebration of his mastery—the culmination of his triumph. The world is his oyster.

For the next few months life will be a practicing and perfecting of what the body-mind has already accomplished. The toddler may add a few flourishes here and there, but essentially the job is done. As far as he's concerned there is nothing more to life than getting better at climbing, carrying, standing up and sitting down, jumping and turning around in circles and naming some names. For the time being, celebration takes over. The baby uses his body to the hilt, wholly innocent of the new beginning that awaits him only months from now.

Though they are captivated by the baby's triumphant mood, parents are of two minds about letting their baby fly away. As he dashes off, they worry about his seeming obliviousness to the dangers that surround him. So they baby-proof the house with tapes on table edges and fortress locks on doors and windows. They cache away their most precious possessions and keep their eyes and ears open. It isn't so much that they occasionally get irritated by all the extra work of putting the household together at the end of a day of exalted rampage or that the mother is exhausted from running after the baby and being on the alert for too much silence or sounds of crashing dishes. For a mother, the baby's uprightness signifies the end of her possession of his body. She can't just pick him up for a hug and haul him off for a bath whenever she chooses. The baby is too much absorbed in himself and what he happens to be doing at the moment.

Every now and then parents worry about the future implications of a baby "standing on his own two feet." They recognize his vulnerability and tremble when they think of the long life ahead with its shattering uncertainties. Sometimes a mother longs for the early months of motherhood, when all she had to do was hold her angel baby and stare into his eyes. In her nostalgia she forgets the remorseless succession of days and nights and her uncertainties about whether she was good enough to hold her baby. She sighs with regret as she takes in the idea that infancy is over and will never return. Celebration keeps these worries and reservations in the background. The mother and father give the baby their blessings. Their celebrating eyes exude confidence in the baby's ability to make it out there: "Look at you, my spectacular walking-away baby!" The baby gets the message and makes the most of his love affair with the world.

The choreography of early conquests radiated from the fixed point of home base. The baby was often more absorbed in checking back and worrying about appearances and disappearances than he was in giving full rein to his urges to explore. Now he is almost totally absorbed by the energies of exploration. The new world, which at birth had been but a narrow shoreline, now turns out to be a vast and limitless continent. When he was a creeping baby he hugged his body to the safety of the earth. Upright, the toddler takes off on the adventure he has been charting since his earliest weeks. True, he once in a while grows nostalgic for home base, but usually he's too much in love with himself to care.

Glimmering in the toddler's self-love is a richer world than he could possibly have imagined when he turned his head to find the nipple he had conjured, when he first slid off his mother's lap to reach and creep away. The world smiles at this conqueror who has had the courage and cunning to discover it.

Soon the toddler can climb extraordinary heights. The top of a dresser, once a remote and unknowable territory, can be reached by tugging one chair over to another chair, climbing from the arm of one to the back of the other, and then clambering onto the top of the dresser. Such acts take a lot of planning and know-how. The alarm in his parents' eyes when they find him sitting atop the world will warn the baby of the dangers of climbing too high. The next time they see him lugging a chair they'll follow him and swoop him away.

Quickly recovering his dignity, the toddler will take off for the living room. There he climbs up the pillows to the arms of the sofa. Then he stands up high on the back of the sofa, turns around on his belly and slides down. Up onto the pillows once more. This time to bounce up and down. He repeats the climbing, sliding and bouncing as though nothing else mattered. Until he spies the hallway leading to the kitchen. He runs up and down the hallway as fast as he can. In the exhilaration of using his leg, chest, back and shoulder muscles all-out, the toddler is unconcerned about the numerous falls and bumps that are the unavoidable mishaps of an adventurer. Nobody has to rescue him when he takes a flop. He rights himself and goes on his way. In fact, it's something of a pleasant excitement to confirm the outlines of the body-self by bumping into the solid outlines of floors and table edges.

Before, the baby spent a lot of time *being* carried from here to there. Now he's the carrier who can clasp a huge pillow to his chest, lug it from the bedroom, and deposit it in the bathroom. The power grip of palm and opposing thumb forms a curl that can encompass small blocks and dishes. With the precision grip of thumb and forefinger pressing together, the toddler can pick up bits of thread and flecks of dust and transfer them from one hand to the other. Nothing is too big or too small to be carried and transported from here to there. The mighty Hercules opens and closes doors, switches lights off and on. Any container, be it a bottle, a box, a drawer, or a cabinet, is an invitation to open and close, empty, spill out and fill up. He pours liquids from one container to another, licking up the spills with his tongue or smearing them around with his fingertips.

The aggression of looking, reaching, tearing, pulling and tugging has paid off in body postures and movements that fit the actual contours of the inside-outside, up-and-down world of vertical space. Being able to control his physical self with such dexterity allows the toddler to suppose that he is in total control of his body and of the world around him.

Several months before he was transformed into an upright conqueror, the little boy's hands discovered his scrotum and penis. He frequently poked into his scrotum and belly button. He pulled and tugged on his penis. Now, from his upright (undiapered) vantage point, the boy toddler bends over to get a good look at his scrotum and penis. To his astonishment, he finds out that his penis is the one visible part of his body that he can't control. It rises and falls according to mysterious laws of its own. Nevertheless, when his parents notice his interest in his penis they give him a name for this newly discovered body part, and once it has a name, the penis is slightly less mysterious. Usually nobody bothers to give the boy a name for his scrotum. The assumption seems to be that the boy toddler experiences his penis and scrotum as one organ.

Several months before she became upright the little girl was fascinated with her belly button. As she was being bathed or diapered, her fingers were just as likely to wander to her vulva as to her belly button. She poked into her vulva and belly button. She rubbed and stroked them both. After she's upright the little girl can't readily see all of her genitals even when she bends over to look between her legs. Yet, her intense exploratory urge would certainly also include an active manual inspection. In addition, many little girls will lean over from a sitting position to visually inspect "the insides" that their hands have already made note of. The combined visual-tactile experience of her genitals is not so easily available to the girl toddler as it is to the boy, but if no one interferes, she makes "the discovery." She is given a name for her belly button. Only rarely does someone give the girl child a name for her vulva or vagina. The unwitting assumption seems to be that because they are hidden a little girl won't realize that she has them.

At the height of the time of body mastery—and largely as a by-product of the exploratory and manipulatory trends that characterize this period of life—it is not unusual for toddlers to fondle their genitals. Before naps and at bedtime many toddlers engage in this early form of genital stimulation. The masturbatory rhythms are quiet and self-soothing. They are not accompanied by the orgastic discharge typical of adult sexuality. Nor are the young toddler's masturbatory body movements vigorous and intense as they often are in the two-and-a-half- or three-year-old. The gestures are a light tapping and pulling of the genitals and a playful tensing and releasing of the perineal muscles. The diffuse, lightly spreading rhythms on the inner walls of the body contrast with the sharp excitements of scaling the heights of vertical space, and thus supplement the vigorous rhythms that come from the aggressive use of the large and small muscles that make up the edges of the toddler's body.

The unleashing of his physical energies could easily obscure the fact that the upright toddler doesn't actually spend all his time climbing and carrying, opening and closing. There are long moments of stillness when he is exercising nothing but his eyes. He becomes totally absorbed in watching his mother hammer nails into wood or staring at children at play. Watching a garbage truck loading is just as powerful a use of the body-self as the actual loading and spilling out of containers. The world the toddler stares at belongs to his eyes. He possesses sights as intensely as he conquers couches and flecks of dust.

Along with his almost absolute mastery of his body, the toddler has been learning the words that will enlarge his mastery of the world. He demonstrates his growing ability to control himself by responding to words. He comprehends and acts accordingly when someone says, "Stop!" "No!" "Don't," "Kiss me," "Say bye-bye," "Bring me the hat," "Hot!" "Put down the hammer."

Except for naming things just for the power of putting labels on the world, and the compliant "please's" and "thank-you's" and other recitals that are sometimes forced on him by overly zealous parents, the beginning toddler chooses for his permanent lexicon the words and word rhythms that are connected to the immediate sensate experiences of his daily life —the words that encourage and give definition to the way a body-mind conquers time and space.

Of the myriad words he has heard, the fifteen-month-old will first choose to utter but a dozen or so. These will be "Mommy" and "Daddy," which are words that later come to be used for all Mommy-like or Daddy-like persons, or even such ideas as "Mommy, get me down from this dresser top." Others are words that stand for the way the toddler supposes his body moves, such as "ball," "doggie," "truck"; other action words such as "go," "up," "down," "look," or "light" (meaning the off-on flashing of light and darkness that happens when the toddler plays with the light switch); descriptive words that he has heard in pleasant circumstances—"big," "pretty," "all-gone"; and perhaps some other basic items such as "belly," "eyes," "cookie," or "pee-pee."

Moreover, at this point in his life the child's confidence in himself is at a high. Unless someone has made him feel that naming is the most important thing, he will not think twice about creating language as he goes along, carrying on a babbling conversation that captures the grammatical rules of the speech he has heard. He invents a story in babbles, with a "doggie" or a "down" thrown in wherever they seem to fit. By now he's learned the alternating rhythm of speaking and then listening, so nothing pleases him more than to have his babble stories answered with another story or sentence. He will listen and then answer with a new babble story.

Using words of his own choosing, labeling for the power of labeling, and creating language as he goes along are as much a part of using the body as climbing and staring.

Choreography—Balancing Acts, Open Spaces, A New Partner When the upright toddler plays catch-me and hide-and-seek (the toddler's version of peek-a-boo) he is utterly entranced by the wonders of running down hallways and becoming invisible behind doorways and couches. He is absolutely certain that he can escape the catcher-of-babies, that the driving free, reckless dash of his madness and joy will last forever.

In his exhilarated certainty, the toddler is relatively unaware of the actual presence of his mother in the flesh. He behaves as though her presence were everywhere. Bodily sensations of mastery combine with a magical feeling of oneness with the world to produce the joyous elation of the love affair with the world.

Before the baby could walk, his body moved toward and away from his mother by molding and stiffening, creeping away and back for refueling. Now that he's upright he stands alone center stage. His mother has been relegated to the role of a protective stagehand, ready to catch the toddler if he goes too near the edge, moving props from here to there so he won't hurt himself, standing by to service his needs. Like an acrobat's assistant, she waits in the wings, attentively watching and listening as the skillful manipulator of space performs his daring balancing acts.

In his way of using his actual mother as a mere appendage, the upright toddler is behaving in a manner suitable to a conquering hero. It is customary for deep-sea divers, pilots, acrobats and mountain climbers to maintain a crew of assistants who are held responsible for the mundane matters of equipment and gear and food and water. Though the security and safety of thrilling exploits and daring feats often depend entirely on the watchful attention of these homey helpers, heroes scarcely mention or remember them. Interestingly, in the British Navy the unmentioned helpers of the submarine heroes are stationed in a depot ship called "Mummy."

Before he becomes entirely proficient at walking, the fifteen-month-old is aware of his need for gear. He carries something in each hand to help balance his upright body and to remind him of hugging close to mother earth. In his early days of walking away on his own two feet, holding on to a blanket or toy takes the place of holding on to mother's hand. Occasionally a toddler will maintain his balance by clasping his own two hands together. He will hold on to himself. But like the tight-rope walker who, with a dramatic flourish, suddenly casts away his balancing pole, the toddler also sooner or later throws off his gear, lets go, and takes off on his own. Once he takes off, the toddler resists any reminders of his continuing need for home base. Thenceforth his actions are designed as a declaration of his emancipation from ties to earthly things. He doesn't look down. He looks ahead to the open expanse before him. When he begins to run he spurns the sedate heel-toe movement that would plant him solidly on earth. Instead he glides trippingly on his toes.

The toddler's pulsating, airborne body is infatuated with the friendly expanse of open spaces. He has found the perfect partner for his love affair. Although he haughtily ignores his mother in the flesh, who reminds him of hugging the earth and holding on, the toddler has discovered a more exciting mother in the world of vertical space through which his body glides. Like his prehuman ancestors who were safely held by the endless sea, like the fetus in the womb who is held by amniotic fluid, like the babe in arms who is held together by the presence of his mother, the upright toddler is encompassed by the limitless open spaces of the new world. He molds his body to its invisible contours, imagining yet again that he is at one with the universe.

Elation Like ecstasy and despair, elation is an intense, overpowering mood which sometimes obscures the subtler moods of ordinary life. However, elation arises out of the exquisite attunement between sensation and motor action. Whenever our bodies move in perfect concert with our senses we experience exhilaration and elation. Thus elation heightens our awareness of some aspects of reality while obscuring others.

The upright toddler is elated. His body is vibrant. His body pulsates with the grandeur of his movements through space, and the outer forms of the world vibrate in the aura of his grandeur. The high-spirited energies of his masterful body spill over onto the world, gathering all of life together in the intense and unexpected release from menace and contradiction.

Elation is joy remembered and a trancelike forgetting of frustration and disappointment. The upright toddler's elation is the joyous climax of a peek-a-boo game that began with worried flutterings. When he looks to the outer forms of the world, they mirror all the spectacular things he feels his body to be. The outer forms caress proud edges onto his body and produce harmony and relaxation inside.

Like Tensing and Hillary in their adoration of Everest, the toddler communes with the outer forms of the world he conquers. He is exhilarated with hallways and the names he names and the cabinets he opens and closes. His current love affair is akin to the dialogue that paved his way into the new world.

In the beginning the newborn had the impression of entering a new world that understood what it was like to be a baby for the first time. The world fit in with his inborn gestures and body movements, affirming what the newborn felt himself to be. Although he was actually totally helpless, the world held him together in serenity and wholeness. But this happened at a time when the baby had a simple mind of tension flutterings inside and sucking mouth and grasping fist and looking eyes facing outward. His mind couldn't know where it began and ended, or where the world began and ended. His body didn't pulsate with elation and vibrate the world. Then it was his mother's presence that lit up the contours of the world.

As he molded his body to his mother's body, the two-month-old was rooting himself with the inner rhythms that would prevent his growth energies from spilling over and exploding. The rhythms at the core of his being would stay with him as reminders of safety and wholeness. Yet even at that early time, the muscles of his mouth, hand and eyes were thrusting and stiffening. The baby's body-mind was being alerted for separateness.

As he started to separate, his mind expanded and pushed away from the mother of oneness. With this wiser mind the baby encountered the appearing and disappearing mother in the flesh, who often reminded him of the disadvantages of separateness. At the same time, the mother's mirroring admiration of his body and the availability of her lap for emotional refueling held the baby together and affirmed his urge to creep over thresholds and conquer the world.

Although the baby might occasionally long for the simple bliss of oneness, his body-self, thrusting outward and upward, began to avoid the enveloping confinement of the actual body of his mother. The baby wanted to do, not to be done to. His mother's lap was comforting, but it also was an unpleasant reminder of helplessness and being done to. So he commenced to prefer illusion to the contradictions and imperfections of lapdom. He created a constantly available mother that he could control absolutely. The baby created a security blanket—an outer form that reflected oneness without reminding the baby of his actual helplessness and vulnerability. Now that he's upright, the toddler goes on communing with his blanket. He communes with his blanket in a mid-realm between waking and dreaming which resembles the not yet fully awake, twilight time of oneness.

Is the toddler awake or asleep when he uses his body to its fullest by dashing, staring and naming? Elation is not the ecstasy of the twilight time of oneness. Yet it too is a blend of wakefulness and sleep. The elated toddler is both fully awake and on the brink of sleep. One side of elation is the "up" of being more alert than ever before. When he handles the world, the toddler knows what he's about. Functioning on his own is a source of real pleasure—not imaginary conjuring. He is exacting in his attention to detail. Furthermore, when he attacks a problem, he sustains his efforts until the problem is solved. There is no hanging back from challenge. The toddler practices and refines until he gets things just right. His clever manipulations of toys and household objects suggest that he is deeply in tune with the rules that govern the outer forms of the sensate world.

He seldom loses track of where he is in the world. When he enters an unfamiliar terrain, he sizes it up, measuring and calculating the obstacles that dot the expanses of space. And though he clambers up a staircase like a mountain goat, as he turns around to go down he views the cliffed-off void of downness with appropriate fear. He ponders the possibilities of creeping down backward or bumping down on his bottom, one step at a time. Perhaps he'll damp his conquering spirit and just sit there howling for assistance.

All in all, the fifteen-month-old appears to be managing the world of inside and outside, up and down, with proficiency and painstaking respect for its rules.

As regards the outer forms of the world he loves, the upright toddler is a realist. He is right to suppose that he has made a world which corresponds to what his muscles can do and what his eyes, nose, skin and ears can take in. He is right to suppose that his mind can manipulate flecks of dust and transport huge pillows; that he can give full play to his aggressive way of handling the world without destroying any part of it. In these respects the toddler's elation is realistic, a wide-awake reaction to events that are actually occurring.

Even his notion of being at one with the world has a ring of truth to it, because in this new version of illusion the baby is reliving events that once actually happened. The baby who was held and satisfied during the early months of oneness has preserved body memories of serenity and wholeness. So he now can create an outer world that holds him.

However, elation also entails falsification and deception. Although the tapestry of the second birth is made up of two inextricably enmeshed threads, one of these threads has been almost totally obscured by the other. Pulled along by the thread of his inborn growth urges, the baby has thrust himself out of the confines of mother-infant oneness and become an independent body-self. But the critical thread of having to reckon with the firm reality of his separateness from his mother has been scarcely remembered.

In the elation of his love affair he supposes that there is no contradiction between oneness and becoming a separate self who functions on his own. He is oblivious to those aspects of oneness that have to do with melting into nothingness, sinking in the snow, drowning in the void, and being held by the catcher of babies. The toddler supposes himself to be fully awake. But he has yet to wake up to the full knowledge of his separateness from his mother in the flesh or to the subtle dangers of absolute oneness. Were he to succumb to the absolute bliss of oneness before carving out his own space in the world, the child would be reabsorbed into the being of his mother. His surrender would be tantamount to ceasing to exist. Later, with constancy, he may risk the merging ecstasies of oneness.

In a few months, a mind that can at least tentatively encompass these awesome realities will claim its ascendency over the innocent body-mind of the fifteen-month-old. But for now, by asserting the full power of his body-self, the toddler is at one with the world. At the same time, he uses his body to separate himself physically from the confines of lapdom.

The baby has had his moods before. Teething and too many don'ts plunged him into icy gray irritability, and the world spiked him with frustration. Often he could be rosy-hued in the glow of his parents' mirroring admiration, and then the world was rosy. However, elation is a more overpowering mood than either irritability or cheerfulness. Elation is the vermilion overstatement that blots out the nuances and tints of ordinary life.

Painters speak of redness and what becomes of it when blended with blue or yellow. "Just as orange is red brought nearer to humanity by yellow, so violet is red withdrawn from humanity by blue," said Kandinsky. Nor did he forget blackness. He thought that when blue "sinks almost to black it echoes a grief that is hardly human." When the toddler's new mind wakes him from his vermilion dream of glory he will be touched by the blue-black mood of sadness. His new awareness of who he is will draw him back to the ordinary tints of earth. If in the process of learning to be true to the earth he can retain a measure of idealism and illusion, the child will have made the most of his first three years in the new world. He will have done the best that any mortal could hope to do.

The full weight of the enigmas of the second birth are held in abeyance by the toddler's elation. Whether or not the child thoroughly partakes of the elated mood typical of this time of life depends on the parents' reactions and on the quality of his interactions with the world up till now. If he has been held well enough during the time of oneness, the toddler will be able to suppose that the world holds him now.

The joy that attends the physical moves away from mother hinges on the magical sense of safety that comes from imagining that the mother's presence is everywhere. If playing alone in the presence of a mother has not been a central experience in the explorations that preceded the attainment of upright locomotion, the elation will be muted. A mother's intrusion on her infant's independent explorations or her abandonment of him totally to his own devices during the early period of conquest will make it difficult for the toddler to experience the true measure of grandeur that comes with uprightness. Walking, running, staring and naming will not be as free or deliciously exhilarated. He will be cautious and more concerned about falling. He will hesitate to name until he's absolutely sure of mirroring admiration. He won't exercise his independent functioning to its fullest.

Sometimes a child achieves upright locomotion and moves away from mother before he has the emotional wherewithal to be separate from her. For this reason a precocious walker always needs special attention. Unless his mother goes on providing him with the orienting beacon of her actual presence, an early walker becomes scattered and unfocused in his body movements. He will continue to lack focus and direction unless he gets enough of the back-and-forth choreography of moving away, refueling and checking back.

On the other hand, some children who are physically capable of walking alone may persist in holding on to the mother. They are preoccupied with the mother's whereabouts and can't let go and walk away on their own two feet. Such children still need the anchoring safety of home base, some additional reassurances about the reliability of the mother's presence. But if a mother is too much there, hovering and worrying every time her child looks as if he might take a step or two, his courage will fade. The best reassurance for a child who is hesitating to walk away is mirroring admiration—the faith and confidence in his mother's eyes—the look that says, "What a magnificent and competent child you are. Go ahead. You can make it."

Also, when a child has been unable to arrive at some beginning understanding of the limits of his natural aggression, he may experience the spurt of assertive aggression that accompanies upright locomotion as destructive. Anxiety about running away with himself overshadows the freedom to become a separate self. Whenever the delicate balance between awareness of separateness and the capacity for independent functioning is upset, the customary high mood is subdued.

Mothers tend to encourage their sons to run away and romp. Moreover, a mother sometimes is even in awe of what she takes to be masculine physical prowess when she sees her son leaping over crib rails and climbing to the top of dressers. She has difficulty keeping her boy toddler safe. Mothers of little boys often complain that "There's no controlling him." "He's all over the place." "I tell him no, but he never listens." The complaints are tinged with more than a little pride at the boy's marvelous independence and masculine bravado. It's almost as though the mother enjoyed being overwhelmed by her spectacular conquering hero.

Little girls are often deprived of the full grandeur of the love affair. The pride that shines on the jumping and leaping boy child does not shine on the little girl who might want to jump and leap. Most mothers worry more about the physical safety of daughters. The worry and hesitation in the mother's face makes the little girl cautious, thus making it hard for her to let go with daring and abandon during this period. The idea that little girls are more fragile than little boys is erroneous. They are, in fact, usually physically stronger, better coordinated, and more masterful in using their bodies.

Girls love to look and they learn to use words earlier than boys. Girls tend to be cuddled and talked to more, so they become easier to socialize, dominate and control than little boys. Because the experience of using the body all-out is not so intense, the edges of the girl's body-self are not as sharp as they might have been. In addition, the being-done-to element in her personality isn't sufficiently balanced by the sense of mastery and active doing-to. Instead of rising and gliding through the expanses of open space, the little girl clings to the safety of the earth. Later, a little girl often is not prepared to face the turmoil of separation. Elation cushions disappointments and disenchantment, and many little girls simply haven't had enough elation.

The mood of elation, with its exotic blend of hyperalert realism and marvelous illusion, is appropriate to this time of human life. It should be the dominant mood. The grandeur and body-buoyancy experienced now will help a child keep in touch with the sensate qualities of the external world for the rest of his life. He will be optimistic about himself. When the world lets him down he will still be able to grab on to the promises it continues to hold out to him.

Low-Keyedness Even during the time of early conquest, when worries about appearances and disappearances held the baby's exploratory urges in check, his mood was often exhilarated. But then only a fifteen-minute separation from mother was sufficient to tone down the baby's mood. Now that he's upright and haughtily forgetful of his actual mother's presence in the world, it should be expected that periods of being away from her would have little impact on his high-spirits. While reactions to separation are less intense during this period than during other phases of the second birth, when the toddler recognizes the possibility that his mother might be departing from the scene for more than a few minutes his mood becomes low-keyed.

The fact is, the upright toddler isn't always high-spirited and elated. Every so often his dialogue with outer forms is interrupted. He forgets about conquering the world of time and space and turns his attention and focus inward. Such interruption of active engagement with the real world is most likely to occur when the toddler becomes aware that his mother is not there.

When he realizes that she has gone away or recognizes as she puts on her coat that she's about to go away, the toddler may protest angrily or cry with anguish as though to prevent her from leaving or to coerce her to return. As soon as he resigns himself to the idea that she has really gone away and won't come back, he calms down and stops protesting. For a while the child may try to find solace playing with his favorite toys or jumping up and down on the couch or rocking on his rocking horse or hugging the book his mother read to him just before she left. But, without her nearby presence the outer forms of the world lose their luster. Within a few minutes the toddler gives up his attempt to restore his lost sense of well-being through active engagement with outer forms. He lowers his sails. His customarily exuberant body curls into a hush of stillness. His bright eyes get a dull, filmy look, as though he were deliberately turning away from the now disappointing visage of the sensate world to commune with an inner world.

At these moments it becomes clear that the presence of the mother has been essential to the toddler's elated mood.

The importance of her role in the choreography stands out vividly when she disappears altogether. The toddler was able to suppose that he was safely held by the world only so long as he could occasionally look around and see his mother standing in the wings. The toddler cannot sustain his bravado when she's gone.

It's not that he is despairing or apathetic while his mother is away. It's merely that his mood is down and that his customary involvement in using his body all-out has been replaced by inwardness. In its most dramatic version, the low-keyed mood of the toddler might be expressed by his settling in at the doorway through which his mother disappeared and seeming to pine away. Another child might tiptoe from room to room, picking up flecks of dust and gazing at them. Still another might snuggle up on the couch next to his grandmother for an afternoon of storytelling and cookies. Grandma will be smugly relieved by the pleasant calm that descends on the household when mother goes away. "He was wonderful while you were gone. He didn't climb all over everything and get into mischief the way he does when you're around. He didn't miss you at all."

Whatever the version of low-keyedness and however it may strike the casual observer, the toddler is always doing something more than he appears to be doing when his mother leaves the scene. Although he sits calmly next to his grandmother, he probably isn't paying much attention to her or to the story she's telling him. He barely glances at the pictures in the book. Nor is the child really engaged or fascinated this afternoon by the power of picking up flecks of dust. Even the pining baby at the doorway, who seems to be doing "nothing at all" in his mother's absence, is privately involved in a very definite something.

Each of these toddlers is working actively at trying to maintain his emotional equilibrium. They aren't passively capitulating to their disappointment. And they aren't being helpless. With their steady inward focus and inwardly curling bodies they are searching for an inner world that will bring back the perfect state of self that got lost when mother walked through the door and disappeared.

As he finally settles in at the doorway or snuggles in on the couch, the toddler is imagining the private inner world he has conjured. His efforts are bent toward holding on to the sensations of well-being and safety that come from communing with this inner world. Since he still has mostly a body-mind, the images the fifteen-month-old holds on to are not ideas or clearly delineated pictures. His images are mostly revived memories of body states of gentle relaxation rhythms and proud edges. The toddler who pines in the doorway is probably not able to recapture a picture of his mother's face, but he can restore the serenity, bliss, wholeness, harmony of the lost world of oneness when her presence was everywhere.

While the mother is gone the toddler is working very hard to keep his focus inward, and all will go well if no one interferes with his efforts. Those well-meaning babysitters and uncles who can't bear the sight of pining or listlessness will surely upset the apple cart if they try to cheer the baby up and do happy exciting things with him. Then the toddler may burst into tears and sob inconsolably for the return of his mother. When his inner world is disturbed, a previously calm baby may suddenly become frantic and dash about the house, searching for his mother. In her way, Grandma has the right idea when she accepts the baby's toned-down mood with relief.

In his gesture of turning away from the outer world to re-create an inner world he can depend on, a baby is managing loss with a competence that should be respected. He doesn't panic and tear his hair out. Nor does he blithely go on with "business as usual," as though his mother counted for nothing. His subdued mood is a sign that he is strong enough to long for what he misses without falling apart when it disappears. His longing is a sign that he cares enough for his actual mother to conjure her as perfect when she's gone.

The mother returns. The toddler hears the key in the lock. He bounds off the couch. His eyes light up with joyous expectation. The door opens. The baby takes one look at his mother's outstretched arms and "happy to see you" face and bursts into tears. Some toddlers start toward their mother's outstretched arms and then turn away from her as though she counted for nothing. "He was just fine until you walked in the door," reports Grandma with a mixture of self-righteousness and irritation at the baby's sudden perverse change of mood. Perhaps the face of the returning mother was a letdown compared with the ideal mothering presence the toddler had been imagining? Perhaps now that she's back and in-the-flesh the toddler feels safe about expressing some of the anger and disappointment he felt when she disappeared? In any case, after a good cry that seems to release the accumulated tension of having to work so hard to keep his balance, the toddler will accept his mother's comforting hugs. He might even welcome her back by dashing to the couch and throwing the pillows around.

Many toddlers need a little emotional refueling before they are able to pick up and go about "business as usual." A quiet snuggle with mother or a good meal from father might be in order to completely restore the baby's lost equilibrium. In a while he will become his usual elated self.

Parents often worry about leaving their baby. They can't face the desperate protests at the door when they leave or the rejections that greet them when they return. The image of their buoyant baby pining away at the door or glumly wandering about, gazing at flecks of dust, spoils the pleasure of their needed time away from the baby. They don't appreciate the competence with which their baby is handling these brief absences. He may not be as energetic or bouncy but neither does he fall apart.

The blue-gray inward mood that goes along with a short

time away from mother and father is good preparation for the disappointments of the months to come. Just around the corner is the new beginning when the toddler will finally have to reckon with the firm reality that he and mother are two separate beings. As his peek-a-boo games and confident walking-away steps help him to master the idea of separateness, so his occasional blue-gray moods leave him with an impression that he can manage loss and separation. By deflecting his attention from the world of outer forms, the child is conjuring an inner world that holds him. The miniature loss-and-longing reaction of low-keyedness indicates that the baby has an ideal mothering-self experience to revive when the world temporarily goes sour on him. If the periods of separation are not prolonged, most toddlers will be able to maintain their equilibrium. Every child has his individual breaking point. For some a full afternoon is too much. Others can tolerate a weekend, provided they are in a familiar home with someone they know and trust.

The low-keyedness of this period is a muted version of the letdown that will follow the love affair with the world. The baby who has never been separated from his mother and therefore never had the experience of being able to comfort himself in her absence is liable to despair when he is finally cast from his Garden of Eden.

The Fall The force of the growth processes that convert a fertilized egg into a newborn baby would overwhelm the universe if its momentum did not abate. And, although the momentum is somewhat slower, the force that converts a newborn into a toddler is equally fierce and unrelenting. During the first fifteen months of life in the new world, the baby's mind and body are continually being shaped and reshaped by this unrelenting force. On any particular day what a baby can comprehend of the world outside the walls of his body will be determined by the current shape of his body-mind. The next day the world that presents itself for looking or grasping will be a somewhat different world, because each day the body-mind is a somewhat different body-mind. One moment inside the body walls there are thundering rumbles, and the next, there may be wild flutterings or calm tension-relaxation rhythms or spikes of dischargeable tension. Each day the child plunges into a new stream of existence.

The outer forms that reach the baby's mind during these first fifteen months are in constant flux. The world is an ever-changing flow of new sensations and new movements which the baby pieces together, takes apart, and then re-pieces. Sometimes he falls apart for a few days while he tries to sort it all out.

Even so, the unrelenting energies of the growth process do not run wild. The presence of his mother lights up the contours of the sensate world and sculpts them into a circle of safety. The baby is held together in a way that allows him to suppose there is wholeness and lawfulness in the midst of flux. He is able to yield himself up to the growth energies that converted him from a limp newborn into an upright toddler whose senses and body movements finally came together in just the right way to absorb and act on the exquisitely changeable sensate world of sounds, colors, motions, odors, couches, tables and castaway toys. With the attainment of uprightness, the world of sensation is delicious and the child is perfectly in touch with it.

In the final coming together of senses and body movements with what is sensed and what may be acted upon, the unrelenting momentum of growth that drove the baby's mind to this pinnacle of perfection slows down.

Thus at around fifteen to eighteen months the toddler's mind undergoes a revolution. The dramatic changes in the quality of his mind wrench the toddler from his sense-motion-action world and cast him into a new world which he cannot immediately comprehend or absorb. For a while he is once more in limbo.

The toddler begins to have a mind that can create symbols, images and concepts. This mind also enables the child to acquire a word language that will be used for communicating with other people. Symbols and word concepts arrest the movement of sensate flux, converting sound, sight and motion into static petrified images.

Before the advent of this new mind, the baby used to have to open and close a box to understand "opening" and "closing." When his mind was just on the threshold of its revolution, the baby could look at a box and conjecture the notion of "opening" by opening his mouth. Very soon afterward he becomes capable of evoking an inner image of "box" or "opening." He can speculate about "inside the box" and "what's inside the box" and "how to get what's inside the box." The outer form of box and its exquisite possibilities are now inner forms that the baby can manipulate without moving his hands or his eyes. He doesn't need to open an actual box or climb an actual couch. The eighteen-month-old can think about boxes and couches and opening and closing without moving a muscle. Of course, he doesn't altogether stop using his body-mind. Nor does he forget what his body-mind taught him about the world of outer forms. He goes on expanding his body-mind and inventing new ways of using it.

Yet, little by little, his thinking mind will take over. Before, a box was a box and a couch was a couch. Now that he can manipulate images the baby also learns that one image can stand for another image. If he chooses, a box can be a couch. An eighteen-month-old can put a block to sleep in a cigar box and make believe it's a baby in a bed. A dump-truck on top of a bowl can become a baby sitting on a potty. The toddler stops banging on his drum for a moment so he can comb his hair with the drumstick.

Occasionally the toddler makes use of his new mind by pretending he's a mommy. He cooks on a table that stands for a stove and serves up a bead meal in ashtray dishes. He puts his bear to sleep on the couch and tucks it in with his precious security blanket. The bear is eased on his way to dreamland with a lullaby. The next day he locks the bear in the bathroom and yells through the door at it, "No." "Stay." With his new mind, a baby doesn't have to have an actual mother right before his eyes in order to follow her example. By acting as though he were a mommy the toddler reveals his initial awareness that he and Mother are different beings. When he's playing at being Mommy, the image of Mother yelling is one image. Mother singing a lullaby is another. There is also the image of a me who is being Mommy.

Innocent though these early manifestations of a new mind may be, the implications are far-reaching. Not only have mother and baby ceased to share the same body boundaries, they now are represented in the toddler's mind as separate images. The mother has her existence, the toddler his. Once the mother can be represented as separate, it's very hard for the toddler to go on supposing that she's a mere appendage or ever-present auxiliary helper. No longer can her presence in the world be taken for granted.

Falling down and bumping into furniture lose their sport. The toddler, who thinks with a mind that can represent, looks about in bewilderment as he finds himself sprawled out alongside the couch from which he has just fallen. "Where is my mother? Why isn't she here to pick me up?" Outrage temporarily blots out the images of a yes-saying mother.

What will the toddler make of his fall from grace? Who will hold him now? He has no way of comprehending that his new mind will go on to empower him with an enlarged capacity for holding himself and managing his body on his own. For the moment, the advantages of his new mind are also stark reminders of the incontrovertible fact of his mother's separate existence.

The plot goes deeper. When the thinking mind first arrives

on the scene, it cannot absorb or accommodate itself to the static world of symbols and words that are meant to communicate with others. The masterful hero who had been at one with the world suddenly is overcome with the sense of his aloneness in the world. He wakes up to another, perhaps even more frightening reality. He is not a conqueror after all. He is a small, vulnerable, helpless and needy self. The next half-year or so of the toddler's existence will be dominated by his struggle to restore his wounded narcissism.

The contradictions of oneness and separateness have come home to roost. There's no getting away from them now. Though the mother will be recognized as an actual mother in the flesh, the toddler will do everything in his power to coerce her back to being an extension of his self. At the same time, a central aspect of his new beginning will be his overriding insistence on claiming possession of what actually belongs to the self. The dilemma of wanting to repossess the mother as a part of the self and yet dreading relinquishing to the mother what rightfully belongs to the self throws the toddler into turmoil. When the self arrives, the acrobat comes down to earth; sometimes gliding gently, sometimes with a thud.

Chapter Six

The New Beginning

Fifteen Months to Three Years
(The Thinking Baby)

The Self Arrives   The earliest signs of the new beginning could hardly be construed as heralds of crisis. On the contrary, in his initial experience of separateness, the fifteen-month-old will gather together the strengths that will enable him to brave the stormy months ahead. The predominant change is his renewed interest in his mother. Upon suspecting the possibility of his mother's separate existence, the child is suddenly overcome with a desire to share his discoveries and achievements with her. He revalues her actual presence in the world. At this turning point, a mother's willingness to share will mitigate the anger and disappointment of the crisis to come.

Whereas it was crucial for the younger toddler to practice body mastery and perfect the skill of uprightness on his own—in a direction away from his mother—his current beginning acquisitions of communicative language, symbolic understanding and social skills are rehearsed and perfected in association with the mother. Her appreciation and stimulation serve as organizers of the child's new level of functioning in the world. She does not take over his activities and possess his mind. Her empathic responsiveness encourages what the child brings to her.

As the mother sits quietly reading, the toddler takes note of her peaceful obliviousness to his presence. He carries his top over to her chair. Tugging on her skirt so that she'll look up, he shows her how pushing the stick makes the top spin around. A few months ago he couldn't have managed that feat. Then, with a calculated winning smile, he offers his mother the toy, his gesture clearly indicating that it's now her turn to make it spin.

Later that day he once again methodically diverts his mother's attention from her book. The toddler makes several trips to his toy chest. One by one, he piles his teddy bear, storybook, crumpled cellophane wrappings, ball, peg bench and assorted blocks onto her lap. Having ascertained her interest in these marvelous gifts, he pulls his storybook out of the pile and commences to entertain and woo his mother with his newly discovered ability to recognize the picture of blocks. He says "block" and points to the picture of the block and then to the real block on her lap. If he is successful in his wooing, he will then methodically remove his toys from his mother's lap. Along with the toys goes the book she has been reading. He climbs up beside her and begins to read to her, naming the other objects pictured in his book. He reads a babble story to her. When he's finished, he reads the story again and then perhaps three or four more times. Then his eyes peer into hers for some mirroring admiration.

Another favorite way of diverting a mother from her personal activities and private existence is ball-tossing. No matter what she might be doing at the moment, the toddler confidently expects that his ball-tossing gestures will result in his mother tossing the ball back to him. The toddler is tireless in his enthusiasm. This ball game might last forever. It is forever to the mother but usually not quite enough for the toddler.

Just recently, the toddler's entire emotional investment was in activity for activity's sake. He couldn't have cared less about who noticed him or watched him or shared with him. Now the world and its treasures are meaningful when he can share them with another person—above all with his mother. Each time his mother joins him or responds positively to his wooing gestures the toddler staves off the full realization that he is alone in the world as a separate person who is expected to stand on his own two feet and do everything on his own.

Pleasure in sharing with mother generalizes to a new kind of interest in other people. The sixteen-month-old is friendly. He confidently walks up to familiar adults and invites them to play with him. He is able to accept their attentions as substitutes for sharing with mother. Imitating another child or adult is the young toddler's way of making friends.

The child is wary, but being like someone else makes approaching them seem safer. If the other child is making a block tower, making a block tower right next to him becomes a gesture of friendship. The social greeting gesture of upraised palm and "Hi!" becomes more prominent than the "Bye-bye" that characterized the creeping-away, walking-away days of the love affair. With people he doesn't know, the toddler indicates his conflict between wariness and a desire to be friendly by offering a half-smile, lowering his head and averting his gaze. The shy-coy smile makes its appearance.

The success of his social overtures alleviates the toddler's anxiety about aloneness in the world. His interest in being with other people and communicating with them further stimulates him to use words in a different way than previously. He discovers that if he says "cookie" or "down" with a special inflection someone will give him a cookie or help him down from his high chair. He gets what he wants by asking for it. And, in addition, people smile at him for telling what he wants in words instead of gestures and grunts. Words have a new kind of power.

Occasionally the toddler surprises himself and everyone else as he squeals with the delight of finding a lost toy, "I got bear!" The surprise is warranted. Only rarely will a fifteen-month-old be heard using the pronoun "I." In fact most children do not use the word "I" consistently until thirty months or so. "I" is the word that means the child has absorbed the meaning of separate identity. Usually before that time the toddler will say, "My bear" or "Got bear." Yet every once in a while that fateful word "I" slips out along with those equally infrequent sentences containing a subject, a verb and an object. A common sentence of this sort is, "I see you."

Along with the new symbolic manifestations of language—this word represents that thing, this phrase brings about that human response—the toddler elaborates the symbolic play that began with using a drumstick for a comb and putting a block baby to sleep in a box bed. Some of these more complicated make-believe play sequences help the toddler to master his anxiety about being helpless and alone. If, for example, he witnesses another child fall off a slide and then look around with bewildered outrage because her mother wasn't right there to pick her up and comfort her, the toddler will take his stuffed animal to the slide, cradle it gently between his knees, slide it safely to earth and then swing it around for a comforting hug and a big kiss. By recapturing his own mother's comforting presence in make-believe, the toddler is comforting himself and assuring himself that aloneness can be managed. Even though he can't entirely possess his actual mother, he has taken a part of her inside him. This inside mother will stay with him and eventually become part of his own self. Though she is not he, he can become like her. Though she is not he, her comforting presence is inside him.

Similarly, on those days when his mother is too preoccupied with her own thoughts to pay much attention to him, the toddler might play with his doll the way he would have liked his mother to play with him. He holds the doll's two hands in his two hands and turns about the floor for a ring-a-rosy game. Or he might put the doll on the rocking horse and give it the reckless ride he had wanted from his mother. On the other hand, if he should take his mother's ignoring of his overtures to share as a rejection, he may throw his doll on the floor, kick it under the couch, and forget about its existence for a day or two.

The more the toddler becomes aware of his mother's separate existence, the more his actual separations from her are fraught with anxiety. When his mother departs from the scene he usually can't find solace in imitations of her comforting presence or in a low-keyed conjuring of her presence or in turning outward to his customary pursuits. His efforts are bent toward avoiding the overpowering blue-black mood of sadness. When his mother leaves, the child runs from here to there, from one activity to another, playing with a toy and then dropping it, leaning on his babysitter and then sullenly pushing her away. In contrast to the well-controlled body movements of the period of elation, the bursts of activity that are designed to avoid sadness are unfocused and scattered. They are restless and manic rather than elated.

At sixteen months a toddler's thinking mind has stimulated many significant emotional and intellectual gains—symbolic play, symbolic use of language, an increased desire and ability to communicate with other human beings, an ability to share real achievements in a real way with an actual mother. These gains are appreciated by the parents. And though they are somewhat aware of the toned-down, slowed-down mood and body activity, parents usually regard with pride and pleasure these initial manifestations of their child's self-awareness. They think of them as signs of his straight-

ahead march out of babyhood and into manageable childhood.

The Crisis Within a month or two, though, the child's
progressive moves toward becoming a separate, independent,
sociable, autonomous self turn the other way. His wooing
of the mother is converted into a remorseless coercive demand that she act as an extension of the self. A desire to
possess the other child's blocks infiltrates the friendly act of
building a tower just like the other child's tower. The battle
of wills begins. The suggestions and nurturing gestures of
the mother are rejected. Whining explosions of "No" and
"Mine" dominate the household. The toddler expects his
mother to be everywhere and yet he pushes her away when
she comes near him. Stormy temper tantrums and intense
mood swings supplant the calm that initially followed the
elated mood of the love affair with the world.

**Choreography—Clinging and Pushing Away, Shadowing
and Darting Away, Holding On and Letting Go** The toddler comes down to earth. He will enact the final episode
of his second birth with a new perspective on the meaning
of space. Although he will not altogether relinquish his love
affair with the vast expanses of the physical world, his overriding concern will be to come to terms with the idea that
his mother's space is not his own. He will be consumed with
a search for a distance that will allow him to be part of
his mother's space while keeping his own space inviolate.
The down-to-earth mother of separateness is a partner in this
final choreography. She is at once longed for and feared.

As in previous months, the child plays out the oneness and
separateness drama in the medium of physical space by
coming close to his mother and moving away from her. But,
now the dilemmas of oneness and separateness are interpreted by a thinking mind. Inner psychological distance is
what the child's consuming search is all about.

Initially the child merely looks around and takes stock of his new situation. He assesses his mighty uprightness and discovers his smallness in relation to his parents, the furniture of his home, the streets of his city. Physical closeness to mother is no longer directly translatable into courage and confidence. The circle of safety which once gave the child rein to measure his place in the world has lost its protective magic. Safety and wholeness now have more to do with the perplexing intangible space between the inner images of the self and the inner images of the mother than with the actual physical distance that separates them. The child strains to reconcile his new inner world of emotional space with his understandings of the familiar outer world of physical space.

As we have seen, the toddler's initial efforts at reconciliation were heroic. He created a circle of shared intimacy. He invited his mother into his circle and thus gained entrance into the space that belonged to her. Mother's lap was no longer the haven of all safety, but it still could be a way station at which the child might stop to woo her with his artful manner of using words, "reading" from books, dancing to music, throwing a ball, scribbling pictures, and imitating Mommy. However, though his mother was infinitely patient and empathically responsive, little by little the toddler came to the realization that his mother's interests were not identical with his own.

As the evidence of separateness mounts, the toddler's confusions intensify. His body movements lose their graceful dignity and sense of purpose, becoming unpredictable and often reckless. His body is electrified by an urgent need to undo the now incontrovertible evidence of separateness. At the same time, his sense of helplessness and deflated grandeur makes him desperate to possess his own selfhood, his body and all its parts both inside and outside. He is driven to own what is his and not surrender to the being-done-to, passive, non-self state of molding oneness. At last the child pushes himself out of the illusory orbit of oneness. The time of preparation is over. The second birth is at hand.

The process is not unlike the first birth, when the mother's uterus contracted and released so as to push the baby out of her dark womb and into the light of the new world. In the second birth, however, it is the child who must do the birth work while his mother and father assist him with all their empathy and emotional availability. In the second birth, the child's body movements are not so predictable or regular as uterine contractions and releases, but the moving-toward and moving-away gestures are analogous.

The self-aware toddler holds on to his mother and then abruptly lets go of her. He runs to the door to greet her and then veers away from her open-armed welcome. He clings to her in order to undo their separateness but then he angrily pushes her away when she responds to his desperate clinging with a comforting hug. If on the next day she should ignore his clinging and not hug him, the toddler may rage at her in furious disappointment, or hit at her book, throw it to the floor, and kick it under the couch.

He tries to coerce his mother into being at one with him. If she gives in to his coercion, he dreads the loss of his self-hood. If she resists and doesn't act as though she and he are part of each other, he comes face to face with his aloneness in the world. Even minor frustrations awaken the longing for oneness and also the dread of oneness.

For several minutes the toddler tries unsuccessfully to ram an unyielding puzzle piece into its proper slot. "Come!" he yells imperiously to his mother. Without so much as a glance at her face or the slightest recognition of her as an actual person, the toddler grabs on to his mother's hand as though it were a mechanical extension of his own, made for no other purpose than to fit puzzle pieces into slots. The mother is supposed to get the piece in but make it seem as though the toddler did it himself.

Perhaps a mother does not comprehend that she's supposed to behave as a magical extension. Instead she decides that it would be wiser to let her child do it on his own. After all, he isn't any longer a helpless baby. Besides, only last week he could do that puzzle himself. Fury strikes. That's not what the child had in mind. He expected his mother to comprehend what he had in mind without having to be told—as any magical extension of the self would automatically do. She failed him again. Aloneness confronts him unmercifully.

Let us suppose the mother catches on that all she need do is act as though her hand and her child's hand were one, and therefore unobtrusively slides the puzzle piece into place. Then the toddler looks up at her and begins to cry. More frightening than reminders of aloneness and separateness are the child's secret longings to be an acted-upon baby of oneness. By understanding his desires with such perfection, the mother has confirmed the very helplessness from which the child had set out to escape. The drama has no happy solutions. It is well nigh impossible for a mother to satisfy a toddler in the throes of the complex dilemmas of his second birth.

Another way a child tries to undo separateness is by shadowing his mother. The shadowing toddler does not have to touch his mother's body in order to bolster his experience of her as an extension of his self. Instead he watches her every move; never lets her disappearances catch him unawares; never takes his eyes off her; never lets her out of his mind. On some days, he turns into a true little shadow, following in his mother's trail but a few inches behind her, oblivious to everything else as he concentrates his being on keeping himself connected to her. Like a suspicious lover who interprets every gesture and detail as a sign of unfaithfulness, the toddler braces himself to shadow his mother at the merest suggestion that she might stand up and walk to another room. He's at her chair before she is aware of her own intention to leave. Furthermore, since the boundaries between his own desires and his mother's desires are still uncertain and permeable, the toddler imagines that his own wishes to be free of the mother are in reality her wishes to be free of him. So just at those rare moments when he might forget his shadowing and allow himself to be carried away with a pleasurable surge of independent mastery, the toddler will look around with panic written across his face—the mother hadn't moved an inch but the child's own wish to be free of her made him imagine that she had disappeared.

Shadowing interferes with the freely generated autonomous activities that would ordinarily ease the child into his own being. To the extent that he is preoccupied with shadowing his mother, his mind is that much less free to grow in its own direction.

Some children are primarily shadowers. Others alternate shadowing with an opposing movement—darting away. Still others are mainly darters away. Darting away is a variation of the catch-me game. This is how it goes: Noting his mother's engagement in conversation with her friend, the toddler abruptly makes a wild dash across the room. He doesn't bother to invite his mother to follow him, nor does he look where he's going or take a moment to assess the obstacles of furniture and toys strewn in his path. He likely will trip or fall, or knock some furniture over. Darting away is reckless. The toddler omnipotently expects to be swooped up and saved from the mishaps of his heedless body movements without having to send out advance notices or invitations to follow. Yet, once he is swooped up, he resists being held. Fiercely, he stems his arms against his mother's chest. He hurls his head backward, forcing his mother to put him down immediately. And then off he darts, once again challenging his mother to undo the separation that he has initiated. Again he will anguish as he is firmly swooped into the encircling safety of mother's arms. Again he strains against her body. This time she gives up and lets the reckless toddler go his way. He falls harder, really hurting himself. "Why isn't she here to catch me?"

Clinging and pushing away, shadowing and darting away, are bound to exasperate even the most patient of mothers. It's easy to think of darting away as a rejection, particularly when the child is so anguished when he's finally caught. Shadowing is experienced as an assault, a possession by a demon lover, a perpetual demandingness that rattles the nerves and invades the space boundaries of the mother's existence. However, the more a mother values her own self-hood and right to boundaries, the more she will empathize with her child's back-and-forth movements into selfhood. On the days when she "goes crazy" from the assault, a part of her will comprehend that it's just temporary insanity. She hasn't truly become a horrible, uncaring mother.

In some instances it's the mother who turns into the shadower. This kind of mother cannot tolerate the increasing evidence that her child is becoming separate from her. So she hovers. She notes his every move; intrudes on his independent activities with constant suggestions for improvement; puts the frustrating puzzle piece in place before the child even has the chance to know he's having trouble; insistently instructs on proper word usage and grammar, not deigning to appreciate the imperfect phrases of her child. She mustn't lose herself in conversation or reading lest her child fall apart from neglect. The shadowing mother has no faith in the growth urges that come from the child.

The child of a shadowing mother often represents everything the mother imagines she never was but wished to be: beautiful, wise, talented, graceful, generous. The shadowing mother shines in the reflected glory of her all-perfect child's superior goodness. She falls apart at her child's no-saying, willfulness, naughtiness, possessive-mineness, greed and other shameful behaviors. She is ever-watchful—on guard lest her child make moves in unpredictable directions which she might not be able to control. Unless such a child has the possibility of alternative dialogues—with an active, strong father, neighbors, grandparents, sisters and brothers—mother and child will possess each other like demon lovers. They alternately cling to each other and then push each other away in angry disappointment, unable to bear the fact of their separateness and terrified of the closeness of merged identities. Unless someone intrudes with an alternative to this tormented dialogue, the child will surrender his narcissistic ambitions, his right to discover his own space in the world. The torments of clinging love are preferable to the dangers of aloneness.

Or a mother might act like an inconstant moon, unexpectedly darting behind the clouds and then not reappearing. Wrapped up in her private reveries, ambitions, self-doubts and despairs, she turns her face away from her child's wooings and willfulness. He gives up caring about her comings and goings. His willfulness becomes an omnipotent demand for unceasing attention and admiration. His wooing intensifies. But now any adoring face will do.

Usually, however, the mother comprehends that her baby is losing the illusions of grandeur which had allowed him to become a mighty conqueror. Even though her responses don't always match up with what the child had in mind, she empathizes with the humiliation that follows the fall from grace, so she doesn't turn her face away. She acts like neither a passive magical extension nor a tormented victim of the child's shadowing and darting away, clinging and pushing away, holding on and letting go. Her less-than-perfect responses demonstate to the child that he can possess his mother's love without having to be a perfect, all-good extension of her self. By not relinquishing the space that rightfully belongs to her, the mother lets her child go and eases him into the space that rightfully belongs to him.

In several months the tempestuous choreography of the crisis of the second birth will calm down, leaving expanded space for growth and further movement into selfhood. At the conclusion of the crisis the child will have found the optimal distance he had been searching for—the distance that allows him to be part of his mother's space while keeping his own space inviolate. The optimal distance will be inside the child as a part of him becomes like the mother, while the rest of him is free to go on enlarging and embellishing the space that belongs to the self.

Willfulness and No-Saying Self-awareness heightens the meanings of desire. The connections between desire and fulfillment are less direct. Previously, if the child was prevented from getting what he wanted or doing what he wanted to do, he might have fallen into a fit of distressful crying. Short-lived moods of crankiness or irritability would have been the direct expressions of his dissatisfaction and frustration. By soothing away the tensions of the child's unfulfilled desires, a mother was able to get him to forget about the prize he had been seeking. She could distract him, offer an alternative solution, a substitute toy, a cookie instead of a bottle. A bit of emotional refueling would do the trick. The pleasures and satisfactions of the moment could wipe away the disappointments of the moments before.

In those days, the child's memories were held together by immediate sensations of pleasure and displeasure. Now, not getting becomes connected to the child's desperate concern to advance his personal power and regain his self-esteem. The issue of helplessness versus power transcends the issue of frustration versus gratification. The child cares much more about his self-worth than about actual gratification or satiation.

With the advent of self-awareness, the child has a mind with memory images that are fixed and lasting. He does not forget the content of his desires or the prizes he seeks. Moreover, because his mind is capable of symbolizing, one memory of disappointment can come to stand for other disappointing memories and ideas. Not getting is another

prick to the balloon of grandeur and omnipotence—a sharp
reminder of helplessness and vulnerability. These deflating
frustrations stimulate the toddler's mind. He becomes cleverer about getting what he wants. He keeps his eye on the
goal. He invents new ways of obtaining the prizes he seeks.

Playing is the serious and gratifying work of toddlerhood.
The toddler is wretched when his play-work is interrupted.
If he should be given a bottle and put away in his crib or
playpen just as he's readied his mind to go to his peg bench
and hammer away, he is not likely to submit and forget. A
bottle will not satisfy a mind that has the idea of hammering
some pegs. He does not start out by raging and crying from
disappointment. He tries to ask for what he wants. He
rattles the bars of his cage and yells, "Mommy, out!" These
direct and reasonable requests are usually countered by, "It's
time for rest now," or "You have to stay there while I make
dinner," or a simple "No."

The toddler will almost automatically associate not getting
what he wants with the ever-present nagging worry that his
mother's wishes and his own do not coincide. "What mother
wants and what I want are not the same." He sits down for
a moment to reflect on the matter. Although his thoughts
cannot be read, the solution that follows his moment of reflection is a clear indication that the child has taken his
mother's desires into account. Once again he stands up.
"Mommy, go!" he announces excitedly—meaning he'd like
to sit on his potty. His mother responds to this signal just
the way he imagined she would. She lifts him out of his crib
and delightedly follows him to the bathroom. After a few
minutes of fakery at the potty, the toddler runs quickly to
his bedroom to hammer some pegs into his peg bench.

This faker is not a mere manipulator whose major intention is to trick his mother. In puzzling through the matter of
how to get his mother to do what *he* wants, the toddler has
achieved a triple triumph. He has confirmed the powers of
his autonomous thinking mind. At the same time, he has

temporarily softened the worry about him and mother as separate beings. Most importantly, he has diminished the anxiety connected to being a helpless, done-to self who must nonetheless stand alone in the world. When he resists the imposition of his mother's will, the toddler bolsters his self-esteem and realizes the power of his own selfhood.

As with willfulness, issues of self-esteem underlie the endless no-saying of the self-aware toddler. When the eight-month-old turned his head away from the last spoonfuls of cereal, his head-turning gesture was easily interpretable as, I don't want any more cereal! Yet even in those simpler times, the body-mind of the baby would occasionally conjecture the analogy between head-turning "no" gestures and the disappearing, reappearing game of peek-a-boo. No-saying already had something to do with mastering the idea of separation from mother. What changes now at eighteeen months is the emotional connotations of the experiences of separateness and separation. Hence the deepened meanings of "No." These profound alterations in emotional meaning bring the themes of the second birth into a new register.

When the baby first began to separate and conquer the world of immediate time and space, his mother's actual disappearances often filled him with nameless apprehensions. Separation from mother meant losing the dialogue that made sense of the baby's energies and excitements; it meant being reminded of emptiness and falling apart; sometimes it also reminded the baby of his powerlessness. But then the baby could take consolation in his illusions and in his low-keyed moods. And although she was then a reminder of the contradictions between oneness and separateness, when the mother reappeared, her actual presence in the world usually gave him courage to go on with his explorations and conquests. At that time, the baby's mind wasn't up to realizing that he and his mother were truly separate beings, with separate desires and existences.

When the eighteen-month-old is separated from his

mother for an afternoon, he isn't afraid of running away with himself or falling apart. By this age he has an idea of where his mother might be going; he can image her face; he can recognize her face in a photograph and talk to it while she's gone; he knows that she hasn't disappeared over the edge of the world and that she will return. He doesn't dread losing her; he dreads the humiliation that wells up inside him when she departs from the scene, leaving him behind as though she had the right to come and go as she pleases. "Being left" is a deflation of self-esteen that infuriates the self-aware toddler. When his mother refuses a request, or imposes her will, or asserts her right to act and do, to come and go as she pleases, this is tantamount to her claiming the right to her separate existence. Physical separation from mother is not the issue. The issue is her claim to the space which rightfully belongs to her.

No-saying is the self-aware toddler's method of trying to approximate the lost omnipotence of his love affair with the world, when he was the masterful conqueror and his mother a mere extension of his desires. "No!" blots out the sense of helplessness, while simultaneously protecting him from his secret longings to move backward to passive oneness. No-saying is the toddler's bravado, the false courage that covers up wishes to be a baby once again. Furthermore, "No!" is a good way to get out some of the anger he feels toward the disappointing mother of separation.

Even if a mother were to empathize with the fear and confusion underlying her child's endless no-saying, there will be days when she is driven mad by it. His "no's" will be viewed as a calculated campaign of defiance and rejection. As she envisions the delinquent schoolchild and violently rebellious adolescent in the making, her proud hopes are dashed, her confidence in mothering demolished. In her panicky helplessness, a mother mounts a campaign of her own, designed to stamp out delinquency and rebelliousness. She redoubles her own no-saying.

Paradoxically, the toddler's "No" is also a preliminary to his saying yes. It is a sign that he is getting ready to convert his mother's restrictions and prohibitions into the rules for behavior that will belong to him. Between eighteen and twenty-four months the child is on the crest of a new mode of organizing life experience. Right now he is in crisis, but in several months he will have found the emotional distance that marks the boundaries between self and other. No-saying helps him to estimate the distance that is optimal for him. Only after he has found his own space and boundaries can the child take in the rules of the other and make them into his own.

Even now, at the height of the crisis, the "No" of the child is a reflection of the "No" of his parents. The toddler is struggling to make sense of his parents' "No." No-saying is the helpless child's way of acting as though he had the power and authority of his parents. The more their "no's" make him feel vulnerable, the more he has to say "No" himself.

In these ceaseless battles of will, the toddler cannot comprehend what it is he's supposed to be winning. He does not want to be abandoned to the omnipotence of his willfulness and no-saying, for such power would leave him alone in the world, and aloneness is the most terrifying thing of all. A child will not emerge victorious unless the grandiosity of his "no's" is toned down by the reasonableness of his parents'.

The child's new thinking mind is a mind of absolutes. In his images of himself, he is either a perfect, all-controlling, all-possessing being or an all-bad monster child whose greed and aggression can eat up the world. When a child cannot make sense of his parents' "no's" the latter image prevails. When he can make sense of them, he gives up the former image too. He gives up imagining that he must be a perfect omnipotent child in order to keep his demons in check.

Many of the toddler's demands are immoderate and impossible to gratify. Others represent his claiming of what rightfully belongs to him—his thoughts, his words, his play-work, his dreams, the insides of his body and its rims and outer markings. A parent's resistance to some demands and acceptance of others will modify the child's all-the-way, all-or-nothing view of himself and the world. He will then acquire a sense of proportion about the self. He will sense he is worthy and valued even though he can't always get what he wants. It would be as disastrous for a child to win all the little battles as it would be for him to lose them all. The child who always wins, the child whose "No" is seldom countered by the "No" of his parents, will emerge from the second birth with an overly extended, overly grand notion of his power. He will not have learned to comprehend the limits and boundaries of his self or the true measure of his love and aggression. He will go on imagining himself as an omnipotent ruler, never knowing when his power has been real and when a sham. And a sham it would be. Such a child then grows up supposing that he will lose his identity and selfhood the moment he finds himself unable to control everything and everybody. His life becomes based on strategies and manipulations that are meant to assure him that he will never be placed in a position of being controlled and dominated. Every frustration or hint of his vulnerability will be interpreted as a threat—as a possibility for humiliation. The only way to be safe and whole is to be all-powerful. And how terrifying it is to be in charge of everything when you can't escape knowing how small and alone you really are!

The child who is given all whenever he demands it is not a confident or courageous child. He treads his way through life perpetually haunted by the dread of being found out for what he really is: an all-bad monster child whose greed and raging aggression can swallow up mothers and fathers, sisters and brothers, friends, lovers and children.

The toddler who loses too many little battles emerges from his second birth with a pervasive experience of humiliation and self-doubt. He learns the lessons that mark out his body boundaries and reveal the measure and extent of love and aggression, but he learns them at the expense of healthy self-assertion and individuality. Every time he gives in and complies with the will of his parents, he hopes to find the look of mirroring admiration that will confirm the goodness of having surrendered his will. But since his desires keep raging inside him with nowhere to go, he is utterly convinced of his badness. In his mother's look of triumphant satisfaction, the child can see only the reflection of his inner badness. A child may be angry when his mother frustrates his wishes, but he cannot imagine for more than a moment that she is really the one in the wrong. Even when she turns into an all-bad mother, the child is convinced that he deserves it, that he is wrong, that his badness has created this bad and disappointing mommy.

When a child continuously complies and gives in, his rightful desire to own himself and be his own master is not entirely squelched or exterminated. It lies buried. Temporarily the child hides his protest behind a wall of dejection and sadness. In later years many of these compliant children take up the battle with vigor. They steal, wet their beds, act like foolish clowns, complain of neglect—all as ways of expressing their self-dissatisfaction and bitter disappointment. Some remain inhibited and depressed. They keep their lusts and angers hidden, totally surrendering their claims to the pleasures and desires that rightfully belong to them. Sometimes they go on to live off the happiness of others, so that they may at least have the vicarious satisfaction of another person's happiness. They hand over their lovers to their brothers and sisters. They dare not be parents, so they care for, teach, nurse and proselytize the children of others. Since they know that underneath their perfect self-sacrificing goodness lurks the monster child whose greed and raging aggression can swallow up mothers and fathers, sisters and brothers, friends, lovers and children, they tread their way through life perpetually haunted with the dread of being found out for what they really are.

Anger, Sadness and Temper Tantrums   Emotions come into existence when the child gets the idea that his bodily sensations and arousals have something to do with the existence of the other. Thus until the dawning of self/other separateness, poundings of the heart, rushings of the blood, quiverings on the inner walls of the body are barely transformed into falling apart, unfathomable dread, storms of rage, explosions, releases of tension, flushes of excitement or pleasure. They are not yet emotions, but simple states of arousal which do not have to do with concern for or interest in other people. One state of bodily arousal blends into another. The rosy flush of pleasure is quickly forgotten as the spikey gray of irritability claims the foreground.

The improved memory of the symbol-making mind is an essential element in transforming heartbeats and adrenaline into true human emotions. Daily life becomes more complicated when the child has a mind that allows him to remember the association between something his mother said or did and what was roused up or quieted down within his body. Life and relationships with other people become richer and more deeply human when the child retains the association between what goes on in his body and what he or the other person did to bring on the arousal.

Whereas the storm of rage is little more than a mad hope of changing things for the better by destroying everything and everybody in the world, anger is an emotion which involves some thoughts about who is responsible and who might do the changing. An angry child is not out to destroy; he wants to improve his lot and right the wrongs he supposes have been done to him. As he tries to fit his mind to the idea that his mother's wishes do not coincide with his own, the toddler is bound to perceive her as the source of all the nasty things that are suddenly beginning to happen to him. He is therefore angry with her and his mind is filled with angry thoughts that do not go away.

Angry thoughts can rouse up heartbeats and adrenaline just as easily as any actual deed. So sometimes the toddler is angry with his mother today for what she did yesterday or what he supposes she might do later or for merely continuing to act as if she can come and go as she pleases.

Some of the child's anger gets expressed in his attempts to coerce his mother into acting as an extension of his own self. He is liable to act the imperious tyrant just when he feels most helpless. Though he's absolutely unjustified in blaming his mother, he's absolutely within his rights to be angry and to try to get her to change. The mother has the power to set things right. If he couldn't be angry with her, he'd suppose he was entirely helpless.

As he studies his mother's reactions to his angry outbursts, the child is discovering another facet of his boundaries. As part of his new beginning he is acquiring an expanded vision of the inner and outer rims of his body-self. He is marking out the edges of the emotional space in the world that will soon belong to him. Through his mother's facial expressions and words and gestures the child gets the sense that his passionate anger has its limits too. Anger can alter some aspects of the world; other aspects are unmovable. And no matter how intense his anger becomes, it cannot annihilate those he counts on for his survival and wholeness. He is on the way to distinguishing which of the rights he claims are due him and which of life's injustices and injuries can't be changed. Eventually he'll realize that the mother he is so angry with now is the same mother who consoles and comforts—the same mother he sometimes loves with a passion equal to the passion of his anger. His anger cannot destroy her wholeness.

Anger is a gesture of protest. It represents the child's hope that the future will be different. Sadness is another sign of the child's continuing hopefulness. Here the disappointments of the present are softened by longing for a past when things were better. Deep sadness is much too painful for a young child. Deep sadness would have to include a *full* recognition that the other is not all that one had imagined. Therefore whenever possible children literally run away from sadness by becoming extra active and lively. Anger is yet another way of avoiding sadness.

However, every once in a while some approximation of sadness cannot be avoided. The letdown that comes from realizing that one is not an omnipotent ruler of the universe, and the transition from the illusions of the love affair to the disillusionments of self-awareness are too painful to be blotted out totally. During the crisis and for months afterward the child will inevitably have moments of being downcast and dejected. Even on days when all appears to be going well and the world is thought to be a cheery place by everyone else, the child is unable to get up his zest and enthusiasm. His face is sober. His movements are lethargic. His eyes have an inward-turning look reminiscent of his low-keyed mood. The contrast between the way things were and the way things are now is too stark for the child to avoid. He is longing for the past, perhaps remembering a touch of that lost experience of ideal mothering-self. Now that life is more complicated by memory and having to link one's bodily states with the actions of a down-to-earth mother, longing is tinged with regret. The child's somber turned-inward emotional experience, his mild form of blue-gray sadness, helps him to reconcile the imperfections of the present with the perfections of the past and to master a small portion of his disillusionment.

Parents find it difficult to witness the child's sadness. They become as dejected and downcast as the child. Some parents find it so painful that they interrupt the child's valiant efforts to confront disillusionment by encouraging him to smile and play games. Being sad thus becomes another proof of his fundamental badness. He conjectures that he ought to look happy so he won't keep on disappointing his parents. "As-if" cheerfulness and false elation cover up sadness. At the core of his being the sadness goes on, while the part of his being that faces outward to the world shows wrinkled eyes, puffed up cheeks, spread-open mouth and gritted teeth. The false smile makes its appearance. The hope of making sense of aloneness and imperfection and the right to own the emotions that are his are lost.

Sometimes a toddler falls apart from the protest raging inside him. He has a temper tantrum. A temper tantrum is a young child's announcement that negotiations are over. Rather than recognize that he has already lost the battle, he finds a way to win.

The temper tantrums of this period resemble the raging storms of early infancy. When the eight-month-old set out to destroy the world and everything in it, his mad protest was a way of restoring goodness and wholeness. When the storm was over, calm and serenity filled his body with warmth and renewed courage. The violence of a temper tantrum is also a way of restoring the peace. But now the violence is associated with ideas, memories, images of the self, images of the mother and father, and reminders of aloneness in the world.

While he is in the throes of his tantrum some of the connections that have just begun to give emotional meaning to life become temporarily uncoupled. Only the present exists. Before and after vanish. Time is now and forever. But the temper tantrum of the ordinary toddler retains an element of emotional relatedness. It is somewhere between a diffuse rage and true emotion. Like diffuse rage, a tantrum provides an avenue for discharging accumulated tension. However, the tantrum is associated with the toddler's fantasies about himself and also with some thoughts concerning the target of his tantrum. With his act of violence, he imagines he is annihilating an all-powerful frustrater. Only moments before, he was on the brink of losing his entire self-esteem. Now the toddler is absolutely omnipotent.

As he's hurling his body to the floor, shrieking, kicking, pounding, hitting, a part of the child wants desperately to stop. He is vaguely aware of the madness of his method. And when he recovers from his tantrum, he won't entirely forget that once again he became the monster child he sometimes imagines himself to be. But he can't stop and he won't stop until all his tensions are gone—until he no longer feels vulnerable and helpless.

When the tantrum is over, the child feels peaceful inside. He has reclaimed possession of his existence. Having reassured himself that the enemy is not so dangerous and that he is not so weak and helpless, he is ready to forgive and be forgiven. After witnessing the violence of their child's temper tantrum, it is difficult for parents to accept his friendly overtures as a genuine act of love. They suppose that if they simply forgive and forget, they will encourage the toddler's violence in the future. Humiliation and fear set tantrums off. A warm hug and some assurance that he is still loved and cherished is what the toddler is asking for now. To humiliate him with a punishment will only set the cycle of tension and need for discharge going again.

Because the temper tantrum often appears to be a response to a much-needed parental "No" or "Don't," parents react to the tantrum with anger, and possibly with shame and humiliation if the tantrum happens to take place in public—at the supermarket or playground, where everyone can see. The spectacle of a raging toddler awakens the parents' memories of their own childhood days, when a "No" or a "Don't" seemed to mean "You are a bad, dirty, ugly monster child." Underneath their anger or shame, parents are often disintegrating and falling apart in sympathy with the child's tantrum.

The child who is having a tantrum counts on his parents

not to disintegrate with him. Although his tantrum is his way of deluding himself that he is capable of punishing an all-powerful frustrater, he does not really want to destroy his actual parents. Nor does he really want to end up feeling like an omnipotent monster child. As frustrating and "bad" as they might sometimes become, the parents are the child's ultimate security. When they fall apart, he is all alone. Parents don't have to demonstrate that they're in control by retaliating and raging back at the child. A child senses strength in his parents when he feels that they understand him. His friendly gestures often mean that he is ready to reopen negotiations. He might even be ready now to go along with the awful "No" that seemed to provoke his tantrum.

The "No" of the parent may have precipitated the tantrum, but the tantrum originates in the strain of the crisis of the second birth, with its inherent frustrations and disappointments and its awesome sense of aloneness. At this time the child has less ability to cope with the simple everyday affairs of life. Fatigue will further weaken this ability. In general, the toddler is experiencing great difficulty in bringing together his new inner world of fantasies, wishes and thoughts with the new demands of the wishes and desires of other people. The strain of relating this new inner reality with external realities is not so easily relieved by illusion as it was in the past, or as it will be again after the crisis is over. A retreat to the perfection of a security blanket or a peaceful reverie will barely alleviate the strain during these awful months.

The crisis holds a greater potential for tantrums than any other period of childhood. Tantrums are to be expected, particularly in children who are high-strung and excitable. Sharing with the parents, clinging and pushing away, anger, willfulness, no-saying, mineness and occasional sad moods are the toddler's bulwarks against temper tantrums. But every now and then the tensions become unbearable. Then an outburst of temper helps to clear the air and restore the peace.

Girls and Boys, Mothers and Fathers   Before birth the sex hormones are already influencing the nervous system, creating sex-typed predispositions for perceiving and responding to the world. Observable sex differences in motor responsiveness, for example, are present from birth. Girls demonstrate less motor activity, yet greater sensitivity to touch and body contact stimulation. By six months girls are more responsive to human faces. After the first year of life boys are more adept at visual-spatial tasks and their play is more aggressive and motor-minded than the play of girls. Their superiority in spatial ability and greater aggressiveness are more pronounced in adolescence. It has been suggested that spatial talent and aggression are sex-linked male traits.

Congenital sex-typed predispositions are the base on which sexual gender identity builds. Nevertheless, differential parental responses will far outweigh biological factors, as parents almost inevitably facilitate certain kinds of learning in their daughters and other kinds in their sons. From the beginning, from the moment parents are aware of the sex of their baby, they behave in subtly different ways depending on whether the newborn is a girl or a boy. And later, although boys and girls will mirror characteristics of both mother and father, a girl's major identification will be with her mother and a boy's with his father. These identifications then further amplify the biological and learned sexual predispositions.

The inborn features of male or female newborns also stimulate different fantasies and different ways of holding. Boys tend to be held upright more often than girls during the first five months. Is this because boys stiffen and push upward and outward, while girls are curled-in molders? Or is it because from the beginning mothers react to boys by stimulating uprightness? Boys tend to be held more frequently than girls in the first three months of life. Is this because they are more irritable and restless? After five months girls are held, cuddled and talked to more, while boy babies are given more encouragement to explore the environment. Surely the differential reactions to boy babies and girl babies are legion. Yet the problem of disentangling what the child stimulates in the parent and what the parent stimulates in the child has not been solved, neither with regard to gender distinctions nor for any other characteristics that make one child turn out differently from another.

Certainly, though, with the advent of self-awareness girls and boys react to the world, to themselves, to their mothers and fathers and other people, and to the issues of the second birth in distinctly masculine and feminine modes.

Profoundly influencing the girl's reactions is her discovery of the anatomical differences between the sexes—a discovery which most often coincides with her recognition of separateness. Though she doesn't at all have a mind that can reckon with ideas such as maleness and femaleness or masculinity and femininity, her discovery that she does not possess what others possess will add a special dimension to the prototypical letdown that follows the elation of the love affair.

A girl's reaction to her discovery that her father or brother or neighbor's little boy has a penis and she has not will put additional strains on the push and pull, clinging and pushing away struggles with the mother. The capacity to symbolize will render this fact of existence susceptible to confused and mistaken psychological interpretation. The girl will associate her "not having" with her disappointments in her mother.

A girl may have previously noticed her father's penis, but her observations will not excite her interest and curiosity until her attention has been drawn to the exciting possibilities of her own genitals. The girl discovers the sexual difference under the impetus of *first* discovering the pleasures of genital self-stimulation. The primarily exploratory and body-boundary-seeking type of genital manipulation of the ten- to twelve-month-old girl has by sixteen months been converted into a focused pleasure-seeking activity. Now, with self/other awareness, the girl connects her frustrations as well as her delights with a person who might be contributing to them. As with the person-associated emotions of joy, anger and sadness, pleasure-seeking genital arousal has the potential of becoming associated with other people. When the self-aware girl rubs and squeezes her vulva and labia, she directs affectionate, erotically tinged looks toward others, particularly her mother. These outward manifestations of erotic love will soon be transformed into the inner erotic fantasies which thenceforth regularly accompany masturbation. As genital pleasure gradually encompasses the connections between pleasurable sensations in the self and the erotic relationship to the other, such pleasure takes on psychological meaning.

This alteration in the experience of her genitals provides the impetus for transforming the anatomical "facts" that have always been there into a discovery with psychological relevance. The discovery of the pleasure possibilities of her own genitals at around fifteen or sixteen months impels the girl to become aware of the genitals of others and to ascribe meaning to this awareness. By seventeen months most little girls have successfully gained entrance to the bathroom to have a good look as their fathers urinated or showered. In today's household almost all children manage to arrange these encounters—even in the most conventional of homes. Also, it is not at all uncommon for girls and boys to bathe together or to observe each other's differences while being diapered or at the toilet. The seventeen-month-old girl is intensely curious about her father's penis. Her curiosity quickly spreads to an active investigation of the genital differences between boys and girls, fathers and mothers, mother and self, and horses, dogs, cats, gorillas in the zoo, cows on the farm. There is a flurry of interest in undressing dolls. The little girl sums up her observations with mistaken algebra. The letdown of separateness is somehow equated with the not-having of an important body part.

Girls clearly demonstrate their distress at the discovery. They paste Band-Aids on themselves, on their toys and on furniture. They become overly concerned with bruises and scratches. Broken crayons and broken cookies are tearfully rejected. Most little girls lose interest in manual exploration and pleasure-seeking touch stimulation of their genitals. Some begin to transfer their interest in their genitals to a preoccupation with rubbing their belly buttons. They inquire, "Why does daddy have two belly buttons?" Soon a preference for indirect stimulation of the genitals begins to appear; rocking horses become possibilities for genital arousal, straddling the mother's or father's legs, rubbing against furniture. The avoidance of direct touch stimulation of the genitals and the preference for indirect pressure stimulation often become permanent features of female eroticism.

In this complex reaction there is no evidence whatsoever that the little girl reacts to her discovery with envy for the penis she does not have. Envy is far too complex an emotion for such a young child. The "not-having" of a body part gets associated with the overall experience of disappointment, not having, not getting, mineness and wanting what others have, typical of the crisis of the second birth. A little girl's anger with her mother might even lead her to imagine that the mother has a penis which she is deliberately withholding and not giving. Since it was the girl's discovery of her own genital pleasures that induced her to investigate the facts of anatomical difference, not the other way around as was once supposed, her discovery eventually can be absorbed in a distinctly feminine mode as the little girl comes into possession of what rightfully belongs to her— her body, including her bowel movements and her inner experience of her genitals, her thinking mind, her play, her fantasy life and her independent selfhood. What is crucial to the girl's eventual acceptance of her femininity and her love for herself is the way her relationship to her mother gets resolved.

All little children will hold themselves responsible for what they perceive as their shortcomings. However, during the crisis they also tend to blame the mother for all their letdowns and frustrations. They associate the mother's separateness with their humiliations, vulnerabilities, helplessness, not getting and not having. In little girls these associations are more pronounced than in little boys; they are accentuated by the girl child's discovery of her supposed anatomical shortcoming. Consequently her anger toward the mother and her disappointments in her are also magnified.

The back-and-forth choreography of clinging and pushing away and shadowing tends to be more pronounced between mothers and daughters than between mothers and sons. As part of her temporary angry reaction to her mother a little girl may revive a feeling that when mother goes away she disappears over the edge of the world. She appears not to recognize the mother when she returns and she often "forgets" how to recognize her face in a photograph. These angry reactions are short lived.

Inevitably a little girl will blame herself for having such bad, destructive feelings about her mother. She turns longingly toward her mother, reaching out to repair the damage she imagines she has wrought with her angry feelings. However, tenderness with mother awakens the dread of merging and thus losing what belongs to the self. So despite her longings the girl pushes her mother away furiously only seconds after she has gone to her for reparation and consolation. She finds herself unable to accept her mother's open-armed willingness to enfold her and comfort her. The girl's coercion of the mother is also a demand that the mother settle her debts; that she give back what she has withheld and taken away, that she repair the little girl's anatomical shortcoming.

Although she is coercive and demanding, the girl continues to long for her mother's comforting arms. But mother can do nothing right; she selects the wrong polo shirt in the morning, serves the wrong dessert, buys the wrong cereal, places the puzzle piece too correctly, dresses the little girl too abruptly, too slowly, holding her too close, too far away.

The crisis of the second birth, then, holds a number of subtle dangers for the future of the mother-daughter relationship and for the girl's image of femininity. A girl may resolve the crisis by remaining a shadow of her mother. She may become a mommy-mirroring nonentity in order to bolster her self-esteem. Since she is unable to cut the mother down to size as a real mother with limited power, she goes through life sharing in what she continues to believe is the mother's omnipotence. She relinquishes her own power. At the other extreme, her anger and fear of merging may make her avoid softness and tenderness in her relations with her mother and all other women. She will emphasize her disappointment at having to be a woman. She becomes a woman by devaluing womanhood, maternity and tenderness. In her later relationships with men she may treat them as though they were disappointing mothers who never settle their debts, rejecting each man in his turn as he fails to give her what she longs for. The little girl may turn desperately to her father, not as a masculine figure who is loved and admired as deeply as the mother, but as a haven from the painful and disappointing relationship with the mother. Thus she remains a helpless girl-child who hides from the devalued but dangerous mother under the protective wings of her all powerful, penis-possessing father. At worst, mother and daughter possess each other like demon lovers, alternately clinging together as one and then separating in furious mutual rejection. They encircle one another in a bond of steel which shuts out all possibility for alternative dialogue —especially with the father. No one dare intrude on their tormented dialogue.

In the best of circumstances the little girl will come to realize that her mother does not wish to possess her or dominate her. A girl who comes into possession of her own selfhood will later perceive her mother as she really is—not as a dangerous, withholding, damaging, all-powerful creature. Then the girl will be free to become something like her mother without fearing that she must relinquish her own self to her mother in the process. The girl will admire her mother's actual power and see in it the strength and power she one day will acquire for herself. Tenderness with the mother and other women will once again become a possibility. The girl will trust her mother's consoling gestures in times of need and worry because she will also trust that her mother will not take advantage of her vulnerabilities in order to repossess and dominate her. As a somewhat older child, the girl may come to envy her mother's real power in the world and thus strive to emulate her in real ways. She may want to achieve power, but she will not necessarily envy the power of men. She will turn to her father not as a haven for frightened little girls but as a masculine counterpart toward whom she can direct her erotic feminine strivings.

One day she may want to have a child of her own, not because she fantasizes a baby as the penis she never had, but because she has made the tenderness and strength of her mother her own and come to value the possibilities of motherhood. Whether or not this solution to the crisis of the second birth occurs is less a matter of feminine destiny than of how the girl is responded to by her mother, her father and the corner of the world in which she lives out her life.

The dangers are different for boys, and their style of response to the recognition of separation also tends to be different. A striking distinction, one which has been prepared for by both the greater motor-mindedness of boys and the reciprocating tendency of mothers to sponsor boys' uprightness and freedom of body movement, is the prolongation of the mood of elation and lively body buoyancy in boys. A boy's continuing delight in running and jumping and asserting the freedom of his body serves to soften his reaction to separateness.

The tempo and direction of the mother-son choreography undoubtedly relate to the boy's prolonged motor-mindedness. A boy might interrupt his running and jumping to shadow the mother and keep track of her every movement and gesture. Some boys may even forget about running around and become literal shadows of their mother, chasing breathlessly behind her as she moves from one room to another. However, the characteristic choreography for boys is reckless darting away. Boys are much more determined and decisive about escaping from the catcher of babies.

Whereas the girl tends to alternately cling and then push away, the boy plays out the crisis of his second birth as though he had no choice but to extricate himself from the bondage of mother-infant oneness. He darts away with the expectation of being swooped up, but he will frantically leap from his mother's arms once she has caught him. What the boy would like is an all-present mother who will automatically rescue him as he recklessly hurls his body through space, but one who nonetheless will never enfold him, cling to him, possess his body, or re-engulf him into the void of oneness. The danger of merging with the mother is the boy's greatest anxiety. If he should surrender himself to his mother's arms, he fears not only the loss of his identity as a separate self but also the loss of his masculinity—his newly awakening gender identity.

When the boy's struggle to disengage from the mother is overly stressful, owing either to the mother's unwillingness to relinquish possession of her boy child or to the unavailability of an idealizable father figure, a boy may have no choice but surrender. He becomes a mirroring momma's boy.

The son of a possessive mother fares somewhat better when he has a father for an ally. Nevertheless he may still construct his image of manhood and masculinity on the basis of devaluing and fearing women. A woman comes to be perceived as a dangerous catcher of men whose entire being is bent toward swooping up, swallowing up, possessing and engulfing. At the climactic moment of erotic surrender such men will quickly extricate themselves rather than linger in the dangerous fold of oneness. As the man moves away to firmly reestablish the boundaries of his masculine selfhood, the woman moves closer hoping to prolong their mirroring passion and merging of boundaries. The choreography of the second birth lives on in the battle between the sexes, the woman once again letdown and the man preoccupied with disengaging himself from bondage and domination.

Fathers play a decisive part in the crisis of the second birth. Even before the crisis, both sons and daughters turn to the father for an alternative to the intense passions of the mother-infant dialogue. The special excitement associated with the father is observable as early as six months of age. When infants are in need of comforting and soothing, they almost invariably turn to the mother. However, when it comes to romping and rough play, the father is the favorite. A father is the centrifugal force that pulls mother and child out of the orbit of oneness. During the crisis, his responses to his daughter or son and to his wife are *crucial*. Now the father is becoming a *masculine* alternative to the *feminine* mother.

At eighteen months a child cannot comprehend the meanings and consequences of sex and gender differences. These will be elaborated throughout his life. But masculinity and femininity have *some* meaning to a child with dawning self-awareness and erotic strivings toward other people. He also has the cognitive capacity to categorize gender and to generalize mother and father as members of separate categories. In addition, the child has begun to accumulate rememberable experiences that correspond to these cognitions.

The feminine is linked to pleasures of bodily needs, comfort, consolation; the masculine to pleasures of motor excitement and risk. Moreover, the family scenario for gender will encourage the female child to locate herself in the category of mother and the male child in the category of father. Such encouragment is subtle but pervasive. Every child senses the restraints and permissions with regard to pleasure, and the approvals and disapprovals with regard to mirroring and imitation. The cognitive capacity to categorize others and to place oneself in a gender category is enhanced by the child's erotic strivings. By two years a child usually has some sense of which parent is supposed to become the object of which erotic strivings.

The father's role in helping his child differentiate self from mother, mother from other, maleness from femaleness, femininity from masculinity continues to be decisive throughout childhood, but especially during the first three years, when differentiation is the central thrust of life. The father's absence in the first three years, although damaging for both sexes, is more deleterious for boys than for girls.

It is essential for a boy to dis-identify with his mother. The crucial movement away from mother begins earlier in boys than in girls. Late in the first year boys already show signs of mirroring the father in their play and body movements. At the beginning of the second year many show a decided preference for the father. However, in homes without fathers, homes where the mother dominates a passive or submissive father, and homes where the father is withdrawn or aloof, the boy has great difficulty in extricating himself from the mirroring one-to-one relationship with his mother. Some never do. They may go on to assert themselves intellectually or artistically or even become heroic soldiers or sportsmen. But their achievements often represent a mirroring identification with the mother's possessive desires, or a continuing struggle to dis-identify with femininity.

For the boy, the father is the other-than-mother figure

who is like himself. Although he is let down at having to give up his infantile omnipotence and grandeur, the boy can strive to be like his father and acquire his power. Then he will be able to woo his mother and receive her tenderness without fearing that she will absorb, humiliate or possess him. A boy relies on a father's presence in his life.

The girl moves less decisively away from her mother and she remains more exclusively tied to her for a longer time. Even with a father in the home a girl will continue to mirror her mother. Typically, she does not react to her father by mirroring his behavior. For the girl, her father is the most deliciously intriguing person outside the mother-infant orbit. At eight months she glances toward her father in a way that could easily be interpreted as coy and flirtatious. Her coyness is a mixture of stranger-wariness, curiosity and longing. Girls have more stranger-wariness than boys and their minds are more sensitive to differences and discrepancies of all kinds. A girl baby will be coy with her father even in homes where mother and father have shared equally in child care right from the beginning.

A daughter's attachment to her father softens the letdown of her new beginning. Gradually she is lured out of the exclusively mirroring relationship with the mother. He is the complement for her femininity. The father's presence in her life mitigates the push-and-pull conflict with the mother. As she focuses her possessive strivings on her father, the girl will be freed to turn to her mother for tenderness and consolation. Her anger and disappointment recede as she comes to sense the value her father places on her. She perks up in the light of his loving admiration. When her selfhood is confirmed in a complementary relationship with her father, a girl gives up dreading that she will lose herself in becoming like her mother. With a father in her life, a girl can begin to experience the possibilities of feminine identity outside the exclusive relationship with the mother. Being feminine doesn't mean being mommy.

But a father's presence is not enough. The father must take an *active* role in the mother-daughter, mother-son choreographies. Some fathers are inclined to withdraw and hide away from the turmoil. They resent the clamor of the child's renewed dependency and endless demands for attention. They throw up their hands and leave it all to the mother. Most significantly, it is not unusual for a father to blame his wife for what he takes to be her inconsistent and confused way of dealing with the child's inconsistent and confused behavior. If he doesn't hide away, he views the struggle from an Olympian height, with contempt for the vulgarity of the powerful passions of ordinary mothers and ordinary boys and girls.

After a hard day "out there in the real world," a father might willingly offer himself to his child as the powerful, all-good alternative to the frustrating and disappointing all-bad mother. It is easy for a father to adopt the role of the protective haven for frightened little girls and to encourage a son's devaluation of women and overvaluation of men. A father may simply find himself unable to empathize with his wife. In her occasionally frantic and inconsistent reactions to his child's willfulness he may see the madness of his own mother. Perhaps the father is the son of a shadowing mother who alternately seduced him into oneness and then terrorized him with her possessive domination. Then it will be hard for him to comprehend that the new kind of madness in the household originates primarily in the child's inner turmoil and not in the tyranny and possessiveness of the mother. Or maybe the father had a mother who turned away from his longings for mirroring admiration and emotional refueling, a mother who just wasn't there to put boundaries on his awesome omnipotence. To such a father—whose children are supposed to be perfect renditions of what he once was, what he is, or what he would like to be—his wife's less-than-perfect responses and his child's passionate clinging and darting away make absolutely no sense at all. A nonempathic father finds it perfectly logical to see his wife as a villainess. As anyone can plainly see, the child responds reasonably and perfectly to him and only acts crazy with the mother.

These are maddening months for a mother, probably the most trying time of her motherhood. She is sometimes perceived as a menace by her child, and that vision of the mother's self is often corroborated by the condemning look in her husband's eyes. And since every human being has demons inside that are only too ready to make their appearance, a mother can easily turn into the satanic creature everyone supposes she is when her ordinary bursts of anxiety and anger are not understood as a reaction to the contradictory and bewildering behavior of her child in crisis.

With regard to the child, a father's passive hiding-in-the corner or hypercritical, haughty attitude toward the mother only serves to heighten and prolong the child's view of the mother as a dangerous creature.

A father who understands what it's like to be a woman and a mother, a father whose vision of motherhood extends beyond the illusion of Madonna-angel oneness, a father who is in touch with the dilemmas of oneness and separateness within himself is a father who is not afraid to offer his masculine tenderness to his wife and child during these maddening months.

Claiming the body   Each phase of the choreography of the second birth makes its specific contribution to the two fundamental sources of the body-self—the rhythms of tension-relaxation inside, and the edges that face out to the new world. The growth processes within the child have in their turn shaped the direction and momentum of the mother-child choreography. The molding and stiffening postures of the lap baby prepared him for the reaching-out, creeping-away time of separation and early conquests. He could give in to the growth urges that energized him to reach out to the new world with his hands, eyes, chest, knees and palms because the invisible bond was a rein that extended from the security of home base. The irresistible currents of growth finally converted the horizontal knee-palm, eyes-hands creeping baby into a vertical walking-away baby who could daringly bounce himself against the corners of the world and through the vast expanses of friendly space as he experienced the full power of his body-self. He began to comprehend that what he could know of the world of space was somehow related to the position and movements of his own body in space. The upright conqueror firmed up the edges of his body, sensed his body as an object in space, and added triumphant elation to the tension-relaxation, courage and confidence, flutterings and quiverings at the core of his body-self.

With a thinking mind the child acquires a new perception of his body. Contributing to his new perception are the growth processes that now convert some of the previously diffuse rhythms and flutterings at the core of the body into the sharp and focused sensations of bladder, rectal and genital pressure. The toddler finds out that he can control the pressures that come from a full bladder and a full rectum. He also learns that he can create intense pleasure by stimulating his genitals. These focused pressures and arousals add a significant dimension to the child's fantasies, thoughts and sensate experiences of self.

However, a thinking mind does not immediately endow the child with the power to comprehend the differences between pressures or flutterings inside and edges facing outside. Rather than clarifying matters, the symbol-making capacity of an immature thinking mind often creates difficulties. For a considerable time, certainly for several months and occasionally for many years to come, the child confuses the products of his body, such as urine and feces and even tears and nasal mucus, with body parts, such as arms and legs. If some parts of the body can fall out or be emptied out or disappear, perhaps arms and legs might also. Sometimes quiverings of worry from inside are experienced as urinary pressures—or the other way around. The stick-like or ball-like appearance of the feces is often confused with a penis or a scrotum or a belly button. The pressure sensations from the rectum tend to spread to the genital area, confirming the mix-up in the child's mind between feces and genitals. With symbol-making and a mind that can associate one event with another, one part of the body or one inner-body pressure can stand for any other part or pressure. The imperfect knowledge that the swollen belly of a pregnant woman has something to do with "having a baby inside" can easily convert the sensations of bowel pressure into "having a baby inside."

The child wonders which parts of his body can fall off and disappear and which stay put. A self-aware child experiments with this problem in his fantasies and make-believe play. Sometimes his experiments are direct. He might, for example, stand before a mirror and drop toys to the floor one by one while scrutinizing his body. Arms and legs and belly buttons don't fall off and drop to the floor like blocks or dolls. But surely this is an incomplete solution to a mighty problem.

Shortly after he began to separate from mother, the child wanted to possess his body as his own. He wanted to be active with his body and not be passive. Now, amplifying the clinging/pushing-away, shadowing/darting-away holding on and letting go of the basic mother-child choreography is the holding on and letting go of the products that come from inside the body.

With these new pressures from inside his body, the child's desire to own his body increases. He is desperate. At times it seems as though his entire selfhood depends on claiming his body as his own—and now this claim includes the products of his body, particularly his bowel movements, the product everyone suddenly cares so much about. The child is as terrified of being robbed of his control over the contents of his body as he is of losing control of his movements into selfhood. Not having the say-so of when and how he urinates or defecates is tantamount to losing a central aspect of the self.

It takes several months for a child to become confident that his bowel movements belong to him; that when they are flushed away he hasn't lost a part of himself or a baby he has made inside; that the loss of pressure inside doesn't mean he's lost his insides. It feels good to hold on because the pressure is like being filled up inside. Some children hold on for days and even prefer constipation or painful bowel movements to the anguish of being emptied out and losing a precious part of the self.

The more a child gets the idea that his body really belongs to him and to no one else, the easier it will be for him to let go of his feces in the proper place and at the right time. Then letting go will mean that he has become the master of some of those mysterious pressures from inside. In the bargain, he'll have gotten the satisfaction of pleasing his mother and father while also doing something he wants to do.

The toddler's consuming involvement with possession of all parts of his body makes him hate being handled—he hates being dressed or diapered or wiped after toileting. Anything that might rob him of power or personal possession frightens and angers him. On the other hand, confidence that his body is his own possession will restore the child's pleasure in using it to the hilt. He will be able to resume his daring explorations of the physical-space world and he won't be ashamed to use his body to show off and dramatize his ideas and fantasies. Pride in the ownership of his body helps a child to accept the fact of his separateness. He gets the idea that maybe he can stand alone on his own two feet and do all right.

A shadowing mother has no belief in the child's urges to grow and manage his body on his own. She imagines she must possess his bowel movements and genitals along with all the rest of the child—his words, fantasies, ideas, games and achievements. While it is possible for such a mother to toilet train her child "in a day" or in a few weeks, her child certainly won't ever arrive at the notion that his bowel movements belong to him. He will probably conjure the fantasy that his arms and legs and genitals and even his fantasies themselves are controlled and dominated by his mother and father.

Resolution—Fear of Loss of Love Replaces Fear of Loss of the Mother Through no-saying, willfulness, mineness, anger, occasional almost-despair and by claiming his body, the child guards himself against surrendering himself into the hands of the other. A child must first absorb the complicated meanings of the difference between "mine" and "yours" before he can come into full possession of the experience of "I" and "you."

The crisis will subside. However, temper tantrums, possessiveness, willfulness, no-saying, separation reactions and battles about rightful ownership of the body and mind can still be expected. These crisis behaviors will diminish in frequency and intensity as the child gradually finds new solutions for maintaining the integrity and boundaries of his self.

The crushing disillusionments of the crisis period will not be replaced by new illusions of omnipotence but by increasingly realistic ways of valuing the self and estimating the power and worth of others. Ideally, the child will retain his capacity for illusion but illusions of omnipotence will have diminishing impact on his everyday ways of getting along in an ordinary down-to-earth world.

As the solutions proceed, the two threads of the second birth continue to interweave and influence one another. The growth urges within the child are, as they always have been, the wellspring of the aggressive momentum which relentlessly drives the child to find his own orbit of existence in the world. The invisible bond between mother and child goes on providing the child with the courage to make the most of his strivings for mastery and separateness. The child who has confidence in the strength and flexibility of the bond is less fearful that his aggressive strivings will rupture it. In this sense psychological birth is fundamentally different from physical birth. Whereas physical birth meant a rupturing of bonds, psychological birth strengthens the bonds of love and attachment between a child and his parents. As the child finds his optimal distance and secures his own space in the world, yes-saying and a desire to please the parents take the place of oppositional no-saying and willfulness. By going along with his parents' wishes the child gains entrance into their space. He will still imagine them as powerful beings, but the contradictions between their wishes and his own are not perceived as unassailable obstacles to his self-esteem. The less the child is concerned with the issues of separateness, the more he can use his aggressive energies for acquiring the emotions, fantasies, language, memory, judgment and learning abilities that will enable him to please his parents and win their love and approval.

With psychological birth, the fear of actual loss of the mother is replaced by a fear of losing her love and the father's love. Experiences of the self as good and holding together are no longer linked to a parent's actual presence in the world but to the parent's approving and disapproving presence in the child's fantasies and thoughts. Although he will continue to rely on his parents' actual yes's and no's, do's and don'ts, admiration and admonition, permissions and restrictions for many years to come, the child will gradually convert these actualities into his personal and unique psychological style of getting along in the world.

The child's belief in his own omnipotence declines rapidly as a result of his psychological birth. However, he continues to believe in his parents' omnipotence, especially when he imagines he has done something they might disapprove of.

For several years the all-or-none, all-bad/all-good view of life continues to bias the child's way of interpreting what he sees and hears, what he does and does not do. When he imagines he's been bad, he supposes he is an all-bad monster child and that his parents have the power of total annihilation. He could be acting precisely the way they expect him to—even better than they ever would have wished—but an angry thought or an aggressive assertion of selfhood could make a child imagine that he's bad.

When he thinks angry thoughts or does "bad things" the child has no way of accurately estimating either how bad he's been or the limits of his parents' retaliatory powers. It is therefore not unusual for two- or three-year-olds to develop sudden fears of Halloween masks, animals, dishwashers and vacuum cleaners. These scary-looking and scary-sounding things can easily come to stand for the awesome punitive powers of the parents. When parents argue with each other, their ordinary yelling voices often sound like the shrieks and growls of scary monsters who are surely sounding that way in response to the badness inside the child. Surrounded by the furious sounds of annihilating punishment, the child is overcome with helplessness. So the next day he makes believe that he's a shrieking witch or a growling monster. Acting like the monster who might be out to get you is a good way of becoming as powerful as the monster and reducing your sense of helplessness.

With his second birth, the child has come into possession of his space in the world. But it is still a very small space. And although he is a separate self with an identity that is his alone, the child is still a helpless and dependent being in relation to his parents. In order to please his parents he must relinquish many of his deepest desires. He does so in the belief that if he pleases his parents he will one day acquire the infinite strength and power he imagines are theirs. He does so because he fears that if he loses their love he will be cut down once again to humiliating aloneness in the world. So at first the child does what he supposes his parents want without understanding *why* they want what they want. The endless why-asking of the three-year-old is a sign of his effort to understand.

Only gradually will the child come to appreciate the down-to-earth humanness of his parents. Self-confidence, courage, bodily exhilaration, pride in his achievements and a sense of contributing in a real way to the real affairs of human life help a child to put his parents in perspective. On the other hand, whenever a child is put in a position of humiliating dependence, his ordinary natural desire to please will be contaminated by fear of aloneness. He will then wish to be as powerful and dangerous as his all-powerful oppressors. Under conditions of oppression a child may remain a child forever. And even after the attainment of separate selfhood, any human being can still be reduced to the position of a helpless child.

Chapter Seven

Coda—The Way of Life

In every adult human there still lives a helpless child who is afraid of aloneness. When the conditions of social life are oppressive and antihuman, the adult is as alone in the world as a helpless child. This would be so even if there were a possibility for perfect babies and perfect mothers.

An ordinary devoted mother cannot flourish in a society where women are humiliated by a self-definition as helplessly dependent. Like a helpless child who strives to be as powerful and dangerous as his all-powerful oppressors, an oppressed woman will protect herself from humiliation and the terror of aloneness by trying to become as dangerous and tyrannical as her oppressors. In becoming just like her own oppressors, a woman selects as the target of her tyranny those who are weaker, more helpless, dependent and vulnerable than she. A woman's hatred and envy of her male oppressors will be reflected in her acts of mothering.

Her male child is adored for his male perfection, but he is adored possessively. As an adult he will never be entirely certain that he has come into full possession of his mind or body. He will feel that they have been appropriated by his envious/adoring mother. The cycle of female oppression will be reinforced as the mother turns away from her daughter when she does not embody the attributes the mother wished to have but never acquired. Should the daughter strive to acquire such envied attributes, her mother will subtly undermine her ambitions. Liberated women who have managed to soar above the commonplace traps of marriage and motherhood exhibit their identification with the oppressor in their lofty contempt for domesticated women.

A man also will identify with his oppressors. A man who was possessed and tyrannized as a child will tyrannize and dominate women. They are thought of as dangerous catchers-of-men. Humiliating the dangerous woman is the screen that protects him from seeing his own vulnerability and helplessness. In politically oppressive societies, women have usually been the most oppressed and humiliated members. Torture and daily threats of annihilation are the lot of the men who live under the domination of the Shah of Iran and his ruthless SAVAK. In Iran it is the male preference to sodomize their women, whom they also beat, cast away, and trade as chattel.

It is said that the women of hunter-gatherer societies were not oppressed because the way of life was good and women's contribution was equal to that of the men. Women's work was essential to the physical survival of the tribal group. However, this notion is a conjecture based on recent anthropological studies of the few surviving hunter-gatherer societies. What is certain is that women have been oppressed in one way or another for 10,000 years, since sedentary agricultural societies began to replace the hunter-gatherer way of life.

Since then there have been ages when women were oppressed by glorification and ages when they were disparaged and denigrated. Usually it has been a bit of both. Nevertheless, it was not until the rise of the capitalist bourgeoisie, when the family realm split off from the social, economic and political realms, that male supremacy over women took its contemporary shape.

With the advent of large-scale industrial production, work, which previously had been the center of family life, became impersonal wage labor. In response to the harsh impersonality of machine technology, the family folded into itself. It became the protective haven that would shelter its members from the crushing indignities of industrial life. The total domestication of women and their isolation from the work world of men were accomplished as women were retired to the home so that they could nurture in their children the human values that the society otherwise no longer fostered. In the sheltered cocoon of the nuclear family, the individual would be foremost. Gradually the values of individualism became supreme: self-interest, self-expression, self-realization, self-consciousness, personal fulfillment and independence. It was not long before these values overshadowed responsibility or commitment to the society or to the world at large.

Since mothers were the source of all goodness in the world, they were idealized and protected from the demeaning sexuality of men. Sexuality was assigned to prostitutes. In the family, sexuality was a secret, its mysteries to be hidden from wives and children. The Victorian family, which had been thought of as a "tent pitch'd in a world not right" became the breeding ground for rivalry, envy, greed, jealousy, self-torment and guilt.

As the society became more inhuman, the family's emphasis on self-realization and individuality intensified. Although the child was eventually handed over to the impersonal State for an education befitting the tyrannies that awaited him, the family tightened its space. What began as a tent pitched against a heartless world became a fortress of confinement and constraint, as the rights of individual family members were pitched against the rights of each other family member. The split between the good family realm and the bad outside world widened. The contradictions deepened between the family's sponsorship of individuality and the emotionally crippling shackles which bound mother, father and children to each other.

Instead of the devotion and loyalty they had been meant

to foster, the intense intimacies of family life gradually began to breed more personal versions of isolation and aloneness in the world. In less than a century individualism and concern for the common good had become irreconcilable. Brought up to believe in self-fulfillment, the contemporary adolescent is thoroughly disenchanted as he begins to step into the adult world. Madness and cynicism undermine the illusions that might change the world for the better. Of what use are illusions in a monolithic, uncaring, impervious society?

In our more enlightened and hopeful contemporary societies, sexual fulfillment is no longer a secret withheld from women. It is acknowledged as one of their fundamental rights. The dramas of the battle between the sexes replace the SAVAK version of tyranny. Here sexual oppression is more personal and the humiliation and aloneness it breeds more individual—and mutual.

One scenario centers on the woman who blames her lack of sexual fulfillment on her less-than-perfect, darting-away, envied, dominating husband. The nagging, unfulfilled longings of the woman are expressed in the nagging, complaining, tormenting, spiteful dialogue between herself and her husband. She envies him his power in the world and hates him for what she takes to be his uncaring, ungiving humiliation of her. However, a man who is alienated from his labor or a man who is a dominating manipulator of other men is actually as powerless as the woman. He has only a temporary delusion of power and supremacy. The godlike controller of other men and the men they control are as alienated from themselves and each other as they are from women and children.

At forty or fifty a man wakes up from his delusion to discover his powerlessness. He will blame his fall from grace on the oppressor who is closest at hand—the weaker his imagined oppressor the better. He looks at his nagging, complaining wife and suddenly realizes that he has wasted his adult lifetime with the tyrannical oppressor he ran from as a child. Husband and wife confront one another in mutual malevolence, reviewing their respective wasted lives. The prophecy of aloneness is fulfilled.

Then where is the hope for partnerships of constancy—devotion, loyalty, camaraderie, admiration, empathy? It seems that wherever one turns, the personal conspires with the social to shatter the reconciliations of oneness and separateness. Does every human baby enter the new world in a partnership with an oppressed oppressor? Are his illusions of harmony and wholeness merely grand deceptions? Are his struggles to claim a separate space in the world merely another version of the same grand deception?

We are told that constancy has not yet perished. It breathes in our genetic predispositions, in the balances we strike between our appetites for attachment and affiliation and our urges to explore and conquer. We are told that these balances are not set immutably during childhood and that a relatively good way of life will afford the opportunity to transform the issues of our second birth.

Ways of life have come and gone. Civilizations have arisen in triumphant glory only to sink beneath the weight of their grandiose omnipotence. Before they perished, each embellished some chord of reconciliation between oneness and separateness. They survived until their less-than-perfect reconciliations were smothered by oppression.

We know that the human dialogue has survived glacial disaster, human pillage and holocaust. We know that some Zhun/twasi, or "real people," hunt and gather for a living as they have always done. In their personal and group loyalties and in their intimate respect for the ways of the animal and vegetable species within their ecological niche, the Zhun/twasi have preserved a way of life that exemplifies some of our possibilities for goodness.

The Zhun/twa woman is an equal contributor to the economy. The vegetables and berries she gathers comprise at least 50 percent of the Zhun/twasi diet. She participates in political and economic decisions and has equal status with men in the society. Though daughters mirror their mothers and sons their fathers, differential socialization of boys and girls is minimal. The man, as hunter, cooperates with other men, each man understanding and valuing the unique skills of his fellow hunters. The spatial and muscular abilities of the Zhun/twa males are superior to those of most men on the face of the earth. Yet Zhun/twa men are not aggressive toward women or children or other men. When disputes arise, those involved go their separate ways, sometimes taking up with another tribe rather than allowing personal animosity to disrupt a way of life in which each person must count on the loyalty of the others.

Except in the prowess of the hunt, the Zhun/twasi discourage aggression. One-year-old infants dig with digging sticks and pound with mortars and pestles. They are encouraged to chase after and bite large insects. The rough-and-tumble play of older children includes play beating with a stick, especially when one child becomes an animal and the other his pursuer. Children beat small animals such as flying insects and lizards as later they will beat their prey to drive them into nets or to kill them after wounding them with poisoned spears.

The tantrum of the Zhun/twa two-year-old is not turned on himself. He beats the ground or throws sticks and pebbles at his mother. He beats his tiny fists on her body. The mother serenely wards off the child's beating gestures, knowing that soon the storm will run its course. She is not angry or vindictive. She does not intimidate her child with her wrath or with the threat of the father's wrath. Authoritarian behavior is avoided by adults of both sexes. The Zhun/twa father is relaxed with his children. He expects them to follow in his way, but he does not require formal respect or deference from them.

However, we learn that as of 1977 less than 5 percent of the Zhun/twasi still live by hunting and gathering. The others are sedentary and live in semi-squatter status near the villages of the Bantu herders and European ranchers. Anthropologists accord to the new Zhun/twasi the rank of an agricultural society and refer to them as the !Kung rather than Zhun/twasi, or "real people." These settled !Kung societies are characterized by rigid sex-typing, vastly dissimilar socialization for girls and boys, competitive wage work by the men, domestication of women, a household privacy that seems to sponsor domineering aggressiveness of men toward women and competitive power strategies by both parents in childrearing.

In two generations the dramatically altered way of life of the !Kung has lowered the age of menarche and first pregnancy, and narrowed the spacing between children. Hunter-gatherers believe that the fetus is formed from the mixture of semen and menstrual blood, so they avoid intercourse during menstruation. However, the mother nurses her child for three or four years and rarely conceives during that time. Sedentary !Kung wean their children a year or two earlier. And like other sedentary agricultural people, they have a preponderance of milk products and grain in their diets. The increased body-fat of the !Kung has been correlated with their earlier menarche. The population of the !Kung is rising rapidly.

The blood pressure of the sedentary !Kung increases with age. Iron and vitamin B deficiencies are not uncommon. Hunter-gatherers live till at least sixty, and some until eighty, free of the usual diseases of the aged. The aged of the sedentary !Kung have already begun to acquire the degenerative diseases typical of the elderly in civilized societies.

Some hunter-gatherers have been less fortunate than the sedentary !Kung. The Ik, once called the Teuso, have come to personify our human propensities for greed, envy, mistrust and aloneness in the world. Once the Teuso roamed the Kidepo Valley between the southeastern mountains of Morungole, the northern mountains of Didinga and the western Niangeas. Early in the 1940s they were confined to the ridge of the Kenya-Uganda escarpment and Mount Morungole—the natural border between Uganda, Sudan and Kenya.

Although the land in which they once lived was neither lush nor easy to traverse, there was always enough to eat. The Teuso knew the land well. They had mobility and could follow the seasonal distribution of game and vegetables. They lived a way of familial and communal loyalty typical of hunter-gatherer cultures. Confined to their mountain ridge and exiled from their traditional hunting grounds, the Ik were soon on the verge of starvation. The way of life of the Ik became each man for himself.

The Ik abandoned all hope, all belief in the mutualities of love and family. They came together solely for self-interest. Their sexual, marital and group associations became temporary and acrimonious. There was no longer any way for affection or trust to flourish. People averted their gazes from one another. One Ik might look at the hands of another engaged in carving wood, but he would never look into his eyes with admiration or devotion. However, if the man should gash his hand while carving, the other Ik would laugh gleefully.

Until he was three, an Ik infant would be nursed by a half-starved, ill-humored mother. Nursing was performed perfunctorily. When they moved from here to there, mothers would carry their infants close to their bodies in a sling. But the infant was put aside abruptly when the mother stopped moving. He was put aside and ignored, sometimes for a full afternoon. It has been reported that many an Ik mother deliberately put her infant aside in a place where a predator would be likely to discover him; that more than once a leopard ate such a baby. The Ik women who knew of this, including the baby's mother, waited for the leopard to finish his meal, knowing that he would soon go to sleep and be easy to capture. The leopard was then killed, cooked, and eaten—baby and all.

At three, Ik children were weaned and put out to fend for themselves. They were relieved to be put out. They slept on the ground in makeshift shelters and wandered in age-bands to scavenge for food and for mutual protection against older age-bands who would often capture the day's take from the younger ones.

In less than three generations the Ik had learned a new way. They had a standard for goodness and a word for it too. The word *marang* meant good; *marangik* was the word for "food" or "possession of food." "A good man" was *iakw anamarang*, or "the man with a full stomach." Mineness was the way.

The elderly Ik, who might still remember the old days, was not surprised to have crumbs of food removed from between his teeth and from under his tongue by his sons and daughters and grandchildren. After all, he put them out before they could learn such things as affection and respect. And when he died, no one would sing his praises or shred their clothes for him.

Between the awful way of the Ik and the noble way of life of the Zhun/twasi Bushmen fall the innumerable ways of the traditional agricultural societies that followed the hunter-gatherers and preceded our recently born industrial and postindustrial societies. Over many generations each worked out a way of relating between a child and his family, a way of balancing physical appetites and emotional desires with the appetites for human attachment and affiliation. Many of these traditional societies no longer exist. Those that remain will be gradually eroded by the individualistic ideals of our contemporary way of life.

The Balinese are a tranquil and graceful people. They control their passions. They are easygoing and good-tempered, expressing neither hostility nor aggressive striving in their everyday behavior. However, it is said that the Balinese tend to brood and that they nurse their grievances. Cockfight gambling is a preoccupation with the men. The women are gossips. Both men and women are vacant-faced, their gaze characterized by "awayness"—an unfocused looking past each other. The everyday mood of the Balinese is an inward-turning mood that precludes full awareness of happenings in the external world.

The inward mood of the Balinese is also reflected in their propensity to fall into trances. In the trance state, however, the Balinese are not entirely away. As they go into a trance, their look is even more remote than usual but they act like little children in the throes of a temper tantrum, crying out to their mothers and fathers, demanding to be satisfied at once, shrieking that they will not be quiet until their desires have been met. Ordinarily such coerciveness is absolutely taboo. By the time they are three or four years old Balinese children have acquired the away look and most have given up coercive tantrums, anger, striving and grief. They are tranquil.

When a Balinese mother nurses her baby she is lost in her gray-blue inward mood. She is away. Soon after her baby can walk away, as he starts to assert himself and demand that his parents pay attention to his desires, he is teased by his impervious mother. She lures him to approach her and when he comes close she mockingly turns away from him. This sequence of seduction and humiliation is more than the child can bear. He has a tantrum. Despite such constant frustration of his advances, the Balinese child may persist for a year or two in this choreography of approaching, being ignored, and falling into a fit. At last he gives up believing that desires are to be consummated.

But the choreography is not altogether halted. It is reenacted repeatedly in cockfight gambling, gossip, trance, and in the exquisite trance-dance performances for which the Balinese are applauded throughout the civilized world.

The *Barong* trance dance, which has many variations from village to village and leaves much room for personal improvisation, is customarily performed when the gods' threat to a village has been removed. Then it is a celebration. Occasionally it is performed when the gods are threatening. Then it is a propitiation—a way of holding disaster in abeyance.

Although it is called *Barong*, in the name of the dragon-lion male god, the most significant character is *Rangda*, the demon female god. The other characters are *Barong* and the followers who are there to aid him in his battle with *Rangda*. *Barong's* followers are unmasked. They wear everyday clothes and carry swords called *kris'*. *Barong* and *Rangda* are masked and they wear the elaborate costumes befitting gods. *Barong's* mask is a gigantic dragon-lion mask, big enough to cover a person's body. Though he is awesome looking, *Barong* is typically portrayed as a somewhat amusing, amiable and lovable protector. *Rangda's* mask is also awesome: huge, bulging, red, staring-ahead eyes; a tongue-like projection that hangs from her mouth down to her knees; and a wild white mane that flows down her sides and back. *Rangda* is impervious and terrifying.

Rangda appears in the temple doorway. The followers of *Barong* move to attack her. She turns away, tempting them to come at her with their *kris'*. Suddenly she turns toward them, casting her bulging eyes in their direction. This scene is repeated many times until at last the followers of *Barong* are overcome by the magic powers of *Rangda*. They then go into the ritual trance dance. Their eyes either closed or unfocused, the trance dancers look at one another with eyes that don't "see." They call out like raging, demanding children; they fall to the ground, crying and shrieking; they beg to be cared for. As the frenzy of their trance fit builds to a climax, the followers of *Barong* stand. They turn their *kris'* against their own bodies, stabbing at their own chests with such passion that the play gestures frequently become real enough to cause actual self-injury.

In the end, the trance dancers are rescued by *Barong*. They are taken into the protective haven of his awesome mask and revived. *Rangda* has disappeared. The gods have been satisfied. The village returns to its usual tranquility.

In the conjugal family a child remains enmeshed in his household until such time as he proclaims his approaching maturity by gradually detaching himself from the intense emotional ties of his childhood. However, as a young child of nine or ten the firstborn son of an aristocratic Rajput household was expected to leave his vast extended family with the express purpose of returning after he had acquired the intellectual and social wherewithal to govern the household. He and his bride, usually a woman he had never seen before, would then move into the orbit of his mother, whose role in the household and what the Rajput son owed to her in the way of devotion and loyalty often counted for more than his intimate love for his wife.

Yet his intimacy with his wife and his personal sense of self were not incompatible with his obligations to his collective family, which may have included as many as five hundred members: servants, clerks, aunts, uncles, mothers-in-law, fathers-in-law, brothers, sisters and many children. As an adult, the Rajput noble usually found a way to be his own self as differentiated from the significant others who were part of his daily existence. Though his attachments were diffuse and spread among many, his obligations bound him to them all. His passions and appetites were intense and varied.

The Rajput of India were warriors who valued the full expression of passion. They ate meat, drank alchohol, and kept concubines and dancing girls. They also valued courage and honor and instilled these values in all members of the family. When a Rajput warrior was defeated, his women were expected to demonstrate their loyalty by performing *johur,* or self-immolation, rather than face the dishonor of capture.

In contrast to the warrior Rajputs, the way of the literate and poetic Brahmins was to transcend passion. Aspiring to purity, they sought to eliminate the appetites. Hot foods and meat were taboo. So were sexuality, anger and grief. Those who were pure were the *brahmachayas,* the twice-born, whose serenity and wholeness was achieved by diminishing the self and withdrawing from the dangerous and contaminating other.

In traditional Japanese societies, adulthood was thought of as the road to an old age that would recapture the exhilaration of youth. The Japanese view of infancy was shaped by this vision of the adult way. Thus the ideal child would develop his selfhood by forming complex interdependent relationships with others in his extended family group. In that way he would become an adult with the qualities of spirit that eventually would release him from the boundaries of the self. He would arrive at an ideal old age, characterized by a perfect blend of *ki* and *kororo.*

The qualities of *ki* and *kororo* (which originated with the ancient Chinese) defined the Japanese way. *Kororo* is the heart, core, essence; the universal spiritual understanding of life. *Kororo* is located in the chest, implying that essential knowing is more than mere cognition. *Ki* is exhibited in alertness and vitality directed to the forms of the outer world. *Ki* is the attitude that expresses one's relationship to practical, commonsensical, tangible, sensate daily life. An alert, self-disciplined posture is an indication of an orderly and well-kept daily existence.

The spiritual insights and universal truths of *kororo* are

arrived at through the disciplines and rituals of daily life. The *kororo,* or essence, of a poem cannot be separated from the vitality of the poet who created it. The sacred is linked to the profane by *ki.* It is *ki* that provides the connection between the down-to-earth self and the eternal truth that lies at its core.

Modern Christianity, which was based on a complex mixture of Judaic, Greek and Roman traditions, has a less harmonious view of maturity. The ideal Christian combines two attributes that are difficult to reconcile: *manhood* and *adulthood.* The concept of manhood comes from classical antiquity, and its ideal is to organize life in terms of the absolute and the static. The word "adult," on the other hand, is derived from the Latin *adolescere,* "to grow up." Adulthood, then, is a process of becoming which encompasses childhood. Manhood is the achievement of absolute and perfect rationality. Unlike adulthood, which is accorded to both sexes, manhood can only be achieved by men.

Looking at childhood from the point of view of manhood, it is a chaotic and unruly state which must be suppressed. From the ideals of manhood come the Christian repression of sexuality, the distrust of spontaneity, the guilt that goes with attraction to lower matters, and the total separation of the man from the child.

The biblical conception of adulthood, however, values the child that resides in every man and woman. In the Bible, God created the universe out of chaos, but he created both heaven and earth. Fearless, godlike man fell to the uncertain earth because he dared to know and to question. The adult Christian way is to seek out the challenges of human life. An adult must risk so that he can grow. The ideal Christian is a pilgrim-wayfarer, a wanderer who voyages into the unknown.

From the adult point of view, a man who believes himself to be the divine center of the universe, a godlike creature who need not grow or change, is less than a fool or a child. A child confidently reaches ont his hands to life. His confidence is the prototype of faith. An adult Christian must renounce his pretended manhood before he can achieve faith and devotion.

While still in the womb, before he takes his first breath in the new world, a human baby is immersed in a "way of life" that will decisively influence the course of his second birth and the range of his later possibilities for constancy. And though each human mother comes to her baby with a unique readiness for mothering and a personal psychological past, her way of being a mother is never entirely "hers." In the most individualistic society a mother is still bound by her biology, the social values she grew up with, and the value her society bestows on her in her role as mother.

Even so, just as each civilization sounds its unique chord, each mother and child will come together and move apart in a unique and personal way—which is why every new generation brings with it the hope of changing things for the better. Though our notions of perfection and the "right way" are infinitely varied, it would seem that we share our devils with all humanity. It takes several generations to work out a "right way." But in a single generation a civilization may fall. A noble way of life can vanish from the earth, leaving only the demonic and antihuman.

There are some who claim that the demonic has triumphed, that our possibilities for human goodness will vanish from the earth. They say that only a concern for the common good might have saved us. The transformations of infantile mineness and individuality into possessiveness, envy, greed and ruthless power have obliterated concern for the common good. The contamination of our earth has proceeded so far that by now there is no way at all to halt the tick of the Doomsday Clock. We ignore and deny such pessimistic assessments. Or we dismiss them as signs of disenchantment and cynicism. Or we resign ourselves to doom.

The youth take these assessments seriously. And many strive to find ways to work for the common good. Yet others view with haughty contempt the disordered planet we have bequeathed to them. Self-righteously, they reject everything it holds. They say that earth and even the very solar system in which it orbits must be abandoned. They believe that human life will survive and begin again in a new solar system. With infinite space and the possibility of infinite new worlds, they will not put their faith in the finite worlds that might emerge from the intimate orbit of human dialogue. As part of their *Star Trek* mystique, what they mistrust most are the binding loyalties of personal intimacy. Nor do they envisage themselves as simple pilgrim wayfarers or daring explorers of Everest. They are the omnipotent conquerors of the universe. They are unhesitating in their commitment to the great beyond, oblivious to the dangers of flinging themselves beyond the boundaries of earth and into their holy paradise.

On his third voyage to the new world, Columbus suddenly withdrew. He fled back to Hispaniola. He returned to home base. It is said that as he confronted the downward-flowing turbulence of the Orinoco he was overcome with the sense that he must be mounting toward the Garden of Eden. He thought that the waters must be running downhill from the highest point on earth. He reckoned that he must have arrived at the foot of the Holy Mountain, the paradise with its forbidden secrets. Columbus wrote to Ferdinand and Isabella, describing his fear of going any farther. His terror of entering paradise was escalated by yet another terror. If this were to be paradise, he would have overthrown the expectations of the authority of the old world. Columbus had undertaken his voyages with the assumption that the world was round like a *"pelota muy redonda."* With the image of the Holy Mountain looming in his mind, Columbus fantasized that the earth on one side must be pear shaped—*"en la forma de una pera"*—that it had a stalk growing toward Heaven, that it was like a breast with a nipple—*"una teta de mujer."* If he proceeded any farther he would find himself alone. He would have destroyed the maps and theories of the old world, where all the learned authorities had asserted that the world was a perfect sphere. So Columbus hesitated.

Only the most exceptional of humans can bear the isolation that comes from discovering a new world that might turn the old one upside down. On the other side of the paradise of a new world—whether it be round or pear-shaped, or a black hole of nothingness, or a swarming, tangled bank of the Galapagos Archipelago, or an unconscious mind swarming with forbidden wishes and awesome punishments —is always the terrible reminder of our aloneness, our soaring away from the familiar, from our beacons of orientation, from our anchors of safety. So with our ordinary humanity most of us create new worlds in more ordinary ways.

And, like Columbus, we also pause at the borders of our new worlds. We hesitate. We return to base. We draw up new maps. We try to reconcile the old geometry with the new calculus that is still only a vision. We chart our journeys with fluttering heartbeats and quivering apprehensions.

A woman and a man awaiting the arrival of their baby thrive on their fantasies of creating a new world in this new human being who will be theirs. He will be free of their imperfections and the imperfections of their own parents. But after the birth very often they are overwhelmed by their awareness of the awesome responsibilities of nurturing an actual infant, who is so vulnerable, so helpless and dependent. In their letdown, the parents imagine that surely they will let down their child, that they will afflict him with their demons, wickedness and personal defects.

It seems that no matter how hard we strive for goodness, our demons refuse to be banished. But when we realize that absolute goodness is as dangerous as absolute evil, our demons can be transformed. Demons are transformed into ordinary human passions by the down-to-earth devotion of one human being for another. As less-than-perfect parents, we endow our children with just enough of the bliss of oneness to allow them to discover the vital rhythms of separateness. We sponsor the courage of their inborn urges to reach out to new worlds. And as life offers them fresh opportunities to transform the issues of their second birth, they will be able to make good use of these opportunities. Their illusions will be balanced by memories of the preciousness of the actual earth. Their journeys will not take them so far that they lose their beacon of orientation. As they step into their own spaces in the world, they will be constant to the earth and protect it from ruthless mineness.

At the conclusion of his second birth, a child is only on his way to constancy. Although he will have arrived at a beginning comprehension of the meanings of "mine" and "yours," "I" and "you," the complex dilemmas of oneness and separateness will haunt him for the rest of his life. The crisis will subside. The reconciliations have just begun.

Notes

Introduction

Mahler's description of the dilemma of the symbiotic psychotic child patient appears in *On Human Symbiosis and the Vicissitudes of Individuation,* Vol. I, *Infantile Psychosis* (New York: International Universities Press, 1968).

Volume II written in collaboration with Fred Pine and Anni Bergman, *The Psychological Birth of the Human Infant* (New York: Basic Books, 1967)* is a report of Mahler's discovery of the normal separation-individuation process—the second or psychological birth. Volume II briefly details the characteristics of the normal autistic ("The Beginnings") and normal symbiotic ("Oneness") phases and then precisely delineates the four subphases of the second birth: (1) differentiation, or hatching ("Beginning Separation ..."); (2) early practicing ("... Early Conquests") and practicing proper ("The Love Affair with the World"); (3) rapprochement ("The New Beginning"); and (4) object constancy ("Constancy"). This second volume also describes the research strategies employed by Mahler and the contributions of the subphases to basic mood, identity formation, separation anxiety and self-boundary formation. There are five case studies that illustrate the unique ways that separation-individuation may be expressed. The opening chapter of *The Psychological Birth of the Human Infant,* "Overview," relates Mahler's research with her psychotic child patients to the normal process of separation-individuation.

* All quotations from Mahler are from *The Psychological Birth of the Human Infant.*

249

I learned of the intimate connection between Mahler's work as a pediatrician with normal babies and her clinical work with psychotic children in a conversation with Mahler. She kindly has permitted me to borrow from the text of her film on separation-individuation to report how her research grew out of her theory of the symbiotic origins of human existence.

Throughout her writings, Mahler has represented the second birth as the child's gradual emergence, or separation, from symbiotic oneness. In this respect *Oneness and Separateness* departs occasionally from Mahler's conceptualization. I have included the symbiotic, or oneness, phase as part of the human psychological birth when technically it precedes the second birth. Although this manner of portraying the second birth does not follow the letter of Mahler's intention, I felt it conveyed the spirit of human oneness and separateness for two reasons: psychological birth can occur only after there is oneness; longings for oneness are a central aspect of the human *psychological* experience.

Mahler's papers on the tic syndrome in children are numerous. In a series of papers, she and her collaborators identified and differentiated ordinary symptomatic tics and the *tic syndrome,* which is referred to in this chapter. Among these papers are: "A Psychosomatic Study of *Maladie des Tics* (Gilles de la Tourette's Disease)," with Leo Rangell (*The Psychiatric Quarterly,* Vol. 17, 1943); "Tics and Impulsions in Children: A Study of Motility" (*The Psychoanalytic Quarterly,* Vol. 13, 1944); "Clinical and Follow-up Study of the Tic Syndrome," with J. A. Luke and W. Daltroff (*American Journal of Orthopsychiatry,* Vol. 15, 1945); "A Psychoanalytic Evaluation of Tic in Psychopathology of Children: Symptomatic Tic and Tic Syndrome" (*The Psychoanalytic Study of the Child,* Vol. III/IV, New York: International Universities Press, 1949).

In 1949 Mahler's definitive paper on childhood psychosis (in collaboration with J. R. Ross and Z. De Fries) appeared; "Clinical Studies in Benign and Malignant Cases of Childhood Psychosis (Schizophrenia-like)" (*American Journal of Orthopsychiatry,* Vol. 19, 1949).

Her subsequent papers on childhood psychosis, which are numerous, include: "On Child Psychosis and Schizophrenia:

Autistic and Symbiotic Infantile Psychoses" (*The Psychoanalytic Study of the Child*, Vol. VII, New York: International Universities Press, 1952); "On Symbiotic Child Psychosis: Genetic, Dynamic and Restitutive Aspects," with B. J. Gosliner (*The Psychoanalytic Study of the Child*, Vol. X, New York: International Universities Press, 1955); "Autism and Symbiosis: Two Extreme Disturbances of Identity" (*International Journal of Psychoanalysis*, Vol. 39, 1958); and with her longtime collaborator on the dynamics and treatment of symbiotic child psychosis, Dr. Manuel Furer, "Observations on Research Regarding the 'Symbiotic Syndrome' of Infantile Psychosis" (*The Psychoanalytic Quarterly*, Vol. 29, 1960).

Chapter One—Constancy

Most of the thoughts in this chapter originated in my paper "Object Constancy in the Light of Piaget's Vertical *Décalage*" (*Bulletin of the Menninger Clinic*, Vol. 36, 1972). That paper and this chapter were influenced by the writings of Mahler, Pine and Bergman and by the work of Jean Piaget. Of Piaget's writings, the major sources were: *Six Psychological Studies* (New York: Random House, 1967); *Play, Dreams and Imitation in Childhood* (New York: Norton, 1962); and *The Psychology of Intelligence* (New York: Harcourt Brace, 1950).

The term "object constancy" was introduced in Heinz Hartmann's 1952 paper, "The mutual influences of ego and id" (in *Essays on Ego Psychology*, New York: International Universities Press, 1964). For almost two decades thereafter, psychoanalysts accepted Hartmann's formulations on object constancy. However, they differed considerably in what they took to be its precise meaning and its timing in development. A common error was to confuse the psychoanalytic term "object constancy," which refers to an emotional variable, with Piaget's "object permanence," a cognitive variable. In my 1972 paper I said:

> This paper will propose a concept of object constancy, as well as memory, structured according to levels of organization, with object constancy having to be reacquired in more complex and integrated ways at successive phases of

development. Thus, in the adult there would be a hierarchy of levels of object constancy which is then not a stage in development but an accompaniment to the significant developments in object relations throughout the life cycle. With this approach, the paper also implies a shift in what has been the trend in the dialogue between psychoanalysis and Piaget [p. 323].

In stating this, I nevertheless agreed with Mahler that emotional constancy represented an aspect of the fourth subphase of separation-individuation. And, as Mahler, Pine and Bergman point out, the normal three-year-old has only achieved a *degree* of object constancy—the phase is open-ended; both individuality and object constancy are embellished throughout the life cycle. Mature object constancy means that a love object is "not rejected or exchanged for another if it can no longer provide satisfaction . . ." (p. 110).

The consequences of the transition from authoritarian to individualistic family structure has been noted by many writers. My reference was Therese Benedek's article, "Fatherhood and Parenting," which appears in *Parenthood: Its Psychology and Psychopathology*, edited by E. James Anthony and Therese Benedek (Boston: Little, Brown and Company, 1970).

The descriptions of splitting are primarily from the writings of Otto Kernberg, particularly his paper, "Borderline Personality Organization" (*Journal of the American Psychoanalytic Association*, Vol. 15, 1967).

Mahler defines the "splitting" of the young child:

A defense mechanism often found during the rapprochement subphase (once a certain measure of ego development has been achieved); the toddler cannot easily tolerate simultaneous love and hate feelings toward the same person. Love and hate are not amalgamated; the mother is experienced alternately as all good or all bad. Another possibility is that the absent mother is felt to be all good, while others become all bad. Hence the toddler may displace aggression onto the nonmother world while exaggerating love for (overidealizing) the absent, longed-for mother. When mother returns she disrupts the ideal image, and reunions with her are often painful, since the young child's synthetic function cannot heal the split. In most cases gradual synthesis of all "good" and all "bad" by the growing ego becomes possible [pp. 292–93].

The contrast between clinging love and narcissistic love is from Sigmund Freud's 1914 paper, "On Narcissism: An Introduction" (*Standard Edition*, Vol. 14, edited by J. Strachey; London: Hogarth Press, 1957). Freud referred to the two types of love as *anaclitic* ("leaning on") and *narcissistic*. Interestingly, Freud considered the narcissistic type to be typical of women and the anaclitic to be typical of men. A number of contemporary thinkers, including myself, would see the situation in reverse. Nevertheless, there is really no such thing as an absolute type of love; one type is emphasized over the other, and each person achieves a balance between them. Even those who employ splitting are not purely one type or the other. Later in this volume I discuss the differences between shadowing love (the clinging, possessive type) and darting-away love (the aloof, narcissistic type). Again, these types are never found in pure form. I have extended the metaphors of shadowing and darting away to convey the spirit of extremely complex issues.

The concept of actual child and fantasy child is from Therese Benedek's paper, "The Family as a Psychologic Field," in *Parenthood*.

The phrase "love affair with the world" is from Phyllis Greenacre's paper, "The Childhood of the Artist: Libidinal Phase Development and Giftedness" (*The Psychoanalytic Study of the Child*, Vol. XII, New York: International Universities Press, 1957). Most of the ideas about the artist's relationship to the world and his special attunement are from her paper. It was Mahler who characterized the triumph and exhilaration of the upright toddler as a love affair with the world. See also Notes to Chapter Five, particularly Lewin and Balint.

The *Nature Morte* is my interpretation of a still life by Cézanne (*vers* 1895).

The story of Gabriel is my rendering of "The Dead," the final story of *Dubliners*, by James Joyce. It has been suggested that Gabriel Conroy is what Joyce would have become if he had stayed in Ireland—not an artist who soared, but an ordinary man paralyzed by the routines of ordinary life.

A note of caution: Although I have stated this point on several occasions in this chapter, I wish to emphasize it yet again. In the life of the adult we see only reflections and hear only echoes of the second birth. It is vital to be in touch with the child in the adult self; however, adult behavior cannot and should not ever be reduced to its childhood origins. What we find in the adult are the many-layered aspects of infancy, childhood, adolescence and later life. The underlying meaning of adult behavior is multi-determined and includes the relationships of the present. The same is true of child and adolescent behavior. Only insofar as the choreography and rhythms of the second birth are common to all humanity can it be said that these events actually occurred. The way they occur is personal and unique, and how they come to be reinterpreted and experienced later in life will also be personal. Similarly, when I write about "cutting loose" and "returning to home base," these are metaphors. The choreography can happen in the mind, and most often it does. A person need not actually leave home and return to have the emotional experiences of the second birth. In fact one could almost say that expansion of selfhood and self-realization can occur only in the mind. Perhaps it is symptomatic of our times that people feel compelled to act out the themes of their second birth rather than experience them internally. Hence the note of caution.

Chapter Two—The Beginnings

In the psychoanalytic literature the first four to six weeks of human life have been designated as the *normal* autistic phase. Some critics have found the use of the term "autistic" unfortunate as a description of normal development, since it is easily associated with the extreme pathology of the autistic child. However, the term refers to the normal turning inward focus of the neonate. Mahler, Pine and Bergman describe this phase as:

> The first weeks of extrauterine life, during which the neonate or young infant appears to be an almost purely biological organism, his instinctual responses to stimuli being on a

reflex and thalamic level. . . . The libido position is predominantly a visceral one with no discrimination between inside and outside, animate and inanimate [p. 290].

In keeping with our increasing knowledge of the early weeks and months of life, Mahler and her collaborators have recognized the relative nature of the normal autistic and symbiotic positions:

> Although the autistic phase is characterized by relative absence of cathexis of external stimuli, this does not mean that there can be no responsiveness to external stimuli. Wolff (1959) and Fantz (1960), among others, have clearly demonstrated such responsivity in the newborn, and Wolff additionally describes the fleeting states of 'alert inactivity' in which it is most likely to occur. It is this fleeting responsivity to external stimuli that makes for the continuity between the normal autistic and later phases [p. 43].

The past fifteen years have seen a revolution in the methodology of infant research. Because the young infant's motor and behavioral coordinations are not developed sufficiently to yield precise information about what he might be attending to or perceiving, prior to this methodological revolution scientists tended to believe that it would be impossible to study infant perception. However, in the early 1960s scientists began to devise a number of ingenious methods for assessing infant perception. Each year, therefore, the public is informed of the newest remarkable feats of visual tracking and visual and auditory discriminations performed by one-week- to two-month-old infants. Moreover, one investigator of infant development, T. G. R. Bower from Scotland, has demonstrated in his lab that these young infants can imitate facial expressions and distinguish between two- and three-dimensional objects within a few weeks after birth. A recent experiment by Andrew N. Meltzoff and N. Keith Moore, "Imitation of Facial and Manual Gestures by Human Neonates" (*Science*, October 7, 1977) would seem to verify Bower's contentions about the neonate's capacity for imitation. However, to interpret these findings as evidence for neonatal "perceptual sophistication" or mediation "by an abstract representational system" is not warranted. A more reasonable interpretation would be that these "neonatal imitations" represent reflexive or innate releasing-mechanism behaviors.

Since the advent of these latest investigations of infant development, some scientists have questioned the psychoanalytic descriptions of the normal autistic and symbiotic phases. However, as Mahler and her collaborators have clearly pointed out, there is evidence of symbiosis in the autistic phase, and likewise in the normal symbiotic phase there is evidence of hatching and differentiation. In speaking of normal autism and normal symbiosis, psychoanalysts are referring to the dominant focus of infant attention—which is inward during the autistic phase, and contained within the mother-infant orbit during the symbiotic phase. Neither is an absolute state of attention. Again, variations among newborns can be observed. Some are more alert and exploration-minded from the beginning. Nevertheless, every normal human newborn will go through at least relative periods of normal autism and symbosis. As with all phases described in *Oneness and Separateness,* there is considerable overlap between one phase and the next, and considerable variation between one infant and another, one mother-infant couple and another.

As the latest laboratory reports of infant feats of perception and awareness have filtered down to the public via TV and popular journals, parents have begun to stimulate their babies prematurely to reach outward, track, focus and discriminate, thereby depriving the infants of their biological right to remain inward for a time and then to be absorbed in the bliss of mother-infant oneness. This state of affairs appears to be particularly evident in upwardly mobile middle-class families. The consequences of such unnatural early stimulation are as yet unknown.

The Mother's Part Although I speak here of the fantasies of the "first coming together," a mother is often unaware of her fantasies until several weeks or months after the birth of her baby. Many mothers are more involved with the physical aftermath of the delivery process than with fantasy exploration. Once having ascertained the "intactness" of the newborn, such mothers remain focused on their own physical state, particularly when the delivery has been less than optimal.

The Mother-to-be The idea of a mother's fantasies shaking her loose from her conventional mode of functioning is from

"Does the Neonate Shape His Environment?" by T. Berry Brazelton, in *The Infant at Risk* (New York: Intercontinental Medical Book Corporation, 1974).

The hormonal influences that reawaken the childhood attitudes of receiving and holding on; the ideas on normal vegetating; the stimulation of hopeful fantasies; the sequence of deprivation, self-hatred and monster fantasies; musing together as deepening the bond between husband and wife; and the fantasies which relate the fetus to the triad of mother-father-child are from "The Psychobiology of Pregnancy," by Therese Benedek, in *Parenthood.*

Although precise in its general outlines, Benedek's presentation of the relationship between hormones and the attitudes of pregnancy is a simplification. Androgens, which many people associate with maleness, also play a role in the pregnancy. Estrogens and androgens are present in both men and women, differing only in their relative balance. The hormone oxytocin also plays a significant role in pregnancy, and during copulation, conception and childbirth. Oxytocin stimulates the uterine contractions that propel the sperm to the ovum, and it also stimulates the contractions of childbirth. An excellent summary of the recent research on the relationships between hormones and behavior appears in Alice Rossi's paper, "A Biosocial Perspective on Parenting," in *The Family, t*he Spring 1977 issue of *Daedalus,* the Journal of the American Academy of Arts and Sciences. As Rossi states:

> Until the fifties, then, cases demonstrating that the nervous system participated in reproductive events were regarded as curious exceptions, while from the mid-fifties on, the endocrine system was demoted to the status of coequal partner with the nervous system in the control of hormonal events in the body. The broader significance of this shift is that it allows us less and less reason to expect a one-way causation between hormones and behavior; the only appropriate model then becomes an interactive-influence model [p. 10].

The Barrier Sigmund Freud first suggested the idea of a stimulus barrier in "Formulations on the Two Principles of Mental Functioning" (*Standard Edition,* Vol. 12, edited by J.

Strachey, London: Hogarth Press, 1958 [1911]). John Benjamin's recent formulations of the concept of stimulus barrier in early infancy are described in "Developmental Biology and Psychoanalysis," in *Psychoanalysis and Current Biological Thought,* edited by Norman S. Greenfield and William C. Lewis (Madison: The University of Wisconsin Press, 1965). Modifications and amplifications of Benjamin's work appear in "The Stimulus Barrier in Early Infancy: An Exploration of Some Formulations of John Benjamin," by Katherine Tennes, Robert Emde, Anthony Kisley and David Metcalf, *Psychoanalysis and Contemporary Science,* Vol. I, edited by Robert R. Holt and Emanuel Peterfreund (New York: The Macmillan Company, 1972).

The Appeal of Helplessness That newbornness, particularly the fat-cheeked look, is a releaser of maternal nurturance was first suggested by Konrad Lorenz in "Die angegorenen Formen möglicher Erfahrun" (Z. *Tierpsychol.,* Vol. 5, 1943). The additional characteristics of newbornness are listed on page 431 of *Ethology: the Biology of Behavior,* by Irenäus Eibl-Eibesfeldt (New York: Holt, Rinehart and Winston, 1970).

The Infant Smile Using a sample of eight infants, Peter H. Wolff investigated the history of infant smiling. His investigation is described in "The Early Development of Smiling," in *Determinants of Infant Behaviour,* Vol. II, edited by B. M. Foss (London: Methuen, 1963). Although there have been numerous subsequent studies of infant smiling, Wolff's formulations have not been contradicted in any significant way. Moreover, his observations correspond to my own. Almost every detail of the descriptions in this section are from Wolff's 1963 paper.

Variations and Uniqueness The differences between neonates from traditional and nontraditional societies, and the description of the Zinacanteco newborn and mother are from, "Does the Neonate Shape His Environment?" by T. Berry Brazelton, in *Infant at Risk.*

The effects of newborn variations on maternal attitudes and the sections that follow on crying, soothing, sleeping and waking and other differences are from "Individual Differences at Birth: Implications for Child-Care Practices," by Anneliese F. Korner, in *Infant at Risk* and, also by Korner, "The Effect of the Infant's

State, Level of Arousal, Sex and Ontogenetic Stage on the Care-giver," in *The Effect of the Infant on its Caregiver,* edited by Michael Lewis and Leonard A. Rosenblum (New York: John Wiley and Sons, Inc., 1974).

Many writers with an ethological-evolutionary perspective on infant-mother interaction have commented on the crying–fear of predators theme. A recent amplification of this perspective is *Human Infancy: An Evolutionary Perspective,* by Daniel G. Freedman (New Jersey: Laurence Erlbaum Associates, John Wiley and Sons, Inc., distributor, 1974). The response to infant crying is on page 29. The volume also includes several chapters describing newborn behavior patterns in traditional groups, Aboriginal, African and Chinese-American.

The states of arousal, and sleeping and waking are described by Peter H. Wolff in *The Causes, Controls and Organization of Behavior in the Neonate* (*Psychological Issues,* Monograph 17, New York: International Universities Press, Inc., 1966).

Wolff's observations of infant states of arousal have been verified by other investigators, among them Janet L. Brown in "States in Newborn Infants" (*Merrill Palmer Quarterly,* Vol. 10, 1964).

Brown's observations led her to conclude that variations in state of arousal are already apparent in one-week-old infants. According to Brown, some infants are in states of prolonged alert inactivity and capable of selective attention as early as one week. Her findings appear to contradict the notion of stimulus barrier. Again, one wonders how much of this early infant reactivity is stimulated by laboratory procedures and would not occur in the natural mother-infant interaction.

The First Dialogue The idea of the early mother-infant dialogue, or "basic dialogue," was first described by Rene Spitz in "Life and the Dialogue," in *Counterpoint: Libidinal Object and Subject,* edited by H. S. Gaskill (New York: International Universities Press, 1963).

The consequences of disruption in basic dialogue appear in Spitz's paper, "The Derailment of Dialogue: Stimulus Overload, Action Cycles, and the Completion Gradient" (*Journal of the American Psychoanalytic Association,* Vol. 12, 1964).

My description of the first dialogue is an integration of Spitz on dialogue and some thoughts of D. W. Winnicott. The notion of the mother acting as an interpreter is from Winnicott.

Several of Spitz's original findings—such as the infant looking at the mother's face while nursing, marasmus in institutionalized infants, his interpretations of stranger-anxiety, and the meaning of the autistic phase described here—have been questioned by developmental researchers. Nevertheless, I believe that the emotional significance Spitz attributes to the beginnings of human dialogue is still valid despite the disagreements with some of his specific observations. Moreover, his early theories of infant development recently have been verified by physiological studies in which EEG findings and REM cycles have correlated with his observations. These studies appear in "Further Prototypes of Ego Formation," in *The Psychoanalytic Study of the Child,* Vol. XXV (New York: International Universities Press, 1970).

Chapter Three—Oneness

Mahler describes the normal symbiotic phase as follows:

> Normal symbiosis is ushered in by the lifting of the innate strong stimulus barrier that protected the young infant from internal and external stimuli up to the third or fourth week of human life.
>
> Symbiosis refers to a stage of sociobiological interdependence between the 1-to-5 month old infant and his mother. . . . From the second month on, the infant behaves and functions as though he and his mother were an omnipotent dual unity within one common boundary ("the symbiotic membrane").
>
> The mother's availability and the infant's innate capacity to engage in the symbiotic relationship are essential at this point. This relationship marks the inception of ego organization by the establishment of intrapsychic connections on the infant's part between memory traces of gratification and the gestalt of the human face; there is a shift of cathexis from inside the body, from the predominantly visceral position of the autistic phase to the periphery, the sensory-perceptive organs [pp. 290–91].

Holding D. W. Winnicott's paper, "The Mother-Infant Experience of Mutuality," in *Parenthood,* is the source of many of the descriptions in this section, particularly those of holding, being let down, and falling to bits. It is in this paper that Winnicott specifically states that mutuality "is dependent on the baby's inherited processes leading toward emotional growth and likewise dependent on the mother and her attitude and her capacity to make real what the baby is ready to reach out for, to discover, to create" (p. 250).

Another paper of Winnicott's that influenced this section is "The Theory of the Parent-Infant Relationship" (*International Journal of Psychoanalysis,* 41, 1960).

The infant's temporary illusion of omnipotence—or of creating the world—is from "Ego Integration in Child Development" (1962) in D. W. Winnicott, *The Maturational Processes and the Facilitating Environment* (New York: International Universities Press, 1965).

The Mother's Presence This section is derived from my own observations and from the writings of Mahler, Spitz and Winnicott. The specific phrase "presence of the mother" is from "The Capacity to Be Alone," by D. W. Winnicott, in *The Maturational Processes. . . .*

Mutual Cueing and Empathy Mutual cueing is described by Mahler as "A circular process of interaction established very early between mother and infant by which they 'empathically' read each other's signs and signals and react to each other." In its essentials, my description of mutual cueing corresponds to Mahler's. However, I emphasize the distinction between sympathy and empathy, the mother reacting with sympathy and empathy, the infant solely with sympathy.

The importance of maintaining the distinction between sympathetic and empathic responsiveness is asserted by Norman L. Paul in "Parental Empathy" (*Parenthood*).

Choreography The description of the molding and stiffening postures is derived from Volume II, *The Psychological Birth of the Human Infant.* The contribution of these postures to the formation of body image is my interpretation of Mahler's writing. I also credit Phyllis Greenacre's paper "Considerations Regarding the Parent-Infant Relationship" *Emotional Growth,* Vol. I (New

York: International Universities Press, 1960), for the concept that inner tension-relaxation rhythms form the core of body awareness. Mahler also cites this reference.

The Baby's Mind The body integrations described in this section are from Chapter II, "The First Acquired Adaptations and the Primary Circular Reaction," in Jean Piaget, *The Origins of Intelligence* (New York: International Universities Press, 1952). I also wish to acknowledge John H. Flavell, *The Developmental Psychology of Jean Piaget* (Princeton, New Jersey: D. Van Nostrand Company, Inc., 1963), for the clarity of his exposition of Piaget's writings.

The psychoanalyst Willie Hoffer also has delineated these core contributions to infant mental organization in "Mouth, Hand, and Ego Integration" (*The Psychoanalytic Study of the Child,* Vol. III/IV, New York: International Universities Press, 1949) and "Development of the Body Ego" (*The Psychoanalytic Study of the Child,* Vol. V, New York: International Universities Press, 1950).

I have emphasized that the infant mind until fifteen or eighteen months is a body-mind. All subsequent references to thought processes such as supposing, recognizing, conjecturing, imagining, pondering, generalizing, Hegelian resolutions, therefore are meant to be understood as produced by a body-mind. With the appearance of symbolic representational intelligence (described in the conclusion of Chapter Four and in Chapter Five) the body-mind is joined by the thinking mind, bringing about a different order of self-awareness and thought process.

Having a Conversation Two papers by Daniel N. Stern are the basis of this section. Most of the details described are from Daniel N. Stern, Joseph Jaffee, Beatrice Beebe and Stephen L. Bennett, "Vocalizing in Unison and in Alternation: Two Modes of Communication within the Mother-Infant Dyad," in *Developmental Psycholinguistics and Communication Disorders,* edited by Doris Aaronson and Robert W. Reiber (New York: The New York Academy of Sciences, 1975). This section was also informed by Stern's paper, "Mother and Infant at Play: The Dyadic Interaction Involving Facial, Vocal and Gaze Behaviors," in *The Effect of the Infant on Its Caregiver,* edited by Michael Lewis and Leonard A. Rosenblum (New York: John Wiley and Sons, Inc., 1974).

The Real Madonna The concepts of the ordinary devoted mother, the baby sucking out what he needs and then throwing away the husk, the incident of the baby meeting the stranger in the park and a mother surviving her hatred for her baby are from D. W. Winnicott, "The Ordinary Devoted Mother and Her Baby: Nine Broadcast Talks," as reprinted in *Mother and Child: A Primer of First Relationships* (New York: Basic Books, 1957).

The idea of the mother feeling that she has failed in two directions appears in Therese Benedek's paper, "Parenthood as a Developmental Phase," in the *Journal of the American Psychoanalytic Association*, Vol. 7, July, 1959.

Separation Begins The difference between the two-month-old smile of recognition and the five-month-old specific smile is drawn from my own observations of infant reactions to the mother. The specific smile and the infant's active longing for the mother as the heralds of beginning separation are described in *The Psychological Birth of the Human Infant*.

The child's specific attachment to the mother has been demonstrated even in children who attended a day care center five days per week from age three and a half months to thirty months. Jerome Kagan describes his study comparing day-care and home-reared infants in "The Child and the Family," in *The Family*, the Spring 1977 issue of *Daedalus*. Kagan cites a Ph.D. dissertation by N. A. Fox which reports that Israeli kibbutzim infants who visited the parents' home for only a few hours a day were more secure when left with a mother and a stranger than with the *metapelet* and a stranger. Children may be attached to a specific substitute caretaker and still prefer the mother for comforting when they are tired or apprehensive. Kagan says, "Both of these studies imply that the number of hours a child is cared for by an adult is not the critical dimension that produces a strong attachment. There is something special about the mother-infant relationship. The parent appears to be more salient than substitute caretakers to the child. It is not clear why this is so" (p. 36).

Chapter Four—Beginning Separation and Early Conquests

The term Mahler uses for beginning separation is "differentiation." Differentiation is the first subphase of separation-individuation:

> Total bodily dependence on mother begins to decrease as the maturation of locomotor partial functions brings about the first tentative moving away from her. Characteristic behaviors that make possible the demarcation of self from nonself are visual and tactile exploration of mother's face and body; pulling away from mother to scan the wider world and look at her; checking back from mother to others. Pleasure in emerging ego functions and the outside world is expressed in close proximity to mother. At the same time, differentiation of a primitive, but distinct, body image seems to occur [p. 289].

Mahler describes the earliest signs of differentiation as *hatching*.

> The hatched infant has left the vague twilight state of symbiosis and has become more permanently alert and perceptive to the stimuli of his environment, rather than to his own bodily sensations, or to sensations emanating within the symbiotic orbit only [p. 290].

Later differentiation overlaps with what Mahler has called *early practicing* ("Early Conquests").

> The differentiation subphase is overlapped by the practicing period. In the course of processing our data we found it useful to think of the practicing period in two parts: (1) the early practicing phase, ushered in by the infant's earliest ability to move away physically from mother by crawling, paddling, climbing and righting himself—yet holding on; and (2) the practicing period proper, phenomenologically characterized by free upright locomotion [p. 65].

In *Oneness and Separateness* the overlaps between early differentiation and symbiosis and between later differentiation and early practicing have been emphasized. Therefore some signs of

hatching appear in the chapter "Oneness," and beginning separation and early practicing appear in this chapter. Practicing
proper, although still part of the second subphase, seemed distinct enough from early practicing for its characteristics to be
delineated separately in the next chapter, "The Love Affair with
the World."

The Invisible Bond "Babies know when to start separating."
Mahler has described the vicissitudes of early and late hatching.
"In cases where the symbiotic process, the creating of the common 'shielding' membrane of the dual unity, has been delayed
or disturbed the process of differentiation seems to be delayed
or premature" (p. 58).

The Mother of Separation The two threads of separation and
individuation are from Volume II. "One track is "individuation,
the evolution of intrapsychic autonomy, perception, memory,
cognition, reality testing." This track, or thread, I describe as the
growth urges within the child. The other "is the intrapsychic
developmental track of separation that runs along differentiation,
distancing, boundary formation and disengagement from mother"
(p. 63). This I describe as the dominant thread of gradual
realization of separateness.

The terms "beacon of orientation" and "anchor of safety" are
from Volume I, *Infantile Psychosis.*

Choreography It is common to use the word "crawling" instead of the technical term "creeping" for hand-knee, trunk-off-
the-floor locomotion. "Crawling" actually refers to movement in
a prone position—belly and chest on the floor.

The various ways of bridging the interlude between reaching
out and creeping can be found in almost any child development
textbook. My major reference was L. Joseph Stone and Joseph
Church, *Childhood and Adolescence,* Third Edition (New York:
Random House, 1973).

When Jean Piaget spoke at the midwinter meeting of the
American Psychoanalytic Association in 1970, he gave the example of adults being unable to describe the motions of creeping.

The checking-back and refueling patterns are described in
Mahler. The term "emotional refueling" was suggested to Mahler
by her colleague Manuel Furer in a personal communication.
The use of the mother as a "home base" for exploration is from

Mahler. The behavior has been observed by numerous child and primate psychologists who also use the term "home base."

"No" and "Don't"—Doing and Being Done To The baby's scrutiny of the mother's face, his exploration of her body, putting food into her mouth, and his fascination with her clothing are behaviors which Mahler views as "tentative experimentation at separation-individuation"—the behavioral signs of beginning separation.

Although Mahler did not state this directly, I have come to believe that the source of the individuation track of separation-individuation is the aggressive momentum of the *growth energies* within the child, and that these energies are largely responsible for transforming him from a being-done-to lap baby into an active conqueror. A similar idea is expressed by Phyllis Greenacre in "The Childhood of the Artist . . .": ". . . the baby of five to six months extending its legs and pushing with its feet against the lap of the mother does so from the aggression of developmental force, not from the aggression of hostility" (p. 63). Heinz Hartmann, Ernst Kris and Rudolph M. Loewenstein, in "Notes on the Theory of Aggression" (*Psychoanalytic Study of the Child*, Vol. III/IV; New York: International Universities Press, 1949) describe how "Musculature and mobility apparatuses for the discharge of aggression contribute decisively to the differentiation between self and environment and through action to the differentiation of the environment itself" (p. 22). They, however, do not attribute aggression to growth energy. And, although Gertrude and Rubin Blanck do not attribute aggression to developmental force or growth energy, two prominent ideas in a recent paper by them are that aggressive drive serves the separation-individuation process, and that it is essential to distinguish affects such as love and hate from the drives of libido and aggression. ("Transference Object and Real Object," *International Journal of Psychoanalysis*, Vol. 58, Part I, 1977.)

Rage The descriptions of rage and its meaning to the young baby are from "Why Do Babies Cry?" by D. W. Winnicott, in *Mother and Child*.

Alternative Dialogues The eight-month-old's reaction to strangers has been described as a developmental landmark by many child psychologists. Rene Spitz began to study eight-month anxiety in the late 1940s. His views are summarized in *The First Year of Life* (New York: International Universities Press, 1965). Spitz thought the reaction signified the full attainment of attachment to a specific mother. And although Spitz clearly states otherwise, his work has been misinterpreted to mean that unless a child demonstrates "anxiety" when confronted by a stranger he has not formed a specific attachment. Mahler has described how the so-called "anxiety" reaction could be a subtle checking back to the mother's face as the baby trustingly plays with the stranger. In recent years the terms "stranger reaction" or "stranger wariness" have replaced "stranger anxiety."

My interpretation of the balance between wariness and exploration, wariness and affiliation, corresponds in its general details with that of Inge Bretherton and Mary D. Salter Ainsworth in "Responses of One-Year-Olds to a Stranger in a Strange Situation," in *The Origins of Fear*, edited by Michael Lewis and Leonard A. Rosenblum (New York: John Wiley and Sons, Inc., 1974).

"Strange dialogues awaken the possibility that the baby might run away with himself" is a paraphrase of Spitz's idea that the stranger reaction represents the child's anxiety about being overwhelmed by his impulses when separated from his mother. The confrontation with the stranger signifies confrontation with strange dialogue. Spitz explains this in "A Note on the Extrapolation of Ethological Findings" (*International Journal of Psychoanalysis,* Vol. 36, 1955): ". . . fear manifestations in presence of the stranger are a reaction to an internal danger. . . ." "It is an apperception, an internal perception of the threat that the ego will be swamped with feelings with which it cannot deal" (p. 164).

The inspection of the stranger is described by Mahler, and also by Sylvia Brody and Sidney Axelrad in *Anxiety and Ego Formation in Infancy* (New York: International Universities Press, 1970). The term "customs inspection" is from Brody and Axelrad. Ainsworth specifically notes that she did not observe such examination of the stranger's face and body in her study. This is probably because she was observing one-year-olds, rather than eight-month-olds who are concerned with the problem of distinguishing mother from other.

The evolutionary-ethological perspective on stranger reactions is mine, not Mahler's. It is a view shared by many writers on the subject. I do not believe that this perspective in any way contradicts Mahler's belief about the species-specific nature of the separation-individuation process.

The dating of the Pleistocene at one million years is approximate. It could be anywhere from 500,000 to two million. The appearance of early man roughly coincides with the Pleistocene. In *Man the Hunter* (Symposium on Man the Hunter, University of Chicago, 1966, edited by Richard B. Lee and Irven De Vore; Chicago: Aldine Publishing Company, 1968) several contributors caution that it may not be possible to reconstruct the conditions of early mankind by studying the way of life of recent hunter-gatherers. Nevertheless, as Sherwood L. Washburn and C. S. Lancaster point out:

> In a very real sense our intellect, interests, emotions and basic social life—all are evolutionary products of the success of the hunting adaptation. When anthropologists speak of the unity of mankind, they are stating that the selection pressures of the hunting and gathering way of life were so similar and the result so successful that populations of *Homo sapiens* are still fundamentally the same everywhere.

Peek-a-boo The descriptions of the passive and active forms of peek-a-boo are from James A. Kleeman's "The Peek-a-Boo Game: Part I. Its Origins, Meanings and Related Phenomena in the First Year" (*The Psychoanalytic Study of the Child*, Vol. XXII, New York: International Universities Press, 1967). The related phenomena of catch-me and tossing-away are also from Kleeman's paper. He connects these games with separation-individuation and also with the appearance of stranger wariness, no-saying, body-image formation, now-here/now-not-here rhythms, and the "me" who acts in harmony with a "not-me" partner.

The Zhun/twasi catch-me game is from M. J. Konner, "Aspects of the Developmental Ethology of a Foraging People," in N. Blurton-Jones, *Ethological Studies of Child Behaviour* (London: Cambridge University Press, 1972).

Illusion—The Security Blanket The creation of the security blanket, its various aspects, and its relationship to illusion in human life is from D. W. Winnicott, "Transitional Objects and Transitional Phenomena" (1951), in *Through Paediatrics to Psychoanalysis* (New York: Basic Books, Inc. 1975). Not all children have a security blanket but some form of transitional (me/not-me) object is usually adopted. It may be a rocking motion, a bottle, a sound, and under certain conditions the mother herself can be transformed for short periods into a transitional object, or security blanket. This is probably true in many places in the world. In this latter instance, the child's posture as he sits on his mother's lap, his inward-turning gaze and his fingering of her hair or clothing clearly indicate that he is re-creating the illusion of oneness. After a few minutes, the mother is transformed back into the ordinary mother in the flesh.

The Baby's Mind—The Visionary Gleam The rules that govern the baby's mind and the specific activities described are derived from Jean Piaget's *Origins of Intelligence,* particularly his illustrations of stage 4 and stage 5 behavior. In general the descriptions are based on his concept of sensori-motor intelligence and his assimilation-accommodation model of intelligence. Some activities are from Stone and Church, *Childhood and Adolescence.*

The idea of the baby being obsessed with verticality, standing in his sleep, and practicing standing in his dreams is from Selma Fraiberg, *The Magic Years* (New York: Charles Scribner's Sons, 1959).

Chapter Five—"The Love Affair with the World"

The phrase "love affair with the world" is from Phyllis Greenacre, "The Childhood of the Artist: Libidinal Phase Development and Giftedness," *The Psychoanalytic Study of the Child,* Vol. XII (New York: International Universities Press, 1957). As Mahler has said, the upright toddler is at the peak of narcissism. Thus, in his exhilaration and mastery of the world he is much like an artist.

Practicing and Using the Body All-Out The activities of the upright toddler are from Stone and Church, *Childhood and*

Adolescence. It should be understood that the love affair overlaps with the events of the second eighteen months of life. Upon attaining uprightness, the toddler does not all at once "climb extraordinary heights" or "glide trippingly on his toes." These accomplishments are spread over the second year of life as the toddler practices and masters uprightness.

The boy's puzzlement and amazement at the mysterious laws of the penis is from Mahler's account of *practicing proper.*

The girl's discovery of her "inside" anatomy and the description of the young toddler's exploratory "masturbation" are from several sources: Judith S. Kestenberg, *Children and Parents* (New York: Aronson, 1967); James A. Kleeman, "Freud's Views on Early Female Sexuality in the Light of Direct Child Observation" (*Journal of the American Psychoanalytic Association,* Vol. 24, 1976); Eleanor Galenson and Herman Roiphie, "Some Suggested Revisions Concerning Early Female Development" (*Journal of the American Psychoanalytic Association,* Vol. 24, 1976).

The young toddler's first use of words is largely from the writings of Katherine Nelson: "Structure and Strategy in Learning to Talk" (*Monographs of the Society for Research in Child Development,* Vol. 38, 1973); "Concept, Word and Sentence: Interrelations in Acquisition and Development" (*Psychological Review,* Vol. 81, 1974); "Individual Differences in Early Semantic and Syntactic Development" (*Developmental Psycholinguistics and Communication Disorders,* 1975).

The emphasis on power words and the child's choosing of words that express the way his body acts in the world is my interpretation of Nelson. The interpretation is consonant with the implications of Nelson's writing on early language acquisition.

Choreography   The ideas expressed in this section are from Michael Balint, *Thrills and Regressions* (New York: International Universities Press, 1959). As I observed the toddlers in my nursery and reexamined Mahler's descriptions of practicing proper, I was reminded of Balint's distinction between *philobatism* and *ocnophilia.* Taking the Greek word "acrobat," which means "he who walks on his toes," Balint° coined the word "philobat" to describe one who enjoys acrobatic thrills and moving away from the earth. "Ocnophil" is also from the Greek and means "to shrink, to hesitate, to cling, to hang back." It seemed to me that the toddler's "love affair," his carefree, abandoned use of his body, could be epitomized by the word "philobat."

Although the upright toddler continues to "refuel," his exhilaration makes him daring and less mindful of home base—less clinging and hesitating.

The partner of the friendly expanses of open space was suggested to me by Balint's book. The Tensing and Hillary metaphor and the illustration of the "Mummy" ships are also from Balint.

Balint was aware of the connections among learning to walk, the love affair with the world, and the philobatic fantasy:

> . . . as our ancestors in phylogenesis were safely held by the sea, or as we ourselves in our ontogenetic past were held by the amniotic fluid in our mother's womb. The philobat regresses in his fantasy to this conception of the world. He firmly believes that the friendly expanses will encompass him safely, just as he was held before the appearance of the untrustworthy and treacherous objects.
>
> In order to indulge in this fantasy, however, he must acquire a high degree of personal skill, and must submit his performance to incessant, exacting reality testing, and to searching self-criticism. Perhaps the first such physical skill, and certainly the prototype for all the later ones, is the erect gait as distinct from crawling on all fours. . . . The underlying fantasy probably is that the whole world, apart from a few accidental hazards, is a kind of loving mother holding her child safely in her arms or, phylogenetically, the structureless sea offering the same friendly environment in limitless expanses [pp. 84–85].

Elation   The primary source for the details on the affect of elation is Bertram Lewin, *The Psychoanalysis of Elation* (New York: *The Psychoanalytic Quarterly*, 1961 [1950]). Lewin located the fountainhead of elation in the early oral (or symbiotic) phase. However, many of his descriptions of elation convey that he probably would have considered the upright toddler in the practicing proper subphase as the prototype of elation. The love affair is, after all, a reliving of the remembered bliss of oneness.

Mahler speaks of the love affair as holding in abeyance the awareness of separateness. Lewin says that the function of elation is to ward off the feeling of anxiety.

The quotations on color are from Wassily Kandinsky, *Concerning the Spiritual in Art* (New York: George Wittenborn, Inc., 1912).

Variations in subphase-specific elation are delineated by Mahler in *The Psychological Birth of the Human Infant.* She also comments on the little girl's greater propensity for disappointment in the next subphase of separation-individuation, rapprochement, and links this to the muting of elation during the practicing proper subphase.

The gender differences were suggested by H. A. Moss, "Sex, Age and State: Determinants of Mother-Infant Interaction" (*Merrill Palmer Quarterly*, Vol. 13, 1967). They are also from Mahler's observations and my own.

Low-Keyedness   The term and the description is from Mahler. Although low-keyedness is more typical for the hesitating early conqueror than for the exhilarated upright toddler, Mahler has recognized that despite his overall good spirits, even the upright toddler will become low-keyed when he is aware that his mother is absent from the room. I chose to put the section on low-keyedness in this chapter in order to contrast this down-spirited mood with the mood of elation.

The imaging of the perfect state of self is in W. G. Joffe and Joseph Sandler, "Notes on Pain, Depression and Individuation," in *The Psychoanalytic Study of the Child*, Vol. XX (New York: International Universities Press, 1965).

The Fall   The idea that "The force of the growth processes that convert a fertilized egg into a newborn baby would overwhelm the universe if its momentum did not slow down" was suggested by Phyllis Greenacre in "The Childhood of the Artist. . . ."

In *The Psychoanalysis of Elation,* Lewin relates the primary decline in elation to the transition from the world of perceptual flux to the world of concepts, and also to the renunciation of orality and pleasure in motion or motility. He refers to William James:

> Amidst the flux of opinions and of physical things, the world of conceptions or things intended to be thought about, stands stiff and immutable, like Plato's World of Ideas. [*The*

Principles of Psychology, New York: Henry Holt and Company, 1890, p. 462].

To understand life by concepts is to arrest its movement, cutting it up into bits as if with scissors, and immobilizing these in our logical herbarium where comparing them as dried specimens, we can ascertain which of them statically includes which other [*A Pluralistic Universe,* New York: Longmans, Green and Co., 1916, p. 244].

William James's turn-of-the-century philosophic position *vis à vis* the transition from the world of sensate flux to the world of concepts has been verified by Jean Piaget's observational studies of infants in the 1950s and 1960s. In Piaget's writings the transition is from sensori-motor to symbolic-representational intelligence—at around sixteen to eighteen months. Sensori-motor intelligence is illustrated in *Origins of Intelligence.* The beginnings of symbolic representational intelligence appear in that volume and primarily in *Play, Dreams and Imitation in Childhood* (New York: Norton, 1951).

The examples of beginning representation are from Piaget and from my own observational studies.

Chapter Six—The New Beginning

The technical term for "the new beginning" is *rapprochement.* Mahler describes this phase as:

> The third subphase of separation-individuation, lasting from 14 or 15 months to about 24 months and even beyond. It is characterized by a rediscovery of mother, now a separate individual, and a returning to her after the obligatory forays of the practicing period [p. 291].

The rapprochement subphase is divided into three periods. In his initial reaction

> The toddler loves to share his experiences and possessions with mother, who is now more clearly perceived as separate and outside. The narcissistic inflation of the practicing subphase is slowly replaced by a growing realization of separateness and, with it, vulnerability. Adverse reactions to brief

separations are common, and mother can no longer be easily substituted for, even by familiar adults [pp. 291–92].

The second period is the rapprochement crisis,

> ... occurring in all children, but with great intensity in some, during which the realization of separateness is acute. The toddler's belief in his omnipotence is severely threatened and the environment is coerced as he tries to restore the *status quo*, which is impossible. Ambitendency, which develops into ambivalence, is often intense; the toddler wants to be united with, and at the same time separate from, mother. Temper tantrums, whining, sad moods and intense separation reactions are at their height [p. 292].

The third period is the resolution of the crisis, which overlaps with the fourth subphase, emotional object constancy. In this chapter, I have emphasized the overlap between the resolution of the crisis and the attainment of constancy. I believe that constancy is achieved only gradually throughout childhood and adolescence—and even beyond. (See Notes, Chapter One.) Mahler says:

> The fourth subphase of separation-individuation, which begins toward the end of the second year, is open-ended. During this period, a degree of object constancy is achieved, and the separation of self and object representations is sufficiently established. Mother is clearly perceived as a separate person in the outside world and at the same time has an existence in the internal representational world of the child [p. 289].

The choreographies of shadowing and darting away were first described by Mahler; her observations have been verified at the New York University observational nursery, particularly when the crisis was intense:

> During the rapprochement subphase the child at times follows his mother's every move ("shadows" her); he cannot let her be out of sight or out of his immediate vicinity. At times we observe the opposite behavior: the child darts away, and waits for and expects mother to swoop him up in her arms and thus for brief moments to undo the "separateness" [p. 292].

Mahler mentions the idea of the shadowing mother, but the emphasis on the shadowing and darting-away mothers is my own. The interpretations of their effects in later life are also mine and are based solely on my observations and my impressions from the preliminary findings of the separation-individuation follow-up study. Moreover, as I have cautioned in the notes to Chapter One, there is rarely a pure type, i.e., either a shadowing or a darting-away child or mother.

Willfulness and No-Saying The description of the sixteen-month-old who gets his mother to remove him from his playpen is from Jean Piaget, *The Construction of Reality in the Child* (New York: Basic Books, 1954 [Obs. 160, 1937]).

The idea that the toddler's "No" is a sign of his efforts to absorb the parents' "No" and then eventually to convert these negations into pleasing the parent and being like the parent is from Rene Spitz. Spitz believed that the "no" gestures and words were signs of the third organizer of infancy, the first two being the smiling response and the stranger reaction. The major references are: *No and Yes: On the Beginnings of Human Communication* (New York: International Universities Press, 1957), and *A Genetic Field Theory of Ego Formation* (New York: International Universities Press, 1959).

The surrender of personal wishes and desires by way of projecting them onto others and then vicariously identifying with the satisfactions of the other is from the chapter "A Form of Altruism," by Anna Freud, in *The Ego and the Mechanisms of Defense* (New York: International Universities Press, 1966).

Anger, Sadness and Temper Tantrums This section is my elaboration and interpretation of Mahler's description of the stormy affects of the rapprochement subphase. They are typical of the period of crisis but often continue until the third year of life. I also wish to thank Mahler for her personal communication to me on the meaning of temper tantrums in the rapprochement toddler. Many child psychologists describe temper tantrums as a total loss of emotional relatedness, a sign of the child's utter hopelessness and disintegration. This may be the case with the tantrums of psychotic and other severely disturbed children, but in the ordinary young child a tantrum still has an element of personal relatedness. As frightening as they may appear to be, tantrums are not danger signals but a child's way of discharging his tension and restoring the peace.

Girls and Boys, Mothers and Fathers The shaping of the nervous system by the sex hormones during the intrauterine period is from Judith N. Bardwick, *Psychology of Women: A Study of Bio-Cultural Conflicts* (New York: Harper & Row, 1971).

Although Bardwick's volume generally assails the psychoanalytic position on gender differences, a recent article by Peter Barglow and Margret Schaefer, "A New Female Psychology?" demonstrates how many of Bardwick's findings are not in contradiction to the psychoanalytic viewpoint. In addition, this paper has an excellent review of recent studies on sex and gender differences between boys and girls. The paper appears in the *Journal of the American Psychoanalytic Association*, Vol. 24, 1976, No. 5. (New York: International Universities Press).

The girl's motoric passivity is from R. Q. Bell, "Relations Between Behavior Manifestations in the Human Neonate" (*Child Development*, Vol. 31, 1960). Her touch sensitivity is from L. P. Lipsitt and N. C. Levy, "Electroactual Threshold in the Human Neonate" (*Child Development*, Vol. 30, 1959). The propensity for aggressive play in boys is from J. Kagan and M. Lewis, *Change and Continuity in Infancy* (New York: John Wiley and Sons, 1971). The sex-linked association between male aggressivity and spatial ability is from E. E. Maccoby and C. N. Jacklin, *Psychology of Sex Differences* (Stanford, California: Stanford University Press, 1975).

A definitive statement on the relationship between genetic factors, sex assignment, parental perceptions and attitudes, and biopsychic factors, such as imprinting and learning, in the determination of gender identity appears in Robert Stoller's paper, "Primary Femininity," in the 1976 issue of the *Journal of the American Psychoanalytic Association*, cited above.

The girl's reaction to the discovery of the anatomical difference is from *The Psychological Birth of the Human Infant*, and also from the paper by Eleanor Galenson and Herman Roiphie, "Some Suggested Revisions Concerning Early Female Development," which also appears in the 1976 issue of the *Journal of the American Psychoanalytic Association*. Although Galenson and Roiphie's theoretical position on the origins of gender awareness is not identical with that of Mahler, Pine and Bergman, in general their observations on the girl's reaction are similar.

The change in the girl's masturbation preferences is from Galenson and Roiphie. Further discussion of female masturbation and female gender awareness appears in "Freud's Views on Early Female Sexuality . . ." by James A. Kleeman, again from the 1976 issue of the *Journal of the American Psychoanalytic Association.* Kleeman's studies also appear in his paper, "Genital Self-stimulation in Infant and Toddler Girls," in *Masturbation: from Infancy to Senescence,* edited by I. Marcus and J. Francis (New York: International Universities Press, 1975).

The relationship among the child's cognitive awareness, his erotic strivings, and his capacity for gender assignment is from a forthcoming volume by William I. Grossman and Donald M. Kaplan, *Female Sexuality: Problems and Paradigms in Psychoanalytic Theory.*

My thoughts on the father's role in separation-individuation were influenced greatly by my discussions with Ernest Abelin and by his writings on the subject. Dr. Abelin has been an associate of Mahler. His papers include "The Role of the Father in the Separation-Individuation Process," in *Separation-Individuation,* edited by John B. McDevitt and Calvin F. Settlage (New York: International Universities Press, 1971), and "The Role of the Father in Core Gender Identity and in Psychological Differentiation," an unpublished paper presented at the American Psychoanalytic Association Meetings in Quebec, Canada, April 29, 1977.

In the 1977 paper Abelin cites a full list of references on the deleterious effects on boys from father-absent, father-passive, father-aloof homes. Among them are: H. B. Biller, *Paternal Deprivation* (Lexington, Mass.: D. C. Heath and Co., 1974); R. V. Burton, "Cross-sex identity in Barbados" (*Developmental Psychology,* Vol. 6, 1972); A. G. Barclay and D. Cusumano, "Father-absence, cross-sex identity, and field dependent behavior in male adolescents" (*Child Development,* Vol. 38, 1967); E. A. Nelson and E. E. Maccoby, "The Relationship Between Social Development and Differential Abilities on the Scholastic Aptitude Test" (*Merrill-Palmer Quarterly,* Vol. 12, 1966).

Claiming the Body   The observations in this section are from Mahler, pp. 222–24, and from studies at the New York University Mother-Infant Nursery.

Resolution—Fear of Loss of Love Replaces Fear of Loss of the Mother   The resolution is described in this fashion by Mahler and is verified by my own observations. The idea of the child's identification with his oppressors is from the chapter "Identification with the Aggressor," by Anna Freud, from *The Ego and the Mechanisms of Defense.*

Chapter Seven—Coda—The Way of Life

Recently a number of writers have commented on the domestication of women and the split between the home and the technological work world—for example, Nancy F. Cott's *The Bonds of Womanhood: Women's Sphere in New England, 1780–1835* (New Haven: Yale University Press, 1977). Cott describes the split between "work" and "home" and the relationship between this split and the desecration of the human spirit by modern work. However, it is my understanding that these ideas and the elaboration of their political and psychological significance first appeared in *Capitalism, The Family and Personal Life* (New York: Harper & Row, Colophon Books, 1976). Eli Zaretsky is the author of this volume and has discussed his concepts with me. His book was my reference. Zaretsky quotes from "The Angel in the Household," by Coventry Patmore, about the "tent pitch'd in a world not right."

The Zhun/twasi and the !Kung   The references for this section were "!Kung Hunter-gatherers: Feminism, Diet, and Birth Control," by Gina Bari Kolata (*Science,* Vol. 185, September 13, 1974), and "!Kung Women: Contrasts in Sexual Egalitarianism in Foraging and Sedentary Contexts," Patricia Draper from *Toward an Anthropology of Women,* edited by Rayna R. Reiter (New York: Monthly Review Press, 1975).

The Ik   My reference was *The Mountain People,* by Colin M. Turnbull (New York: Simon and Schuster, Touchstone, 1972). Neither I nor Turnbull is certain the Ik were once called the Teuso. Turnbull only suggests this. I also understand that some anthropologists consider Turnbull's descriptions of the Ik to be exaggerated. However, from what I know of the fragility of human morality, Turnbull's work seems entirely plausible.

The Balinese My references were *Trance in Bali*, by Jane Belo (New York: Columbia University Press, 1960), and also the classic by Gregory Bateson and Margaret Mead, *Balinese Character: A Photographic Analysis* (New York: New York Academy of Sciences, 1942).

The Rajput, The Brahmin, The Japanese and the Christian Way As I was nearing the conclusion of this volume I remembered my mental note to reread the Spring 1976 issue of *Daedalus*, entitled *Adulthood*. The Rajput and Brahmin ways are from "Rajput Adulthood: Reflections on the Amar Singh Diary," by Susanne Hoeber Rudolph and Lloyd I. Rudolph. The Japanese way is from "The Promise of Adulthood in Japanese Spiritualism," by Thomas P. Rohlen. The Christian way is from "Christian Adulthood," by William J. Bouwsma.

The Doomsday Clock There was an actual Doomsday Clock. It appeared monthly on the cover of the *Bulletin of the Atomic Scientists*. The clock was first set in 1947. It began ticking at 8 minutes to 12. In 1953, after both atomic powers had successfully detonated thermonuclear devices the Doomsday Clock was set forward to 2 minutes to midnight. "In January, 1960, to the relief of subscribers to the *Bulletin,* the Doomsday Clock was set back 5 minutes. This was the year Nikita Khrushchev made the pages of *Life,* a tourist in America, turning up on the movie set of *Can-Can.* . . . The clock remained stationary at 7 minutes to 12 through both the Russian and American bomb series of 1961 and 1962. The atomic scientists make no claim to being expert at running clocks." From *The Domesday Dictionary*, by Donald M. Kaplan, Armand Schwerner and Louise J. Kaplan (New York: Simon and Schuster, 1963).

The Third Voyage of Columbus is from pp. 117–19 of "Sketch for a Natural History of Paradise," by Frank E. Manuel and Fritzie P. Manuel, *Daedalus*, Winter, 1972. In their conclusion, the Manuels state:

> But if paradise was born of that mystical union between
> mother and child, is it not man's fate to oscillate forever be-
> tween a longing for the return to that state and disillusion

when it finally arrives? The flux and reflux of belief in paradise then becomes part of the order itself, and do what you
may, destroy its traditional religious foundations, abolish
Eden and the world to come, paradise will reappear in a
new place, still drawing its children to Joachim's reign of
the Holy Ghost on earth, to the third state of Auguste Comte,
to Marx's Highest Stage of Communism, to Teilhard's Noö-
sphere and even, caricature of caricatures, to Consciousness
III [p. 123].

Index

Absence of mother: effect on toddler, 176–81; images of body-mind during, 179; and later letdowns, 181

Adaptation problems, 25–26

Adolescence, adolescents: bodily and emotional changes, 55–57; disenchantment with world, 234; thoughts of, 56–57

Adult(s): confrontation of death, mourning, 45–47; echoes, reflection of second birth, 254; emotional depths, heights, 40–43; helpless child within, 31–32, 33, 230, 231; illusion in, 156; importance of creativity, 39–40, 53–54; search for perfect partner, 43; *see also* Father; Mother

Adulthood: Christian concepts of, 244–45; in Japanese society, 243; *see also* Adult(s)

Aggression: and walking, 175; absence of, *see* Zhun/twasi

Alcoholics, 51

Alienation: and biological roots, 26, 55; of father-to-be, 66–67

Aloneness, 231; and Columbus' third voyage, 247; as dread or pleasure, 40; toddler and, 189–90, 194

Androgens, 257

Angel-madonna images, illusions, 116, 117, 119, 223

Anger: child's, 205–07; and resentment toward baby, 113–17; *see also* Rage; Temper tantrums

Artist, acts of creation analogous to child's discovery of world, 53–54

Baby: aspects of rage, 134–37; dialogue with father, relatives, 138–140; *see also* Body-mind; Infant; "Lap baby"; 2 to 5 months; 4 to 11 months; other entries by age

Balinese society, 240–42

Ball-tossing, 187

Belly button, 164, 165; girls and, 214

Biological readiness of newborn, 68–69

Biological roots, alienation from, 26, 55

Birth, 59; analogous to second birth, 193; *see also* Second birth

Biting, 131–32

Bladder pressures, 55

Body: alienation from, 55; basic subject matter for infant, 104–08; child's desire to own, 225–26; confusion with body's products, 224–25; "stiffening," of "lap baby," 102; toddler's mastery of, 166; two skin surfaces of, 101 (*see also* Molding); *see also* Body-mind; Body-self

Body-mind, 104–05, 262; attuned to world of time, space, 57–58; components, 50; in flux, 181–82; early alerting for separateness, 170–71; of 4-month-old, 48–49; images during mother's absence, 179; and oneness, 36, 89; and peek-a-boo,